The Heart of Self-Care

A Woman's Guide to Joyful Living and Well-Being

LINDA TUMBARELLO

ISBN: 978-0-9995003-0-9
Library of Congress Control Number: 2018903801

Printed in the United States of America

Editing by JoAnne O'Brien Levin
Book Design by Deana Riddle
All photographs by Jacki Jacobs

Published by Joyful Living Press linda@lindatumbarello.com

Visit www.lindatumbarello.com

TABLE OF CONTENTS

Dedication

I dedicate this book to the heart in all of us: to the heart that beats every moment of our lives.

The heart that knows who and what you really love, what brings you joy and beauty; the heart that knows you deeply, for the blood she circulates has traveled through all of you to feed you before returning to be replenished.

The heart that knows that joy is good for both you and her— inviting the happy chemicals that open your blood vessels, making it easier for your heart to send out blood everywhere.

The heart that knows she needs to pause and rest in between beats. One beat, one pause, one beat, one pause…

The heart that knows that, in order to keep doing the non-stop job of nourishing every cell to keep you alive, she needs to nourish herself first.

The heart that knew that, despite obstacles, discouragement and huge sacrifices, I needed to write this book and share it with you. The heart that helped me to keep going, just like her.

Your heart, my heart; this is our touchstone.

Introduction

Your heart is an amazing part of you and a source of deep wisdom. And in its wisdom, your heart knows to care for herself first.

As women, we are often taught that we are here to care for others and that focusing on our own needs and nurturance is selfish. (That dreaded word!) The implication is that our caring for ourselves would diminish our ability to care for others. But this is a false belief. To see how this is so, you need but turn to the wisdom of your body, and especially, to that of your heart. This is how your heart does it: Your heart and lungs are directly connected. When you breathe, the oxygen you inhale goes directly to your lungs. There, it is absorbed into your blood and then travels to your heart. Your heart then pumps that life-sustaining, oxygen-rich blood to every cell in your body. Where do you think your heart sends this blood first?

You might guess that this fresh blood goes directly to your brain, but this is not so. Your heart sends the freshest, most oxygen-rich blood to her own cells —that is, she sends it to herself first. You see, your heart knows how to prioritize: to keep nourishing the rest of the body, she knows that she needs to be nourished first.

It is that wisdom that we, as women, need to emulate. Caring for ourselves is not being selfish or indulgent; nor is it a luxury, for we women are the hearts of our families, our communities, and our world. When we follow the wisdom of the heart, tending to our own needs in a satisfactory way, we have more energy to be truly loving and caring towards others. When we move towards our own dreams, we can really inspire others to move toward theirs.

Can you follow the example of your own heart?

I know that following the example of your heart can be challenging. As both a Psychotherapist and a Therapeutic Hands-On bodywork therapist for over 35 years, I have seen many women struggling with issues concerning their self-care. Why, I kept wondering, was it so difficult for us women to take care of ourselves? Why was it so hard for us to think that self-care is okay, let alone necessary? While our concern for the well-being of others may arise naturally, our social conditioning seems to promote our putting others first—often at the expense of ourselves. This is a false belief, and it does not serve anyone.

Furthermore, rather than being supported to *care for ourselves,* women are continuously receiving messages telling us that we need to *improve* ourselves in order to meet some external standard. The messages we get from our culture, and particularly the media, tell us that what is most important is how we *look.* The emphasis is on our outward, physical appearance, not what's inside. This conditioning is so relentless that we, too, begin to view ourselves from the outside. Then, when we scrutinize ourselves this way, very few of us feel we look the way we "should." In general, regardless of our body shape, size or features, most women feel their bodies are problematic; we think we are too fat, too thin, too tall or too short, that our breasts are too big, or too small. This thinking has consequences. It is not only that we feel deeply inadequate, but that we also become *disconnected from our inner experience and our bodies.* Just as a plant will bend towards life-sustaining light, most of us have a special part inside of us that moves us toward greater well-being, health and vitality. I call the source of this impulse the Wisdom of the Body. If we attune to our body's Wisdom, it will guide us unfailingly. But how can we trust our body if all the media images are telling us that our body is not good enough?

Unfortunately, whether intending to or not, most self-help programs still reinforce that message. Much of the self-help industry has been formed on the basis of telling women how we should be and look, and then promising to help us fix whatever is terribly wrong with us. In short, we live in a society full of experts who tell us how to improve ourselves, how we should exercise and eat, and how we should look and feel. The implication, of course, is that *we are not good enough as we are.* And because of all these messages, many women tend to be hyper-self-critical or, at the least, vulnerable to the judgments and evaluations of others. Do you see how all of this becomes a self-reinforcing, downward spiral, taking us farther and farther away from our bodies, our self-care, and ourselves? In fact, the conditioning around us is so strong that many of us often fail to even *recognize* our own self-care needs, let alone, fulfill them.

I want to tell a different story.

I strongly believe that we can—and must—make the switch from focusing on how we *look from the outside* to how we *feel inside.* When we stop giving others the power to tell us how we should look, we reclaim our own inner experience—and the wisdom that is innate to our bodies. When we learn to listen deeply to our bodies and to ourselves, we will discover what really nurtures and sustains us.

This book was born of my fervent desire to tell that different story, and to share what I have learned as a therapist, teacher and woman of a "certain age," working to enhance the well-being and joy of women just like you. I wanted to articulate an approach to self-care that rests on the assumption that we *are* good enough as we are. This approach encourages us to not *improve* ourselves, but to *love and nurture* ourselves—and to make that self-nurturance a priority, just as our heart does.

But before I could write this book, I discovered that I needed to embark on a journey to the heart of my own self-care.

About 10 years ago I spent three weeks alone—for the very first time in my life. I had never before had that much time where I could be concerned with only my desires, needs and feelings. In fact, I had just spent a long period focusing on my husband's health and recovery. After his prostate cancer diagnosis, I supported him as he made some agonizing decisions about treatment and then helped him to recover, both physically and emotionally, from surgery. Along the way, I had to find a way to deal with my own fears and concerns as well. All through this difficult time, I had a busy work life, and I was also writing a book about movement/exercise in whatever spare moments I could find. Suddenly, when it was all over, I realized that I felt totally wrung out. I absolutely HAD to get away. I felt as if I'd die if I did not. While that was not literally true, I knew from my own previous life experiences, and from those of clients and friends, that I could easily become ill if I did not stop and take care of myself.

I decided that what I wanted most deeply was time, time to be alone and to focus on writing. But then came the obstacles: I had no idea how I could make room in my schedule for something as seemingly luxurious as a writing retreat. And how could I afford it? How would I find the right setting? Yet, instead of resigning myself to the idea that it couldn't happen, as I might have done previously, I became even more resolved. Then, almost immediately thereafter, my husband's brother telephoned, saying that he and his wife were soon going away for three weeks. When I heard this, I called and asked if I could housesit for them. They were thrilled at the idea because their dog was in need of special care. I had to move more quickly than I imagined, and I was anxious about the long drive, but I was determined to go.

After I arrived and began to settle in, another magical thing happened. My concerns and thoughts about everyone else in my life slowly began to empty out of my body and mind. With nowhere to go and no one else's needs to be concerned about, I began to experience a wonderful, deep sense of myself. Slowly, I began asking myself more what I *wanted and needed*, what I thought was important, and what would support me all through each day.

Yet, even as I did his, another kind of awareness began to set in. I began seeing the many ways in which I did *not* always listen to myself, how I tended to put others needs first. In fact, it was amazing to realize how I tended to literally "carry" everyone I loved with me.

I became aware of the harsh ways in which I habitually pushed, prodded and criticized myself, thinking that was the only way to get things done, but causing myself much unnecessary stress and pain. I noticed how I rushed through my daily tasks, as if needing to get them over as quickly as possible, even though now, especially, there was no real urgency. Spending significant time alone also helped me become more aware of how I often spoke to myself very critically and unkindly, rather than supportively.

Even though I had worked on deepening my self-care for many years, I still saw ways in which I doubted that *I* was good enough, or that *my* needs really mattered. I saw how easy it was for me to give up attending to or supporting myself.

This got me wondering if I could shift out of these unhelpful habits. My time alone gave me the space and I gave myself the permission to begin listening more deeply to myself. I developed a little practice to help me do this. First, I would pause and breathe deeply. Then, putting my hand on my heart, I began asking myself questions, such as: *What do I really want right now, in this moment?* and *What would bring me joy now?*

At first, no answers came. But I kept asking and listening, and before too long I began to feel a knowing. I knew that my meals would feel more nourishing if I took a few extra minutes to find the most beautiful place to eat, and then breathed deeply and relaxed before eating. I knew that music could make even cleaning fun, so I cranked up some upbeat songs and sang along. I already knew that physical activity really supported me, and I had a habit of walking every day, but I discovered that walking to music brought an added joy. Then, when I felt a longing to join a dance class, magic again prevailed, and I found a wonderful class and teacher nearby. In addition, I was in the process of writing a book about alternative types of exercises I had created using large, exercise balls. Now, with the space to focus, I developed much more appreciation for these movement activities; I saw how rich they really were and how they helped me to feel my body more deeply.

I began to see that I had fallen into certain habits and hadn't thought to ever check in with myself about whether or not these still worked for me. For example, most of my life, I tended to wake up early, and so for many years I had filled my morning hours with classes and clients. Now, though, I found my rhythms had changed. After rising, I treasured being alone with my thoughts and feelings. My days flowed more easily when I took the time to do nurturing things for myself first thing in the morning. Once I saw this, I put off everything, including calling home, until later in the day. Perhaps even more importantly, I began shifting my self-talk. I noticed I had a tendency to criticize or nag myself. So, I decided to find a way to change that. I started to speak to myself in a kind and loving way instead—and noticed my life changing for the better. I turned this into a daily practice, and began thinking of it as my Inner Support System.

Soon my tasks and then my days began to transform, bit by bit. In fact, my retreat time was so transformative that when it was finally drawing to a close, I did not want it to end. So again, I became curious. I wondered how I might bring all the goodness and joy I had experienced back with me into my daily life. That's when I realized that I'd already been shown the way: my own heart was my touchstone. All I had to do was pause, breathe, tune in, and listen to my own heart.

Once I understood that, I knew I had something worthwhile to share. That's what gave birth to this book.

Into the Heart of Self-Care

I knew I wanted to write about a book about genuine self-care, which is absolutely *not* self-improvement. It is not about "fixing" the things that are "wrong" with you, nor is it about trying to become perfect according to some external criteria. No, the heart of genuine self-care is about accepting, valuing and loving yourself exactly as you are. It is about being kind and compassionate towards yourself, and about treating yourself gently and with respect. This is at the very foundation of both my work with my clients and this book. I view each and every woman as innately whole, no matter what their physical injuries, illnesses, emotional distresses, histories of childhood abuse or adult life difficulties. I encourage every woman to acknowledge her innate goodness and to become more loving of herself; when I see this blossoming, I encourage her to celebrate. This is the spirit I hope to convey in this book.

The heart of genuine self-care begins with *you and your wants and needs*. Not the views or opinions of an expert or a guru— you. You don't need more messages from outside telling you to improve yourself in order to meet some external standard in ways that may be ineffective or damaging.

Yes, I draw upon what I have learned from my 35 years of experience as a body-mind practitioner and psychotherapist, but I write not as an "expert" trying to impose her program or structure on you, dear reader. Always, in my work, I have resisted the idea that "one size fits all," for we are each unique and special. Genuine self-care also has to be about *what really works for you*, what you can fit into your life and lifestyle. So, rather than adhering to certain techniques and approaches, I have always tailored my work to my client's specific requests and needs. I ask my clients what is already working for them in their lives, and then we go from there, building upon that. This book embodies that approach. It takes you on a journey to discover what is supportive to you, what renews *your* vitality *at this time.*

In this way, I hope to inspire, empower and gently lead you to find your own way to self-care, encouraging you to become your own expert about what feels good to you and enhances your well-being. That's why, throughout this book, I will invite you to trust your own instincts, your inner wisdom and your life experience. In this large book, we will explore many aspects of self-care and I will offer many helpful suggestions and tools. Let your inner wisdom guide you; choose those that speak to you and offer you the support you need.

The heart of self-care is about attending to yourself in all of your many dimensions. Mine is a body-mind-spirit approach because *everything really is all connected.* Our bodies, minds and spirits really are meant to work together to guide us toward greater well-being and joy. Tending to the needs of our body lifts our spirits; tending to the well-being of our heart and mind opens the door to caring for our bodies.

The approach to self-care articulated here is both powerful and gentle. It doesn't rebel against aging, as many others do, but recognizes growing older as a natural process that we benefit from acknowledging rather than denying. That said, we have it within our power to grow older with grace and vitality. I'm happier than I have ever been. I have learned how to create the energy I need, to move more freely in my body and in my life, and to enjoy my days more than ever. The circumstances of my life in the last few years have been easy at times and very difficult at others. I have learned that I can choose how I respond to life's circumstances, using the tools in this book. I have learned that developing resiliency in order to adapt to life changes eases suffering. Staying flexible and juicy is lots more fun than feeling rigid and uptight!

You may still wonder: Do I really need all this tending and care? Yes! Sometimes we can get in the habit of treating ourselves like a machine that can keep going and going without maintenance and care. Treating ourselves like a machine is a habit—one that our society still reinforces—but this is neither accurate nor sustainable. If we continue to treat ourselves this way, especially as we grow older, we risk injury, illness and burnout—and we certainly won't experience much joy. That's why it's so important to learn to listen to your body and to your heart, which this book will guide you to do.

So, with this book, I invite you into the very heart of your own self-care. I ask you now to imagine caring for yourself, prioritizing your own needs and tending to them, just as your heart does. Can you imagine:

- *Having a nourishing and caring relationship with yourself and your body?*
- *Savoring all the joy and pleasure possible in your life?*
- *Enjoying physical activity?*
- *Having a more comfortable, relaxed relationship with food?*
- *Feeling your body as a source of wisdom, comfort and pleasure?*
- *Taking time for yourself, time to be, time to dream?*

This is what true self-care looks and feels like. This is the journey we will take together.

How This Book Is Organized

Genuine self-care begins on the inside. So, I begin with be-liefs and assumptions, with your habitual ways of thinking and acting, including the ways you talk to yourself and manage your emotions. Here I introduce five Practices designed to strengthen and empower you from the inside out. These Prac-tices will help you to tune out external messages and tune into the one who really counts: you. These Practices are:

- *Cultivate Inner Kindness and Love*
- *Cultivate Joy*
- *Discover What You Really Want and Need*
- *Listen to the Wisdom of your Body*
- *Cultivate Inner Support*

In the second part of the book I address the many dimen-sions of self-care. Some may surprise you. Of course, I will talk about physical activity and exercise, food, rest and renewal, but I also aspire to awaken your awareness of self-care needs that are less obvious, but no less important, such as smoothing the many transitions you go through each and every day, taking time for yourself, returning to balance, growing older and sex-uality.

Bringing more self-care into your life will involve making some changes. Because there are so many false beliefs about change, I want to approach this topic realistically. Have you tried a self-improvement program, only to fail, drop out, or even injure yourself, and feel worse than before? The truth is that *most* of these programs fail. They fail because they are just too big and complicated. They tend to set you up for failure by encouraging unrealistic expectations, perhaps a complete transformation. In addition, most are "one size fits all;" adaptations that take into consideration your specific background, age and actual physical condition are seldom offered. Then, if you fail to meet your expectations, you are often made to feel that something is terribly wrong with you, *not* with the program. It doesn't matter that the expert behind the program might be a 30-year-old male athlete suggesting exercises that don't fit your 50-, 60- or 70-year-old female body, a body that perhaps hasn't moved much in years.

Genuine self-care is most certainly *not* a recipe for some sort of massive overhaul. It's not about creating unrealistic expectations, and it's not about trying to make radical change all at once. In life, there are no instant makeovers—not really, and radical change is rarely sustainable. True, lasting change comes from going slow and steady; that's what works for real. Change that lasts is most often achieved by taking small steps; it's incremental, gentle and compatible with our current lives and lifestyles. That's why, in my practice, I always ask my clients in our very first session what they *already* do for their self-care. Then, I help them build upon those things already in place to derive even more benefit.

To help you create sustainable change, I suggest five essential Guidelines designed to help you bring more self-care into your life easily, sustainably, and with joy:

- *Keep It Small*
- *Make It as Enjoyable as Possible*
- *Find Your Own Way*
- *Make Your Day Work for You*
- *Appreciate All Your Efforts*

Genuine self-care is joyful. So, all along the way I have included many practical tools and practices designed to help you enhance the quality of your life. They're all simple, do-able and efficient, because I know your time is precious. Some of the most user-friendly are my **5-Minute Helpers:** ten quick, easy, fun and effective tools to help you relieve stress and tension, shift and lift your energy and mood, stop unhelpful thinking and re-balance your body and mind. Each takes just a few minutes, and yet they can make a huge difference! You'll see these Helpers referred to throughout the book, and an overview of all the Helpers can be found in the chapter called Coming into Balance.

As you engage in this journey to the heart of your self-care, I'll be here with you, as a friend and guide. Though I am not in the same room with you as I am with my clients, I hope that my heartfelt words will reassure and inspire you to appreciate all your efforts to enjoy life more fully each day. I will be your encouraging inner voice, the voice that says: "Let's get out for a walk today. The sun is shining. You have time." Then later, I will encourage you to appreciate your efforts, however humble: "It's so great that you walked today!" or "I'm so glad that you let yourself rest 10 minutes today—you really needed it," or "You deserve self-care, so breathe out any false beliefs that say you don't."

What I say in this book may not be entirely new to you, but the quality—the feeling of kindness I encourage you to feel toward yourself—may be just right for you now.

Lastly, *how* I wrote this book was very important to me. I wanted it to reflect what I had learned on my retreat; I wanted to live what I was writing, to truly embody it. I wanted to know that these ideas and tools worked, not only in my practice, but also in my own life, before passing them on to you. That required a lot of unlearning and relearning, which took courage and time—and humility. I learned, for example, that when I pushed myself to work harder or faster, I might have some momentary success, but it wasn't sustainable; I either got very little done, or I felt stressed, which made it harder to think clearly. I realized that I worked best when I felt good, and I learned not to force myself, but to inspire and encourage myself, just as I hope to inspire and encourage you to lovingly care for yourself and do what nourishes you.

Looking back, I am shocked that writing this book took so long. However, I know there was a reason. My life experiences during these years—which included losing both of my parents as well as a younger friend, recuperating from a car accident, and dealing with my own and others' health issues—all contributed to this book because, over and over again, they took me back to the heart of my self-care. They taught me how to become more joyful, how to keep going despite great discouragement, and especially how to become kinder and much more nurturing to myself. Everything I am sharing with you in this book was absolutely essential to my getting this book done, and it all became part of my approach to self-care. That's why I feel this approach will work for you.

I confess that I am actually surprised that I wrote this book. I don't like to sit, especially at a computer. I didn't used to like to write either. And to say "Yes" to this book, I had to say "No" to more people and activities than I ever imagined. But completing this book was a long-held goal, and being able to accomplish that goal was a very powerful experience for me. I did it! Here it is!

I'm so glad to share this book with you. Your journey to a more joyful life awaits, and I can't wait to travel there with you.

Let's Begin!

Part One:
Embracing Self-Care

Imagine for a moment that you are standing in the middle of a lovely, bountiful garden. There, in the center of the garden is the most beautiful plant, one you really love to look at. Now imagine that it was you who first planted it. Perhaps it was just a seed or seedling. You tended that beautiful plant, making sure it received what it needed to thrive, to send out roots, bud, unfurl, and blossom. Now it is in gorgeous full-bloom, healthy and vigorous, and you feel your heart swell.

Now imagine: What if that beautiful plant were you? Take a moment to breathe that in. That is exactly how you deserve to feel.

In many ways, we are just like that beautiful plant. We thrive when we receive the kind of care and tending we need, and our lives are a lot like gardens. Here are just a few of the similarities:

- Every plant is distinct and has different care needs.

- Only you can really know what you want to plant in the garden of your life.

- Just as plants give you clues about their needs, your unique body gives you clues about your wants and needs.

- Like a plant you, too, need a supportive environment.

- Some plants need a long time to establish their roots before they flower.

And this is not merely a metaphor. We do need to tend to ourselves just as lovingly.

I want to encourage you to embrace tending to yourself as you would that beloved plant.

This book is about self-care, and takes an "inside-out" approach. So, we begin on the inside, at the heart of the matter: with your beliefs and assumptions, your habitual ways of thinking and acting, including the ways you talk to yourself and manage your emotions, for these lie at the root of your self-care.

1

Find the Heart of Self-Care:
The Five Practices

Five Practices lie at the heart of self-care. These practices—ways of consciously directing your thinking, being and acting—are like keys to the garden within. They are designed to help build your capacity for self-love, self-awareness and joy in small, easy, day-to-day ways. As you practice them, they will unlock any inner resistances, freeing you up to care for yourself and showing you how.

Each Practice builds upon the next to help you build a strong foundation to support you in caring for yourself now and for the years to come. These Practices are:

1. Cultivate Inner Kindness and Love

2. Cultivate Joy

3. Discover What You Want and Need

4. Listen to the Wisdom of Your Body

5. Cultivate Inner Support

I call these "Practices" because, like other things you practice, they yield results through repetition. And as you repeat them, they become second nature. But unlike practicing an instrument or meditating at a certain time each day, these Practices are innate to us; we have just forgotten them. Imagine that you carry these Practices in your heart; that they are always with you as you go about your life. For example, you can pause at any time to ask yourself how you might cultivate joy, or to check in with your body. In this chapter, we'll look at these Practices in depth. Let's begin:

Cultivate Inner Kindness and Love

I invite you to imagine having a loving relationship with yourself. As women, we tend to think about our relationships with others—the people in our lives, our pets—but not so much about creating a loving relationship with ourselves. However, your connection, your bond, to yourself is actually the most important. It is the foundation for all your other relationships; it shapes all those other relationships, whether you are aware of it or not. But how do we develop a loving relationship with ourselves—especially if we have not been taught or encouraged to?

I believe that the heart of self-care is self-nurturance, self-compassion, self-love. I am here to encourage you to love yourself, for this is where our self-care begins.

A friend asked me what it feels like for me to be self-caring and self-loving. It means listening to my desires and my needs. It especially means believing that it is possible for me to have what I want, that I deserve it, and that my receiving what I need or want takes nothing away from anyone else—in fact, quite the opposite. Receiving what I want and need is what enables me to care for and share with others. It fills the well. With that in mind, I begin each morning by asking myself questions such as: *What will bring me more joy?* and *How can I make whatever I do more enjoyable?* In this way, I continuously sow the seeds of self-love and self-nurturance. I have to sow these seeds again and again and again because it's all too easy to forget my own care and needs.

I realize that the very idea of self-care can sometimes seem daunting, impossible, or self-indulgent. If you ever feel that way, you're not alone. Many women have received messages that make us doubt our worthiness, and these doubts can get in the way of our fully embracing our self-care. These are false beliefs, however, and they need to be cleared away. My approach will help you do this.

Self-care isn't one-dimensional. It is not only about tending to your physical needs; it is about recognizing and nurturing *all* the aspects of who you are—physical, mental, emotional and spiritual. That's why, in my view, self-care includes taking time to cultivate joy, to play and dream about what we want, as well as time to just be. These needs, too, are asking to be acknowledged, so I've written a whole chapter to address them. In addition, our self-care needs evolve over time, so it's important to pay attention to those changes and respond to what is calling to us.

As I said, this book is about encouraging a kinder, more self-compassionate way to relate to and care for you. Only *you* can do that. No one else can. That's why an important part of this approach is encouraging you to find your own way to explore, experiment and discover what works for you. We discover our own way by attending to our needs and wants, by listening to our bodies and to the small still voice within, and by proceeding one small step at a time. A caring relationship with yourself is nurtured through all the ways, both large and small, in which you care for yourself daily.

I realize that, for some, the idea of self-love may seem too far a stretch, given all the judgments we tend to have about our all-too-human selves. It's true that, as women, we have received many messages about perfection. We have been taught to pursue perfection, and many of us have tried to do so—or given up. But perfection is an illusion; no matter what the images in magazines tell us, none of us are perfect; nor will we ever be, no matter what we do. Instead we must learn to love ourselves as we are. For some, it may not be easy to imagine developing a kind and caring relationship with your body/yourself. You may feel that you have tried before and failed, or feel regretful that you didn't get a chance before. To you I say, it's not too late. It may take time, but that's okay. And you are beginning right now by reading this book.

Another way to give yourself an experience of kindness or self-appreciation, and to connect deeply to yourself, is by taking a few moments to do the activity I call *Touchstone*:

Place your hand on your breastbone— the bone in the middle of your chest, near your heart. Exhale out any tension. Now breathe in, and let yourself be nurtured by your in-breath. Remember your heart's wisdom: I need to nurture myself before I give to others."

Don't expect that learning to love yourself will be like flipping a switch; for most, self-love will develop slowly, beneath your awareness. Just begin where you are. Just try having a bit more compassion for yourself, especially around your difficulties. Just listen in a bit closer to your body and spirit. Just embrace the idea of beginning to care for yourself. Each time you attend to yourself in these ways you are sowing the seeds of self-love and compassion. And then, one day when you least expect it, you will recognize it: *Oh, yes, this is what it feels like to love myself!*

Cultivate Joy

I invite you to awaken to the idea that life can be joyful, for this, too, is at the heart of self-care. The truth is that fun, play and joy are essential to your health and well-being. When you experience joy and pleasure, your body creates chemicals that actually improve your physical and mental health. Joy feels good because it is good for you! What could be better? I invite you to cultivate whatever inspires joy in you!

You may wonder: Why is it so important to *cultivate* joy? Doesn't joy just happen—or not? No! Does good sex just happen by itself? Sometimes, but very often it, too, needs to be cultivated. The seeds of a joyful life are already within us; we just need to tend to them. Now let's look at some of the ways we can cultivate more joy.

Have fun and play—it's good for you!

The importance of play, especially as we grow older, is being written about more and more. In *Free Play*, Nachmanovitch states: "Our play fosters richness of response and adaptive flexibility . . . play makes us flexible."[1] Flexibility, as I will emphasize throughout this book, is key to our quality of life, especially as we grow older. Rigidity of any sort advances the aging process, but flexibility keeps us feeling youthful and vital. This shows us clearly how interrelated our body, mind and spirit really are. When our bodies are flexible, our minds and spirits tend to be as well—and vice versa. The fact that play enhances flexibility makes it a crucial aspect of caring for you. But what do we mean by "play"?

Pathways to Playfulness

"Play," writes Nachmanovitch, "is always a matter of context. It is not what we do, but how we do it. Play is the free spirit of exploration, doing and being for its own pure joy."[2] In other words, play is not separate from life; there's no need to create a special category in your mind called play. In sum, playfulness is a state of mind; it's an attitude that we can apply to *all* of life.

Nothing helps bring an attitude of playfulness toward life more than having a great sense of humor. Life brings many difficult situations; I don't want to minimize that. But, as I'm sure you have experienced, difficult situations seem easier if we can laugh about them. Seek the humor in any situation—it's there! —and laugh often. And yes, one's sense of humor can be cultivated. I now have a good sense of humor, but I didn't always. Being around people who can laugh at themselves helped a great deal. Over time, I did cultivate my sense of humor, and I'm glad I did!

Another way to access playfulness is to invite our playful inner child to come out. As Nachmanovitch writes, "The most potent muse of all is our own inner child. The poet, musician, artist continues throughout life to contact this child, the self who still knows how to play."[3] So if you're looking for more vitality this is a great place to start. Think about how much energy children have! Somehow, we have the idea that being an adult means not being silly or not singing as we walk down the streets and lots of other unnecessary restrictions that dampen our energy. Remember the movie, "Singing in the Rain"? Gene Kelly dancing with his umbrella, splashing in puddles, is one of the most magical moments in the history of cinema. Almost everyone responds to it because it reminds us of the childlike delight we have suppressed. Right now, is a good time to change that. Can you make some silly sounds, or make funny faces in the mirror? Can you sing as you walk down the street? Can you remember a simple moment from your childhood and how much joy it brought you? Is there a way to bring that same joy into your life now?

As I write this, I'm remembering when I was swimming this summer, blowing bubbles and jumping up and down in the water, just like a little kid.

Cultivate Joy by Setting an Intention

Each and every morning, I try to ask myself this question: *What will bring me joy today?* I ask myself this question right before I get out of bed, or while having a cup of tea. Whenever I do so, it sets a tone, an intention, for the day, and those days do, in fact, seem to be more joyful.

When I ask: *What will bring me joy today?* I pause and wait for an answer to come. On a busy day, the answer might suggest that I work as calmly as I can, that I breathe out my tension, and that I renew my energy throughout the day by taking frequent, short breaks. On another demanding day, I might get the suggestion to take an extra five minutes to walk along a nicer street to an appointment, or to put on music and dance around for five minutes before I start my day. On a day when I have more time for myself, the answer might be to dance, to spend more time out-of-doors, to write, or to call a friend whom I miss. Many times, the answers surprise me. One day, for example, the answer was to clean my desk. I had no idea that doing so would bring me such great pleasure!

When I forget to ask what will bring me joy, I often get so caught up in my tasks that I take them (and myself) way too seriously. I lose my sense of humor, and forget to bring in more playful moments. Inevitably, the more I push on in this way; *the less I actually accomplish*, and I certainly don't enjoy myself! You see, many of us hold the belief that "all work and no play" is more productive—but most often, it isn't. This is certainly true for me.

Cultivate Joy by Being in Nature

Being in Nature feeds our souls in myriad ways. Wherever we are we can find a bit of nature. Growing up in a big city, I looked to the sky to feel space and beauty. Feeling connected to nature also helps us to feel not so alone, but rather that we are a part of something bigger than ourselves. When I lead guided meditations, and ask people to imagine a peaceful place where they can truly be themselves, most pick a place in nature. It might be a beach, the woods, a mountain top vista, or listening to a stream going over rocks. There is a place in Utah on top of a small canyon that truly feeds my soul.

Looking at the sunrise or sunset is so nourishing to my body, mind and spirit. In *Growing Up in Old Age*, author Peggy Freydberg shares: "My own happiness—I can even call it joy—is the passion of looking at and reacting to and assimilating the life of this earth. It derives from such commonplace things as breathing sea air, setting one foot in front of the other, feeling well, hearing birds sounding…thinking back on the events of the day before and knowing that even though they were unremarkable I would love to live them over again."[4]

Cultivate Joy by Appreciating the Gifts in Your Lives

You have probably already heard about the value of gratitude and appreciation. Many spiritual books and practices recognize how important these are to health and well-being. It is all too easy to habitually focus on what is NOT going right in our lives, to see the glass as half-empty. But when we look at life through the lens of appreciation, when we notice what *is* working and what feels right, this has a very powerful, joyful effect on our entire being.

Practicing gratitude is not difficult to do. We can simply appreciate the goodness of the moment, or perhaps thank a higher power for whatever gifts we are receiving. Enjoy those moments and those gifts thoroughly, for they are blessings. Let yourself really drink in and savor each and every morsel of their deliciousness for as long as you can.

You see, appreciating and savoring life go hand-in-hand. As Frederickson states in her book *Positivity*, "Savoring is a mental habit you can develop . . . it is a resource you can build. Beyond merely accepting goodness, you can learn to relish it, deeply appreciating each facet of its pleasantness . . . To savor simply means considering good events in such a way that you willfully generate, intensify, and prolong your heartfelt enjoyment of them."[5]

Cultivate Joy by Staying Present

Have you ever looked down and noticed, for example, an apple core in your hand or on the table, and realized that you must have eaten the apple, but had no memory of having done so? I certainly have, and it is shocking. It makes me wonder:

Where was my attention? Was the apple sweet? What else am I missing in my life?

The poet Mary Oliver tells us of her "willingness to be attentive," to notice the beauty around her and to fan the "flame of appreciation" for life. In her poem "A summer day" she tells us, "I try not to miss anything, especially a kiss."[6] To truly savor a pleasurable activity, it is essential to focus on that activity with our body and our mind. It is all too easy to let moments of pleasure fly by without noticing them. If you are eating a favorite, special meal, but all you can think about is the next "to do" on your list, then you might as well be eating any old boring meal!

I'm also going to suggest you learn to savor something that you might not have ever thought about savoring: your breathing. We tend to take breathing for granted; it's so automatic, that we never even think about it. However, our breath is truly a wonderful gift, one that's available every moment of our lives to help us balance and so much more. The breath is so remarkable that there's a whole chapter on breathing coming up. For now, though:

Let's enjoy the miracle of breathing just for this moment...Slowly exhale out a few times. Feel tension draining out of your muscles as you blow the air out. Drink in nourishing oxygen into your cells as you inhale. This oxygen is freely available to you every moment of your life.

Cultivate Joy by Cultivating Friendships

*You can't stay in your corner of the Forest waiting for others to come
to you. You have to go to them sometimes.*

— *A. A. Milne, Winnie-the-Pooh*

Much of this Practice has focused on how we can cultivate joy
for ourselves, by ourselves. But there is another important way
to cultivate joy, and that's through connection with others.
We cultivate joy by having good relationships with the people in our lives, mutually supportive friends, neighbors and/
or acquaintances with whom we can talk, exercise, travel and
do creative and/or volunteer activities. Seek community. Encourage yourself to reach out; don't hold back. Kindred spirits
really are all around. Sometimes we just have to be willing to
take a little risk and do the legwork:

> *I gave a copy of my sexuality book to a sex educator whom
> I wanted to get to know. After two weeks had gone by and
> I hadn't heard from her, I heard a voice in my head saying,
> "She probably hated the book that's why she didn't get back to
> me." To stop this discouraging self-talk from gaining a foot-
> hold, I emailed her. She thanked me for "taking the first step"
> and invited me to get together. We had a wonderful time ex-
> changing ideas and we hope to collaborate and support each
> other in our work. It was definitely worth my stepping out
> of my comfort zone!*

Cultivate Joy by Sharing It

You can amplify your good experiences by telling friends and
family about them, and by reliving them in your memories.
Write about events and moments that have especially pleased

you to remind yourself to re-tell them, and to create more of these kinds of experiences. Alternatively, you can ask others about their most joyful experiences or read books that recount other's joyful adventures.

Cultivate Joy by Bringing the Qualities and Activities of a Vacation into Your Everyday Life

On vacation, you usually feel that you finally have permission to have fun, relax, or be adventurous, whatever it was that you wanted to do. When you're in a vacation frame of mind, you tend to focus on things that bring you pleasure. In this setting, you can allow yourself the opportunity to play and do whatever you choose. What if you could bring in some of the qualities you enjoy on vacation into your daily life?

Here are some of the vacation-like qualities I try to bring into my daily life: sitting and being in nature, being physically active in a variety of ways and, especially important, giving myself permission to move at my own, slowed-down pace. When I allow myself to not rush and to do just one thing at a time, I can truly enjoy anything and everything I do, even household tasks that I usually dislike. I feel more connected, both to myself and to whatever I am doing.

What about you? What qualities of vacation time would you like to bring into your daily life?

Cultivate Joy – Maximize the Most Pleasant Aspects of What You Like

Swimming is one of my favorite activities! I always loved to swim, but I absolutely HATED wearing a wet bathing suit afterwards. I got chilled no matter the temperature. I just endured this until one day I finally realized that if I could immediately change out of my wet suit, I wouldn't get chilled. I started experimenting. I tried a number of large dresses until I found one that worked as my "personal changing tent." Now I always pack an extra suit or two, so I can change into a dry one right away. Friends at the lake where I often swim began to notice my changing suits and would jokingly ask: "Is today a 2 or 3 bathing suit day?" Soon, on cooler days, they began to change out of their wet bathing suits right after swimming, too!

Can you do something similar to minimize the unpleasant parts of activities that you love to do?

Clear Away Obstacles to Joy

Now that we've identified a few ways to cultivate more joy, let's look at some of the obstacles that can get in our way and prevent us from experiencing joy. If we are aware of these, we can move more easily through them.

We have a strong work ethic in our culture. We are used to spending the majority of our time getting things done—and quickly. Unfortunately, that means that we have little time for play. Play, just having fun, is often postponed until the to-do list is done; we put it off until "someday" in the future, or until the weekend, if we are lucky. What beliefs drive this habitual way of being? Are they true or false?

In addition to our feeling almost constant internal pressure to get things done, there are other obstacles that interfere with cultivating joy, such as the habit of putting other's needs first; the mistaken belief that that there is only so much joy to go around, so our joy must be taking away another's; or the inner voice that says we don't deserve to feel good.

Notice that these obstacles involve either habits or beliefs—and sometimes both! To cultivate more joy, then, we'll want to learn some new habits and beliefs, and also let go of false or limiting beliefs and habits that don't serve us. Discovering and releasing false beliefs and unhelpful habits is a repeated theme in this book, as you will see.

Old habits and beliefs can be stubborn—but not insurmountable. Each time we sprinkle more moments of joy into our daily lives, it helps us to slowly overcome those false beliefs and create new helpful habits. Each time we appreciate ourselves for the efforts we're making to cultivate joy, it reinforces these new habits, and helps to establish them. It's so easy to become discouraged or impatient with ourselves. Many times, for example, I have asked myself why I don't just give myself 15 minutes every morning to dance, as I enjoy my whole day much more when I do. Or why don't I take the extra minute to put on some fun music while I clean up the house, rather than just pushing through, making it yet another unpleasant chore? At these moments, I practice patience with myself. I take a deep breath and remind myself that it takes time to learn new habits. So, I forgive myself when I fall short, and I appreciate myself when I succeed. For instance, each time I do take the time to dance in the morning or do other joy-inspiring activities, I pause and remember how good I felt, both then and for the rest of the day. Remembering that pleasure not only feels good, it reinforces that new, joyful pattern.

Resource Page for Cultivating Joy

Here are more ways to "say yes to life," to appreciate and delight in small moments:

Appreciate beauty and nature:

- Inhale the fragrance of a bouquet of flowers.

- Drink in the beauty of a bird, a tree, or the face of someone you love.

- Breathe in wonderful fresh air.

- Feel a delicious cool breeze.

Try something new:

- Take a different route to a place that you usually visit.

- Go on an adventure – Explore an area that is new to you.

- Dress up at home and dance in your living room.

- Wear something outrageous when you go out.

- Find humor in unusual moments.

- Create new anniversaries or your own special holidays.

For joyful eating:

- Cook a favorite dish.

- Enjoy an outdoor meal.

- Select a special plate.

- Light candles.

- Linger a moment to enjoy the aroma and color of food.

- Eat something luscious and messy like a mango or pineapple.

In bed:

- Snuggle under a warm blanket.

- Fully enjoy that now you can finally rest in your cozy bed.

- Allow your body to be fully supported by your bed. Let your muscles release – no more to do now.

Anytime:

- Feel gratitude for your body's wisdom, the wonder of breath and blood that nourish your every cell.

- Appreciate all that is working well in your body right now.

- Pet a purring cat, or a happy dog.

- Listen to a favorite song.

- Call or visit with a friend.

- Celebrate everything that you can!

In sum, you cultivate more joy when you:

1. Start your day by asking: What would bring me joy today?
2. Say yes to life's pleasures!
3. Treasure every moment you can.
4. Have fun and play.
5. Live life as if you were on vacation.

Do any of these ideas or suggestions appeal to you?

Discover What You Really Want and Need

Knowing what we want and need is key to living a joyful and fulfilling life. After all, how can we bring what we want into our lives if we don't know what it is?

When we have a clear picture of what we need and want, it propels us in the direction of our true desires. Those desires might be a nicely painted bedroom, a whole day just to relax, or something more expansive, such as creating more vitality, more meaningful work, or more community. When we're clear about what we need and want, we're more able to see opportunities that can lead us towards those things. Often those opportunities are right there, but we need to recognize them, catch them as they occur—and that requires us to know what we want. In fact, many times I have experienced helpful opportunities that fall into my lap once I am really clear about what I want.

Some of you may feel you don't have a clue right now as to what you want regarding self-care, movement, or much of anything. You are not alone!

Many women have focused much of their lives on fulfilling others' needs or wants or on doing what they think a "good" mother, wife, partner, daughter, boss, sister or employee should do. As women, we are taught to respond to signals and cues from others. We ask ourselves lots of questions about others' needs. We notice, for example, when children are hungry, bored or need more activity because we pick up on their signals: they are cranky, antsy or agitated. But do we pick up on our own signals?

I invite you to use that highly developed ability to notice, feel, hear and see the needs and wants of others, to discover your own. I know that it is not an easy task to discover what you want and need. It's a skill that needs to be developed, cultivated, over time—that's why we call it a practice. Each time you take a moment to ask yourself what you want, you get a little better at it. Each time you ask, you move closer to knowing the answer. Here's a story you might relate to:

A good friend who is in her early 70's longed to more deeply know what she wants. For most of her life she had done what had to be done. Working full-time, raising two daughters, running a household, and going to school left little time to even consider asking the question: What do I want?

Whenever we got together, I provided the music since I had experience using music in my classes. However, sometimes I would be at a loss as to what to play. I would feel frustrated when I asked her what kind of music she might like, or even if she liked what I was playing. She would say things like

"Whatever you want," or "I really don't know."

One night, however, she became acutely aware that none of the music I'd played felt quite right to her. I put on music of different types and tempos and then asked her whether she liked it or not. Sometimes she knew right away; other times, she couldn't tell—but it was a start. Learning to know what you want is a process. It can feel like learning to work a muscle you haven't used in a long time—you won't become strong or proficient at it immediately, but if you keep at it, you will see a change.

How Can I Learn to Know What I Want?

This Practice is really about getting to know yourself, and about developing an intimate, caring and loving relationship with yourself. A good way to begin is by remembering a time when you knew exactly what you wanted, and you actually got it. Perhaps a time when you knew exactly what you wanted to eat, and then got to thoroughly enjoy eating it. It might have been a special cake or simply a tuna fish sandwich made your favorite way—with pickles. Remember how satisfied you felt? Or think of a time when your muscles ached and you wanted a hot bath with your favorite bath oil. Do you remember how good you felt when your muscles relaxed in the tub? What about the time when you had fun dancing around your living room? Yes! You can have your cake (or tuna fish) and eat it too!

The next step is to ground yourself in those things you *already know* that you need, like and want. All of us have certain areas of our lives where we're very clear. Perhaps, for example, you know what colors are most soothing to you in a room, or make you feel most vibrant when you wear them. In addition, most of us have some capacity to listen and respond to our body's signals. For example, I usually feel clear signs when I need to eat. I have hunger pangs, or I begin to feel fatigue and moodiness. If I'm busy, or out of touch with my body's signals, I might only notice that I am feeling cranky or overwhelmed, but when I pause to check in with myself, I know I need to eat.

Notice, also, how you choose what you do. Are you choosing to do certain things simply out of habit? Are you just doing what you think you *should* do?

Each day we make lots of choices, both small and large: what clothes to wear, what to eat, how to spend our time, who to connect to. These choices may seem insignificant at the time, but they accumulate; they become the sum of our lives.

Often, we choose things unconsciously, out of habit. We put on the same pair of jeans or eat the same breakfast without checking in to see if that's what we really want today. Each time we stop to consider our choices we have the opportunity to make a more satisfying choice. For example, instead of the same old jeans, you might choose to wear bright colored pants or a red skirt to lift your spirits. You might choose to eat a different breakfast, one that gives you more sustained energy.

Here's how to begin discovering what you want:

- Pause; give yourself a few moments just for you.

- Do *Touchstone*: Place your hand on your sternum bone, the bone in the front of your chest. This bone can be your touchstone to help you tune into your needs and wants. Sigh and exhale out tension a few times. Let yourself be nurtured by your in- breath.

- Then ask yourself a simple question, such as: *"What do I want right now"* or *"What would feel good to do for myself in the next 15 minutes.* Then, as you develop this practice, you can ask questions involving longer time spans, such as: *What do I want in the next month?*

- Allow space for an answer to come. Don't work too hard to figure out an answer. If no clear answers come now, just allow the question to float around in your mind while you are doing other things—commuting to work, out walking, washing dishes etc.—and notice what arises. If the answer you get still isn't clear, ask again. Or ask in a different way, just as you would in a conversation with someone else. Often, this means asking some follow-up questions like: *What would I enjoy doing now? What would I like to eat now?* or *Would moving or exercise feel good? If so what kind?* or *Would I enjoy talking to a friend?* Just keep asking questions. Even if there are no clear answers as of yet, you are starting the process. Your inner self is hearing you, and she is pleased. "Wow," she might say, "she asked me what I wanted!"

- Lastly, give yourself what you want. This is extremely important! Because you are only asking about what you want right now or in the next 15 minutes, whatever you want is likely to be very do-able. So, do it! Then, as you ask yourself questions about what you want over a longer span of time, or around larger parts of your life, know that you will not be able to do everything right away. It may take several steps to get there. That's okay, just start.

Here's a story from my own life that illustrates how important knowing what we want is to our well-being:

After my mother died, I was surprised to receive a small amount of money, as I thought it had all been used for her care. Since I missed my mother so much, I wanted to do something that would have a lasting effect, so I decided to use the money to paint the upstairs of my house. But then, suddenly, I came face-to-face with my own challenges around knowing what I wanted.

Years before, I had taken out a loan to finish the upstairs of my house with the intention of creating a large studio space to dance in. I had dreamed of having a space like this since I was a young child living in a small city apartment. But, sadly, after it was done, I didn't really use the space much because something didn't feel right. By asking myself again and again, I came to realize that the dark exposed ceiling beams made the room uninviting. Almost immediately after having that realization, I heard about a special decorative painter. Under her direction, I explored colors to discover those I liked and those I didn't. Then, when she asked me to think about my favorite natural settings, I didn't hesitate for a moment: I showed her a photo of my favorite canyon in the Southwest. She responded by saying that she could make my studio look like a canyon by painting the ceiling and the oppressive beams to look like the sky, and the rest like canyon walls. From the moment it was done, the studio became the expansive, magical space I had always dreamed of. It is more wonderful than I could ever have imagined! This room became the place where most of the book that you are reading was written. It took me time to get it right, but I did!

Ask: What *Don't* I Want?

Just as it was helpful for me to identify the colors I didn't want in my studio, sometimes it's easier to learn what we want by asking first what we don't want. When I first started gardening, for instance, I found it difficult to know which plants I wanted in my garden because I couldn't imagine how certain plants would look years later. So, I started to ask myself what I *didn't* want. I knew I did not want one particular plant in the center of my garden because it only bloomed for a week and then looked like an ugly mess. That gave me a clue, so I looked for plants that flowered all season. Also, I discovered that I couldn't balance a large garden with a demanding summer teaching commitment, so I moved towards a small, easy-to-care-for garden. That way I could use whatever little free time I had to swim, which I loved to do!

Knowing what you don't want can be a good place to begin. For example, you may not yet know what you want, but you may be very clear that you hate to wear orange or pink, eat grapefruit, lift weights or watch violent movies. That's a start!

I've also found it helpful to pay attention to how I'm feeling when doing things related to the question of what I want (or don't want), as my feelings give me clues. For example, if you're dreaming about a vacation, but every time you research information about it, you feel exhausted, that might mean that that particular trip will demand too much of your energy at this time. Now you know more about what you *don't* want.

As we get to the end of this topic I ask you to be gentle with yourself, especially if you feel you don't have a clue about what you want regarding your self-care, or about much of anything. That's okay. Just keep asking yourself, over and over: *What do I want?* This question is essential to fulfillment on any level. It will likely take some time and practice, but answers *will* begin to come.

Each time you ask a question, you get better at knowing what you want and don't want.

Again, *Touchstone* can help you to connect to your heart's desire: Pause, feel your breath, place your hand on your chest bone and ask yourself a question. Remember: Each day is a new opportunity. Take it! Learning what you want leads to rewards beyond your wildest dreams! Dream! Dream wildly!

Listen to the Wisdom of Your Body

Listening to your body's wisdom is actually a very big topic. It's also a foundation that you come back to every time you do Touchstone or check in with yourself. But for now, let's use your Body's Wisdom to help you discover what you want and to know yourself more deeply.

Most of us know very little about how our bodies work or how to access our bodies' wisdom, but we can learn. All we truly need to do is listen—our bodies are constantly talking! Every day, our bodies send signals meant to inform us about how we feel physically and emotionally. These signals include fatigue, hunger, high or low energy, a feeling of stiffness, a desire to stretch, or a gut feeling about what feels right or wrong. These signals are intended to warn and guide us, to move us away from potential injury and toward greater well-being; they let us know when we need to rest, or when we can't sit still a moment longer and need to move. When we don't notice and attend to the more subtle signals, our bodies will send even stronger ones, like twinges of back pain when you bend down or do a certain exercise.

I invite you to tune into your body's wisdom and listen just as deeply as you would to a good friend who is telling you about something deeply important to her. It's that heart-to-heart conversation in which each person speaks, listens, asks questions, and leaves space for the other's answers.

You can begin by simply pausing to check in. Just asking yourself, "How have you been doing lately?" can give you crucial information. For example, when you pay attention to your body's sensations and reactions before and after doing an activity, you can get to know if this activity helps you to feel better or not, or if it might lead to an injury. You also get to know which activities suit you best at this time.

When you check in, you may notice, for example, that a part of your body is signaling discomfort. Perhaps your neck is signaling stiffness. If that's the case, you can take a break to check in further by asking yourself some additional questions, such as: *"Is my neck always this stiff? What was I doing that made my neck so stiff? What can I do to make it better?"*

As you further inquire, you may realize that your neck is trying to tell you, "I need some stretching," or "I need you to spend less time on the phone with me all tilted over to one side. Use the speaker phone!" If you listen even further, you might also "hear" "I would love you to massage me for a couple of minutes in the morning, or put heat on me at bedtime when I'm sore." This is how you can begin to hear your body pointing out what's happening inside and out, so you can address issues as they arise.

At first, conversing with your body may feel silly and awkward. After all, it may feel strange to ask your neck "What would help you loosen up or have less pain?" However, you may be surprised by what you hear. And, over time, it gets easier to hear your body's responses to the activities, events and people in your life.

Let's have that heart-to-heart conversation with your body now. Similar to doing *Touchstone*, here's a simple way to pause, check in, and ask questions to clarify your body sensations now:

> *Close your eyes. Feel your breathing.*
>
> *Notice if you are holding your breath.*
>
> *Can you feel the movement of your torso as you breathe?*
>
> *Is your jaw tight? Are your shoulders tight?*
>
> *Now sigh a few times as you let out your breath.*
>
> *With each sigh allow your muscles to relax.*
>
> *Gently stretch out your arms above your head or in any way that feels comfortable. Gently shake your shoulders. Move your neck s-l-o-w-l-y in different directions.*
>
> *Do your shoulders feel looser now?*
>
> *Does your breath feel freer?*

Would it feel good to stretch or move easily in any way? Can you do that now?

You can repeat this check-in whenever you need to listen to the signals your body is giving you, especially when you feel stressed or the need to relax, or stretch or move around.

Remember you can also do *Touchstone* to connect deeply to your body, mind and spirit, anywhere, anytime.

Cultivate Inner Support

In the introduction, we spoke about how we, as women, often direct our attention and energy toward caring for the needs of others. That has value, of course, but what about our own needs? This chapter speaks to the need to direct those skilled nurturing abilities toward someone equally deserving: *yourself.*

I invite you now to imagine how good it would feel to receive some of the attention, nurturing, tending, concern and support that you are so good at giving to others. Can you feel what this would be like? It might feel like taking a hot bath on a cold day, receiving a loving head massage, or being with a good friend, someone who:

- Sees our innate goodness and appreciates our strengths.

- Encourages us to move towards what we wish for.

- Is there for us during the difficult times, providing

49

support and encouragement when we most need it.

• Celebrates our joys and successes.

Becoming that good friend to oneself is an important pathway to inner support. Doing so will help sustain your efforts to care for yourself and to cultivate greater well-being and joy. When we know how to support ourselves, we become more self-reliant. Support from others is wonderful, of course, but we really have no control over whether or not we receive it. We do have control over whether we give it to ourselves.

Yet, for many of the reasons we've already discussed, we might not be doing that so well. We might have a tendency to be self-critical; we may tell ourselves that our self-care doesn't matter, that we're being self-indulgent, or that we don't have the time or energy for it.

If that's the case, let's give your inner support system a tune-up. Here are two important ways to strengthen, fortify and boost your inner support:

• Transform Your Self-Talk
• Release False Beliefs

Let's explore these now.

Transform Your Self-Talk

The foundation of inner support is what you say to yourself every day. This is called self-talk. Simply put, self-talk is what you say to yourself about anything and everything that occurs in your life. Whether you live alone or in a household of ten or more, you regularly carry on such inner conversations. They continue all day long and even as you try to sleep. For example, have you ever awakened in the middle of the night to hear an inner dialogue running through your head? Maybe you're reminding yourself all the things you have to do the next day or lecturing yourself about what you did wrong the day before. That's your self-talk in action.

You may have become so used to your self-talk that you no longer even notice it. However, it's essential to pay attention, because the kind of self-talk you engage in can deeply affect the quality of your life. That's because there are essentially two kinds of self-talk: supportive or unsupportive, encouraging or discouraging.

How you talk to yourself—whether you tend to encourage or discourage yourself—is a very important contributor to whether or not you accomplish your goals and dreams. It will also either support your self-care or stop it dead in its tracks. It can even often determine whether or not you get a good night's sleep. *It is the key to whether you feel good or miserable on a given day.* Take a moment to reflect on your self-talk. What kinds of things do you tend to say to yourself? Are you likely to say things such as: "What a great job I did on that project!" or "I enjoyed walking yesterday. Let's go out again today." Or is it more likely that you will say things like: "I should not have done that. That was stupid," or "I'll never exercise regularly. It's hopeless!"

As I said, our self-talk can be largely supportive or unsupportive. Unsupportive self-talk can easily slide into self-criticism. When we engage in self-criticism, we nearly always sabotage our self-care efforts. Imagine, for example, that you've finally begun exercising, perhaps after a long time, by simply going

- Say: "*Stop, I'm not listening to you.*" To give this more power, say it aloud. In my ongoing search for making self-care more fun, I recently started singing the refrain from an old song while I make a stopping hand gesture: "Stop in the name of love." That shifts my mind.

- Change your direction physically. Pivot or turn around to signal a shift in your thinking.

- Choose a more encouraging self-talk: In this case, with regard to the bath, you might say: *"Honey, your back hurts.   You know that you'll feel better and sleep better if you take a bath now.   It's easy. Just get the water started and add that nice smelling bath oil."*

Because so many of us have internalized discouraging—even deeply critical—self-talk, learning to talk to ourselves in an encouraging way will take practice. Fortunately, being with ourselves 24/7/365 means we have many opportunities! I, too, need to practice.

Here is an example showing how my learning to shift into encouraging self-talk made this book possible:

After I returned from a writing retreat, a good friend who is a writer asked, "Was your retreat successful for you?" "Yes," I replied without a trace of hesitancy. "I developed a wonderful new exercise, and I worked on . . ." But then, when someone else asked how many chapters I had finished, I felt cornered and began getting defensive. Pretty soon, I was berating myself for falling short.

Luckily, my encouraging self-talk came to the rescue or you wouldn't be reading this book!

I had never before worked on such a large project, one that would not just take months, but years, so I really had to learn to beef up my inner support to see it through. For example, there were times when I hoped to write all day, but didn't.

At those moments, I had to learn to push away discouraging self-talk such as: "At the rate of only an hour a day, you'll never finish this book," and transform it into encouraging self-talk, like: "Great! You wrote for an hour!"

Every day presents lots of opportunities to practice self-talk that truly supports you.

At the end of this chapter you'll find more resources, including some suggestions for supportive statements you can say to yourself throughout the day. I encourage you to use them to help transform your self-talk.

Release false beliefs, the inner obstacles to self-care

Every gardener knows that in the spring, before we can plant new things in our garden, we have to clear away all the debris that's accumulated during the winter, and till the soil to receive new life. Each of us may need to do something very similar before we can truly embrace self-care: we have to clear away whatever gets in the way.

The biggest obstacles to self-care are our false beliefs about it. Certain beliefs, the products of conditioning and life experiences, can keep us locked into neglecting our self-care and ourselves. Consider, for example, this false belief: *Any self-care beyond the bare minimum is selfish.* We may not realize it, but many of us hold that belief because the conditioning around it has been so strong. From the time we were little girls, we were taught to be aware of the needs of others and to care for the things and people around us, starting with our dolls and our stuffed animals.

Not only were we taught to share everything, from our toys to the attentions of those caring for us, we were supposed to *want to*. Repeatedly, we received the message that thinking of ourselves or wanting things for ourselves was selfish, and that being selfish is bad or wrong. Few of us received the equally important message that we are worthy and deserving of self-care.

That's the bad news. Here's the good news: we can break free! These false beliefs can be cleared away. In fact, just becoming aware of them helps begin to diminish their power. And later in this chapter, I'll show you some tools you can use to help you release false beliefs that no longer serve you. Of course, this too is a process. You'll need to take actions based on new, more truthful beliefs about yourself and your self-care, and to support yourself with encouraging self-talk. Doesn't that sound good? Let's not waste any time. Let's start discovering—and dissolving—those false beliefs!

Another common false belief is: *I don't deserve joy and pleasure.* Here's a story you might relate to:

> *I brought some mangos with me when I went to visit a good friend. As we ate them, we both re-discovered how much we liked them, but realized that we had put them in the category of "special foods"—not for everyday consumption! Then, as my friend was eating just part of one, she realized she really wanted the whole thing. But she stopped herself because it seemed selfish, even though we had plenty for both*

of us. As she explained this to me, she recalled the pain of her mother calling her selfish. Upon hearing this, I encouraged her to eat as much as she wanted. We got napkins so that we could make even more of a mess as we each ate a second mango. We realized that there was no good reason to eat mangoes only on special occasions. We could eat them every day if we chose. Why would we deny ourselves this simple pleasure?

Thinking we don't deserve joy and denying ourselves pleasure is often part of a deep pattern of beliefs that work together to convince us that we don't deserve to have what we want. This is especially true if people we love and feel responsible for also have needs or are hurting in any way:

At one of my workshops I asked the participants to imagine whatever they would like to bring into their lives. As one of the women in the group began to imagine her desires, she began to feel some guilt creep in because those desires were only about her and did not include her 13-year-old son. When she shared this with me, I encouraged her to keep going. I reassured her by telling her that it was okay to have her own desires, just as her son had plenty of his own wishes and wants. One did not exclude the other.

For many women, tuning into our own wants and needs is still difficult because of beliefs about being undeserving or selfish. If this feels like you, the *Touchstone* activity will support you.

Pause with your hand on your heart and breathe out that false belief. Remember how your heart feeds herself first, and breathe in the truth: *I am worthy and deserving of self-care.*

Release Your Inner Obstacles to Self-Care

Below are some more examples of beliefs that create inner obstacles to self-care. As you read them, ask yourself: Do any of these feel like *my* beliefs? If so, take a moment to read the solutions I offer.

To start, here's a BIG ONE!

1. **"I can take care of myself and rest only when all my tasks are done."**

HA! Have you ever finished all your tasks? The reality is that your tasks will never, never be finished!

New tasks emerge all the time. We eat and then we need to clean up. Later, we get hungry again, and the cycle continues. We dust and more dust is created. We pay bills and there are more to pay next month. That's the reality for most of us. Unless we have a personal chef, a live-in housekeeper, a full-time secretary, and more, our tasks never end. We need to let go of the belief that we have to wait until they do end to pay attention to our own care. How to do this? Changing your self-talk can help. You can say things to yourself such as: "Linda, you know your tasks will never end—so now is the time to take a break and do something nice for you." Or, "You're tired. Would it be more renewing to rest or to walk for 15 minutes now?"

2. **"Self-Care is a chore."**

We like to categorize things. It helps us navigate a complicated world. Unfortunately, self-care activities frequently get filed under the category called "Work." When we lump it in with all our other chores, self-care becomes just one more thing in an endless list of things we *should or must do*. It becomes a burden, rather than something nurturing.

The tendency to think of self-care in such a daunting way is an issue many women share. Here's what to do to help shift this belief: Take a moment right now and create another category in your mind called "Care." Think of some things you might want to put under that category, like naps, sunset walks or bubble baths. When you think in terms of a "Care" category, something shifts; that shift makes it possible to care for yourself in a nurturing, and ultimately more successful way.

3. "I have to want to do self-care—and I don't want to!"

Resistance to self-care often arises when we believe that we are going to *feel like* doing activities that we know will help us to feel good. Unfortunately, this just isn't true. It is *guaranteed* that you will not always feel like taking your vitamins, soaking in a bath to ease your back pain, stretching, or devoting five extra minutes to eating something that feels healthier for you—even though these things will make you feel good! Still, it's hard to ignore that discouraging self-talk that says, "I just don't feel like exercising or doing any self-care. In fact, I don't feel like moving at all!" So, what do you do?

Tactics like pushing, prodding or yelling at yourself, as in: "You must do this or else!" won't work for long, if at all. (That's the old stick approach.) You could, of course, promise yourself a reward afterwards (i.e., the carrot approach). That might work sometimes. But I suggest trying this instead: coax and inspire yourself, like that good friend I mentioned earlier. Imagine taking your own hand and saying to yourself, with great kindness: *Let's go for a walk. The sun is shining, and it's a beautiful day.* Continue with more encouraging self-talk: *I may not feel like it, but it's important to take care of myself. Even though it is hard to walk sometimes, I know I feel better and have more energy when I do. Plus, maybe those beautiful pink flowers down the street are blooming, and I could walk to some favorite music. That might be fun.*

If any resistant or negative feelings arise, just let them be, and keep going. You don't have to wait until they go away. If you accept those feelings, and keep going anyway, they'll transform—it just takes a little time! (I'll talk much more about how you can motivate and inspire yourself in Chapter 3, Five Guidelines for Joyful Living.)

4. "Nothing helps me feel better—what's the point?"

If you hold the belief that your situation is hopeless, that you will always have stiff joints or be in pain, no matter what you do or don't do, it will be hard to take 15—or even 5—minutes a day to do something that might help to alleviate it.

Feeling frustrated in the face of certain physical challenges is very understandable, especially if nothing you've tried so far seems to have made a difference. But please resist hardening that frustration into a belief. One way to dissolve that belief and build trust that your self-care will make a difference is to take a scientific approach. By this I mean stay open to new approaches and ideas. Conduct little experiments. Then evaluate the evidence. If, for example, your issue is related to joint stiffness or pain, I've developed a number of very effective movements that can help you keep or regain joint flexibility and ease pain. You'll find them in the chapter about your joints.

Try doing one or more for just 5 minutes a day for a least a week, and note if it helps you. Or look back on things you've tried in the past. Did they yield good results? If so, can you build upon them?

5. "She doesn't have to do as much self-care stuff as I do!"

Have you ever heard yourself saying things like this? That's the "Comparison Gremlin" at work. It's easy to compare ourselves negatively to others, especially to people who seem to be able to eat anything or love to exercise or never get stressed out or have teeth as strong as boulders. A relative of mine never gets cavities and rarely goes to the dentist. It is easy for me to whine: "It's not fair! I have to spend all this money and time to repair my teeth, and he does nothing and hasn't a cavity." Perhaps we do this because we believe it is somehow useful or productive to do so, that it leads somewhere. The truth, however, is that engaging in comparison only leads us away from joy, away from appreciating ourselves (and others).

Here's another way that the "Comparison Gremlin" gets us: We can slip into comparing how we are now to how we were when we were younger. For example, you might find yourself saying things like: *"I can't spend so much time taking care of myself,"* or *"I never needed to take 5 minutes to warm up before walking. I never had to take 5 minutes after exercising to loosen up my hips,"* or *"I never needed to rest during the day to keep up my energy. It's just not fair!"*

When these voices arise—and they will—you might find it helpful to take a moment to recall how energized and relaxed you feel *after* walking, resting or doing other kinds of self-care. Stay with that feeling, and release the urge to compare; it's stressful, unproductive, and tends to trigger critical self-talk.

6. "I haven't the time (or money) to take care of myself!"

If we hold the belief that self-care has to be costly, we can start to dissolve it by acknowledging that many things we can do to care for ourselves are simple and inexpensive. It might entail sipping a quiet cup of tea, or making a special meal just for you, resting when you're tired, or buying (or picking) some flowers to brighten up the day. None of these things are costly, and they can make a substantial difference in your life.

Self-care doesn't necessarily require more time either; it may be more about doing things differently. Here's an example: A busy college professor with two young children had a serious neck problem that was interfering with her sleep and most of her daily activities. As we explored the problem together, she realized that her habit of carrying tons of books and papers up and down stairs to classes was aggravating her condition, so we brainstormed a solution. She switched to using a bag with wheels, and started to use the elevator. As she did so, her neck pain slowly decreased. She also began to use a hot water bag under her neck and shoulders at bedtime, which helped even more. She also told me that she liked baths, but said she did not have the time. Instead of always stuffing one more task into an already busy schedule, she began to look for 10 or 15 minutes here and there to take a bath, to use a hot water bag, or simply to lay down to relieve neck tightness.

Become a detective for solutions to your self-care needs.

Discover creative ways to counter the belief that you don't have time or money. If you can't afford something like a membership to a gym or a swimming pool, problem solve until you find a way. Can you try a short trial membership?

Can you ask friends or relatives to chip in toward that instead of buying a birthday or holiday present, or in exchange for help they might need?

When a friend asked what I most wanted for my 50th birthday, I told her I really wanted a new bicycle. She decided to contact all the folks I had invited to my party to ask if they wanted to contribute. Most were more than happy to do so. I still enjoy my bike today!

And remember: we may tell ourselves that we can't engage in self-care because we don't have the time or the money, but this may not be the real reason. We may be denying ourselves self-care because of an underlying belief that we are undeserving. If you think this may be the case with you, keep doing *Touchstone*. As you do so, add a self-support statement, such as one of those at the end of this chapter, or just say, "I deserve to feel good."

In sum, it's taken a while for these obstacles, these false beliefs and self-critical ways of talking to ourselves, to accumulate and shape our lives, but they can be changed.

Tools to Help Release False Beliefs

Ask yourself now: "*Am I acting in ways that no longer work for me because of false beliefs?*" As I said earlier in the chapter, false beliefs can be cleared away. Just by becoming aware of them, we begin to diminish their power. If you are holding on to beliefs that no longer serve you, here are some things you can do to begin to release them:

- Turn to your breath and do *Blow It Out/Let it Go*, one of my 5-Minute Helpers. Exhale, blowing out as much air as possible. Send out any false beliefs with your exhale. Open your mouth wide and yawn as you inhale. Imagine that this deep inhalation fills you with calmness. Repeat *Blow it Out* as much as you need. Every time you breathe out a false belief, you let go of it a little more.

• Alternatively, write each false belief down on a piece of paper. Then rip them up, burn them or flush them down the toilet.

• Bring your imagination into play a little as you blow out or rip up your false beliefs. Maybe you were a Harry Potter fan. If so, you can imagine using banishing liquid, a magic wand, or whatever feels like fun or magic to dissolve your false beliefs.

• Now, plant a new belief. You can do that by telling yourself the truth, such as *I deserve to feel good,* or use a self-support statement, such as those at the end of this chapter. New beliefs are like planting a seed. It takes time but if you keep nurturing that seed it will grow!

As I said, releasing false beliefs and replacing them with more truthful and nurturing beliefs is a process. (In fact, we'll be talking about this topic again in the chapters on Food and Growing Older.) Meantime, remember that *each new day* presents an opportunity to release anything that makes us feel discouraged and disempowered, and interferes with our joy. Each day brings us the opportunity to bring more self-care and joy into our lives a little bit at a time.

In closing, here are more tips to help you develop your Inner Support System:

- Talk to yourself as you would talk to someone you love.

- Transform your obstacles to self-care by using the tools above to release false beliefs.

- As you go through this book, practice using encouraging self-talk, particularly around your self-care.

Resources for Cultivating Inner Support

How to Transform Your Self-Talk to Support Your Self-Care

As you read through the examples below of discouraging self-talk, see if any feel familiar. If so, note the accompanying example of encouraging self-talk. Try an experiment! Practice making the switch and notice what happens.

Here's an example that challenges beliefs that caring for you is not a good use of time.

When you want to take a few moments to do something nice for yourself during a particularly busy day:

- Discouraging self-talk: *"You don't have time for this now. You'd better check your email or balance your checkbook."*

- Encouraging self-talk: *"I'll feel better and think more clearly if I do something to build up my energy now. I deserve time focused on my well-being. It's important."*

When you don't appreciate your efforts to care for you:

- Discouraging self-talk: *"You call that exercise? All you did was roll around on the ball for a few minutes."*
- Encouraging self-talk: *"I'm learning to enjoy exercising. Moving on the ball was fun!"*

When you are distracted during your stretching or movement time:

- Discouraging self-talk: *"Look at all the dust bunnies on the floor. I need to clean now."*
- Encouraging self-talk: *"Honey, you don't need to clean that now. This is time for you. How about doing those movements to release tight shoulders that felt so good yesterday?"*

When you feel that nothing will help you:

- Discouraging self-talk: *"It's too hard. This movement stuff doesn't work anyway."*
- Encouraging self-talk: *"Remember when you did some gentle moving and stretching for 10 minutes last week? You felt more relaxed and had less pain the rest of the day. Let's try that again."*

Self-Support Statements

It's important that we give ourselves encouragement frequently, and especially during difficult times. That's what a good friend would do. To help with that, I've created some self-support statements, short and simple statements that act like reminders or slogans. Below are a few of my personal favorites, and ones I have created with my clients:

- *When I care for myself, everyone benefits.*
- *I deserve self-care. I deserve to feel good.*
- *I can choose what brings me joy.*
- *Each day is a new opportunity.*
- *Small steps matter. Each step takes me further towards where I want to go.*
- *Things have a way of working out. (This is one of my favorites. I've made it into a song by adding ". . . even if I don't know how right now.")*

Please choose a few that resonate for you, or come up with your own. Write them down so you don't forget, and put them in places where you will see them often and/or where you can find them easily when you need them. *Remember you can repeat these phrases as many times as you need.* I love that we can support ourselves any time of day or night, beginning right now! So, take a moment now to appreciate yourself for reading this chapter.

2

Five Guidelines for Joyful Living

As you've seen, the focus in this book is not only *what you do* to care for yourself, but also *how you do it*. How we attend to our self-care can create a sense of feeling nurtured and tended to— or, conversely, we can turn each of these activities into just one more boring chore to do. For example, we can hurriedly wash our bodies as if we were cleaning the sink, or we can wash ourselves gently and lovingly with nicely scented soap or a special washcloth. Remember: you are as worthy of attention and care as all the other loved ones in your life.

When you provide care that nurtures and honors your needs, you feel cared for and valued. This "gentler" approach may take little or no extra time, but the experience will be much more pleasant, and the results will be far reaching. You will be tending to yourself, and your body and spirit will respond, just like a plant that is being tended to with care.

Does this nurturing approach seem more appealing to you than the way you have been doing things up until now?

I suggest that you take a moment to seriously consider that putting a little more focus on the *how* of your self-care could make a huge difference in your daily life. So, take a moment now to ask yourself: *How do I currently approach my self-care? Do I tend to rush through my self-care? Can I slow down? How would that feel?*

My hope is that, by reading through this book, you become more aware of your habits, especially those that pertain to self-care, and recognize whether or not they are still supporting you. Habits are shortcuts or routines. Like taking the same tramped down path over and over through the woods instead of trying different routes, they're easy and automatic. I love habits because I don't have to decide *if* or *how* I'm going to do something; I just do it, automatically. But habits have a downside: Not thinking about how we do an activity can lead to doing it in the exact same way, whether or not it still feels good or is actually helpful for our well-being *at this time*. This is especially true with respect to self-care. For example, some of us may have an exercise routine that we have been doing for a long time. While this series of exercises might have been great ten years ago, they may not be right today. It's not just important to exercise; it's also important to discover what exercise really works for you, now.

Awareness provides the motivation to make changes. But, you might ask, isn't it difficult to change? No! We can outwit old habits by approaching change in a way that will help ensure our success. Remember: we learned our habits over time—not in a flash. Even brushing your teeth took time and repetition to learn to do it automatically as a daily habit. So it's important that we *give ourselves time*. Don't expect change to happen overnight—but *do* expect it to happen!

A Few Words about Motivation

When it comes to making changes in our lives, motivation is key. What really motivates us? How can we sustain our motivation so we keep going? I want to note here that we are all different. Some women thrive on discipline and structure and don't have a hard time motivating themselves with respect to their self-care. In this section I am addressing those of us who have a harder time with motivation.

Most of us are probably familiar with two common approaches to motivation, often referred to as the "carrot" or the "stick." These approaches are widespread, but how effective are they?

The stick method has a sense of arm–twisting to it: "You *should* do this, or else!" It can feel like being disciplined by a harsh taskmaster who is trying to force us to do something. This can have strong, negative associations, and so it often backfires; we find ourselves rebelling and avoiding the activity, even though it might benefit us. But then, if we don't do what we're told we should do, we may be filled with self-recrimination: we may call ourselves names or label ourselves with unflattering traits, like "sloth," or think of ourselves negatively, telling ourselves we are undisciplined or weak willed. Can you see how this can spiral down?

In sum, the stick approach does not usually set us up for success.

The carrot method, on the other hand, promises to reward us for our efforts after the fact: "After I start walking regularly, I'll buy music for my phone so that I can listen to music when I walk." Another example: "After I get back to my photo project, I'll invite a friend over because I'd love to show my photos to her." Are you familiar with the carrot method? Has it worked for you?

Doctor's Advice

We may experience the stick method when we are advised to take better care of our health. Your doctor might advise you to exercise more or eat differently because of an increase in blood pressure, blood sugar levels, or other medical conditions or health issues. A chiropractor, physical therapist, exercise coach or teacher may notice that your back has increased stiffness, or that you have lost some of your ability to move your shoulder joint. They might suggest that you address these issues before they become more problematic.

When this happens, it can be easy to say to ourselves: Here I am being told what I *should* do—yet again. But rather than just reacting rebelliously, I find it useful to receive this important advice in the spirit in which it is given. Then I challenge myself to find the carrot aspect within the stick. In other words, I tell myself that if I do these things, I will enjoy improved health and well-being.

The Inner Source of Motivation: Find the Joy

While the carrot is a much more caring method than the stick, I would like to suggest an alternative approach to motivating yourself, one that goes even beyond the carrot. I want to help you to find the pure joy that arises naturally when you care for yourself in the ways that are right for you. I want to help you discover how to move, eat, relax, attend to your personal hygiene, et cetera, in the ways that are most nurturing and fun for you, and to experience—and savor—the pure joy that arises naturally from these experiences. You can then remember these satisfying experiences to support and encourage yourself to do them again and again.

This is the key to lasting motivation; it never comes not from the outside, but from deep within oneself.

Can you see the distinction between forcing yourself (the "stick" approach), rewarding yourself with something external (the "carrot" approach), and coaxing and inspiring yourself to do a self-care activity because it feels good?

Here's an example: Imagine that you are with a child who has been happily drawing. She suddenly wants to stop drawing, but you would like her to continue for a little longer. You know that saying to her "You *must* keep drawing for 15 more minutes" won't work. It *might* work to say, "If you draw for 15 more minutes, you can have a cookie." However, consider asking her a question like this: "Would you like to use your brand new multicolored crayon to draw on your super big pad now?" Do you see how that might just do the trick because it reminds her of the sheer joy she experiences when drawing? That's the best motivation of all!

Not only is it important for that little girl to experience that type of intrinsic motivation—it's important for us big girls, too. Here's an example of how a client moved beyond the stick to discover a source of motivation within that helped her get back to moving and exercising again:

Susie had accumulated an impressive collection of exercise videos. She kept them arranged neatly in a row on a shelf in her living room. Unfortunately, every time she walked by this line-up, she felt guilty. Even though she actually enjoyed some of them, the overwhelming feeling was that she should be using them more. So, she shamed herself—a common "stick" strategy—but it wasn't working. Neither did telling herself that she looked fat motivate her to go to a dance class, or to go for a bike ride.

As we worked together to help her listen to her body, she finally found a source of motivation that went beyond the stick or the carrot. It came when she remembered the wonderful sense of vitality and aliveness she used to feel at the end of a dance class. She had loved the experience of feeling her muscles working and her blood circulating, and she wanted to feel this way again. She discovered that her strong, inherent desire to move had gotten buried under her guilt about not exercising and gaining weight. Once she got in touch with her own joy, the joy she derived from moving in this way, she decided to go back to classes again.

The Pause That Re-Sets

Now that we've looked at motivation, let's look at how we can leverage that innate joy to help change some of our less desirable self-care habits.

The first step in changing an old habit is to stop and notice when you are falling into it. Noticing is very important because that's what creates the space for change. It's like hitting the pause button on a remote control. Then, with the pause button on, ask yourself: Is this a choice that supports my health and well-being now? If not, it's time to say no to that old, unhealthy or unhelpful habit and say yes to something new—something, ideally, that enlivens you and brings you more joy. When you keep choosing a new way of doing something, it too will soon become automatic.

I suggest you think about changing your self-care habits not as trying to "fix" something "wrong," but as embarking on a new adventure, an adventure where you're going to learn more about yourself, what you like, what you want, what works for you, what gives you joy, an adventure where you may even have fun! To help with that, I've developed five Key Guidelines: *Keep it Small, Make It Enjoyable, Find Your Own Way, Make Your Day Work for You* and *Appreciate all your Efforts.* These five little rules of thumb may seem simple, but they're kind of like a secret formula. If you use them, they will support you in bringing new, healthy, nurturing habits into your life—with ease and joy. They can help you achieve other desires as well. Think of these like gardening tools you love to use; you can just pick them up whenever you need them.

Before we review the Guidelines, I'd like to talk a little about language. You may have noticed that I don't use the words "success" or "failure." Likewise, I don't use the terms "positive" or "negative." That's because those words have become so loaded. So many of us have engaged in a great deal of self-judgment about not living up to ridiculous standards of perfection, and I don't want to add to this. When we think in black-or-white terms, like success/failure or positive/negative, we set ourselves up; we tell ourselves that if we're not amazingly successful by some external standard, then we must be a dismal failure—but that's just not true. There is a lot of space in between. That's why I believe it's more helpful to use words like "helpful/unhelpful" or "encouraging/discouraging," as in the chapter on Inner Support. I prefer to use language that helps you visualize yourself walking a path, making strides in the direction you want to go while also including more joy and well-being in your life. I sincerely hope that the following Guidelines will help you move towards what you truly want in ways that are both gentle and realistic.

Keep It Small

The *Keep It Small* guideline will support you to begin to move, rest, and care for yourself in easy and manageable ways. You need not start big or perfectly. Just begin.

The *Keep It Small* guideline applies to whatever you would like to add to your life now, whether you want to exercise more, tackle your to-dos, or complete a life's work. *In fact, this Guideline made it possible for me to finish this book.*

Start small. It's easier to keep going that way. To successfully build a new habit, or complete a large project it is essential that you begin in a way that you can manage. For example, if you want to create a garden, but you work full-time or have a back problem, it is best to begin by cultivating only a very small area. The same applies to self-care. If you want to add more self-care to your life, it's best not to embark on a complete makeover—and set yourself up for failure or disappointment. Instead start small. Walk, stretch, release stress, have more fun or breathe deeply and freely for just 5 or 10 minutes a day!

That way there's no tumbling into discouragement because we dropped out of the gym or the program or we failed to transform ourselves completely. Sure, you may have stopped—or never quite begun—to bring self-care activities into your life. You might like to get back to moving/exercising, taking relaxing breaks, or picking up a project or favorite hobby again. The good news is that you can start today.

So often, we search for the quick fix, but, unfortunately, quick fixes are illusions. To unlearn an entrenched habit or to acquire a new, healthier one requires a process, and that process involves a commitment as well as repetition and time. Yes, change does take time and effort, but here's the saving grace: We can *start small*.

Every day presents an opportunity to make small changes that will make a big difference. It's never too late to feel better in some way! Each new day offers an opportunity for a fresh start, to unlearn an old habit or create a new, healthy one.

The *Keep It Small* guideline has three aspects.

- **Just Begin.** Five minutes a day is a great way to start. Focus on one activity, for five minutes—whether that five minutes is dedicated to walking, relaxing or reducing stress. Then, when you are ready, experiment with crafting one day. Move through that day with as much well-being, joy and ease as possible. It is far less overwhelming to commit to enriching one day—today—than to embark on the project of improving the quality of your entire life. The days do add up!

- **Accept your starting point.** Where you are is okay, because that is where you are. *Real lasting change begins when you honor what is already in place.*

- **Set realistic goals and expectations for yourself.** Realistic expectations are important in all parts of your life. When you are realistic about what you can accomplish at work or at home, you will have more success. *My former unrealistic daily to-do lists would have taken me 24-hours-a-day until I learned to modify them with manageable goals.*

Consider these realistic expectations:

- Expect that on some days it will be easy to do what you choose, on other days it will be difficult.

- Expect to get sidetracked, especially when trying to add new self-care activities into your life. This is time when encouraging self-talk really helps. When you are gentle with yourself, it will be easier to find your way back. Here's an example: "We all get off-track. Today's another opportunity to begin again." (See *Inner Support Practice* for more examples of encouraging self-talk.)

Keep It Small discourages you from putting obstacles in your way. For example, you might tell yourself that you need to wait until you have the money, time or inclination to join a gym before beginning to exercise more. This is one of the primary ways we procrastinate. And it's just not true! You can *start small*. You can start walking or doing another self-care activity today.

Make It Enjoyable

As I said earlier when discussing the Practice called *Cultivating Joy*, fun, play and pleasure is good for your body, mind and spirit. Each year more research supports this claim. There are two parts to this. One is to enjoy your life by making each day as joyful as possible. The other is to make whatever you do as enjoyable as possible. This is especially important for self-care activities, because that will inspire you to keep doing them.

Very few people will keep exercising if they find it unpleasant or boring, hence all the unused exercise machines. So, you see, fun and play are essential for the success of your self-care.

Now here's a little secret that can make all the difference: When it comes to self-care, it's not only about *what* we do; it is also about *how* we do it. This is very important to understand. We tend to think in black-or-white terms; we think that some things are intrinsically fun, pleasant, joyful, and others aren't. But what if it isn't the activity itself that is enjoyable or unpleasant? What if the difference lies in how we do it, or even how we think about it?

How we approach an activity can make it playful and fun, or turn it into one more unpleasant chore. Children know this almost instinctively; they know how to create a game out of almost any activity. As they go about their day, they may hum or sing songs or simply babble. They may weave a fantasy story.

> *I remember a game I played as a child. When I washed dishes,*
> *I pretended that the dishes were people who were going to a*
> *very special party. I loved cleaning them up so they would*
> *look nice for their event.*

Then, as an adult, I forgot this game. I hated washing dishes until one day when I realized that I was always rushing through the task. What was the rush? I have no idea. Often, I rushed even when I had time, even holding my breath and practically gritting my teeth because I just "had" to do it fast. No wonder I dreaded washing the dishes!

In both cases, I was doing the same task, but the experience was completely different, all because of how I related to it. It's all about bringing a fresh, childlike creativity to every task or activity, or enjoying how it feels in our body. A friend of mine loves to wash dishes because she delights in the feeling of the warm water on her hands.

We can remind ourselves to do that by asking ourselves questions like: *How can I make this task more enjoyable or fun?*

Remember the old saying: variety is the spice of life? It's true! Routines can be dull, so it is helpful to think up and try different ways to do the repetitive things we all have to do like cleaning and tidying up. Here's an example:

> *One day, I found a CD of show tunes that I had loved as a child. I had a blast singing to those tunes as I cooked and cleaned my home. Music really makes tasks more enjoyable for me. What about you?*

When you apply the guideline of *Make It Enjoyable* to your self-care, it really makes a difference. For example, exercising is often the part of self-care that is most challenging for many of us. If you're challenged, like I am, to get enough movement and exercise into your life, look for ways to make it as enjoyable as possible, so that it becomes something you actually look forward to, instead of dread:

> *I love to dance but need some inspiration to do so at times. I have a fun top with flowing material that I can quickly put on over whatever I am wearing. When I put it on, I feel inspired to dance around my living room. It works especially well on dreary days!*

More ideas for how to make everyday activities and tasks more fun:

- Make a game out of the task, as a child would.

- Wear a fun outfit to stretch, dance or exercise in, or even while you tidy your home.

- Sing your heart out to a show tune or an opera as you do your cleaning chores.

- Listen to audio stories, the radio, or podcasts as you do tasks.

- Reward yourself with a few minutes rest, a walk, a crafts activity, or your favorite cup of tea after you complete a task or part of it.

- Make your walks more enjoyable. For suggestions as to how, see my chapter on *Walking*.

In sum, we all need to play more. That means not only giving ourselves permission to do more things that are intrinsically fun, but also doing everyday things—including our self-care activities—more playfully. (For more, see the Practice of *Cultivating Joy*)

Can you think of ways to make your daily activities more playful and game-like so you can enjoy them more?

Find Your Own Way

This guideline encourages you to find your best way of caring for yourself. It has two important aspects:

- Become your own expert on your well-being.

- Learn what works for you and adapt programs, exercises and tools to fit your unique needs.

instructor about how you might adapt or modify it to better suit your needs. In fact, I routinely speak to the instructor before starting any new exercise class. I tell her that I have some physical issues, and that I may not do all the exercises—in fact, I may even leave the class if it isn't right for me that day. Having this conversation frees me up to take care of my own needs, which often include adapting exercises to make them work better for me. Here is a personal experience:

I love to walk, but during the winter there are just too many days that don't support walking safely. Also, I wanted a more social situation, such as a class. However, I was tired of going to movement classes where I was twice the age of most of the other women there. So, I was pleased to hear about a dance class being offered at the senior center—something I never considered before. I assumed that since this was a class for older women it would be okay for me. However, although I loved the music, the class involved too much fast and fancy footwork, and even though I tried to adapt the movement, I strained my knee. I was disheartened, so I took a break. The next time, I told the teacher I wanted to continue to attend, but that I would be greatly adapting the movements— doing less fancy footwork—so that I could enjoy the class and not hurt myself. Even so, it's not really as fun as I'd like, so I will keep looking for something more enjoyable.

If you are ever in a situation similar to this, don't be intimidated into doing things that aren't right for you Don't hesitate to talk with the teacher about your concerns. If she or he is not responsive, please find another class!

Here is a suggestion. Try a bite-size sample to help you discover what appeals to you.

While looking at a menu, have you ever wished that you could taste a few different foods to help you be sure of what you wanted? I sure have! You can apply the same principle to activities or exercise movements: Sample before making a commitment. Think about trying on possibilities for different activities as you would try on clothes. In the dressing room, you might ask yourself a whole series of questions, such as: *Do these pants fit well? Do they look good? Are they comfortable? Do I like this color?* Be just as discriminating when sampling an exercise routine or program.

When you "try on" different activities in your mind, look for feelings similar to those you experience when you wear your favorite clothes: You just feel good in them. You want to feel the same way about things you do for your self-care. And you want to avoid the feeling of too tight pants that make it hard to breathe, or the stiff-feeling fabric of a dress that you bought for a special occasion and will never wear again. Those feelings are clues; tune into them.

Remember: What you choose does not have to be perfect or right for the rest of your life; it is just what you choose today. You will learn from that choice. If, for example, you return from a walk feeling energized and in better spirits, that's great! If you come back tired and wish you had rested, then chalk it up to a learning experience. And be aware that your whatever worked well today might not work quite as well tomorrow. Our bodies, our moods, our energy, our ability to think clearly, these can change from day to day, whether because of what we ate, how we slept, the weather, or the cycles of the moon. Who knows?

Let's try taking a bite-size sample of different activities. Give yourself the next 5 minutes. If you can give yourself 15 minutes now that would be wonderful, but please do what works. Five minutes of a helpful activity that you actually do is lots better than 15 minutes of an activity that you never do!

- Try a small stretch with your arms just a bit above your head. Feel your body's response as you stretch.

- Then try the same stretch with your arms all the way up to the ceiling.

- Ask yourself how that "taste" felt: *Did I enjoy the smaller stretch or the bigger one? Do I want to stretch other parts of my body?*

- "Try on" or imagine a moment of resting, then one of moving/exercising.

- Let's say that you prefer moving. Then ask yourself: *What kind of movement do I want to do now? Do I want to go outside for a walk or would I like to stretch or do another activity?*

- If you choose walking, imagine going for a walk. Still not sure if this is what you want? Open a window, or go outside to feel the fresh air. Take a deep breath. Does the outdoors beckon to you? Still not sure? Go for a short walk today.

Find Your Own Way includes such things as discovering the time of day that works best for you to exercise, meditate, get your work done, etc. You'll get more ideas about this in the next guideline *Make Your Day Work for You. Finding your own way* also means *not* doing things just out of habit or inertia. It's important to recognize that our bodies and our needs change over time. What worked for us five years, or even just two months, ago might not work now. Don't be afraid to re-evaluate. What works for you *now*?

Find Your Own Way is important when we are healthy, and even more important when we are not. If we are faced with a serious condition, we may have to decide about different treatment options. We need to ask: "Will this treatment option really work for me, given my temperament and my lifestyle?"

Find Your Own Way even pertains to this book. Here, I invite you to try suggestions and exercises that I have found helpful during my 30+ years of experience. At the same time, I encourage you to adapt these suggestions to fit your own, specific lifestyle and needs.

Remember only you can really know what is best for you.

Make Your Day Work for You

As women, we have a tendency to focus on making sure things work for others, but we often forget about ourselves. This can lead to fatigue, or even exhaustion. Often, we give ourselves over to the needs and wants of others. When we do this, we abdicate responsibility for our own lives. We may do this because we feel we don't have a say in how things go, which leads to feelings of helplessness or victimhood. Instead, take each precious day as a new opportunity to nurture yourself. Let's design each day to be as fulfilling and joyful for us as possible. The Guideline of *Make Your Day Work for You* has three aspects: Start Your Day Out Right, Structure Your Days for Well-being, and Anticipate Your Needs.

Start Your Day Out Right

You've no doubt heard that old expression about getting out on the "wrong side of the bed." Well, it's still around because there's a lot of truth in it. Whatever we do first thing in the morning can cascade until it affects our whole day. In short, how you start your day can make a big difference. Here's a story to illustrate:

A good friend had the habit of checking her bank balance the first thing every morning. No matter how much she had in her account, the very act of checking would initiate a flood of anxiety, which affected the whole rest of her day.

When I asked why she did this, she told me that, years ago, at a time when money was really tight, she was fearful that she might bounce a check—so she developed the habit of checking her account the moment she opened her eyes. On hearing this, I pointed out that her financial circumstances had certainly changed for the better in the years since, and that even if she still needed to keep her eye on the balance, there was no reason to check it first thing. Because she always awoke very early, hours before the bank opened, she had plenty of time to do something nice for herself first.

Since my friend loved sea birds and many flew near her home, I encouraged her to step outside when she awoke to enjoy the birds and the morning sky before doing any tasks—especially money -related ones. Soon this became a pleasurable habit. As this new habit grew, she still checked her bank balance, but now she waited till later in the morning to do so. Even though she only spent a few minutes outside the first thing in the morning, it made a huge difference in her day. She experienced more calmness and peace throughout the day.

Before long she realized that it served no real purpose to check her balance more than once a week.

Whatever you do the first thing in the morning sets the tone for the whole day, so why not start your day doing something that makes you feel really good? This is especially important if you tend to wake up feeling stiff, achy, in pain, or otherwise not well rested. Furthermore, it's one of the best ways to insure that you actually do the activities that help you feel most joyful and alive. We all have good intentions, and we genuinely think we'll find time later in the day to stretch or meditate (or whatever our chosen self-care activity), but the unfortunate reality is that, nine times out of ten, we don't. That's why it often helps to make a habit of doing these things first thing in the morning. Not only does this help insure that we actually do them, but it also starts your day on a high note, setting it on a course to bring you more joy and well-being. Here are some examples of the kinds of things you can do to help start your day out right:

- Gaze at things that delight you, such as looking at the sky, a tree, etc., or at a lovely object in your home and appreciating its beauty.

- Take a moment to feel gratitude for another day and the opportunities it brings you.

- Stretch or do gentle movements of any kind. (Check out the chapter on *Joints* for some great movement suggestions to relieve morning stiffness.)

- Meditate, become aware of your breathing, or do *Touchstone*.

These things take but a few minutes. What a good use of your time! And remember, whatever feel-good thing you choose to do, it's likely to have the biggest, most positive impact on your day if you do it the very first thing in the morning. Remember that five minutes in the morning of actual stretching is a lot better than a mythical 30 minutes in the afternoon that never quite seems to happen!

Now let's put the guideline of *Make It Enjoyable* together with the guideline of *Make Your Day Work for You* Remember how, in Chapter 2, we put things in a special category called "Care"? Now, choose one thing from your Care category. Choose something that you already enjoy doing, or find a way to turn it into a game or otherwise make it as enjoyable as possible. Then, do this activity first thing in the morning. At first, do it for just 5 minutes. Then, if you want, continue for more time. Continue to do this every morning. Pretty soon, you're starting each day out right —and feeling good!

Structure Your Day for Well-being

Another part of *Make Your Day Work for You* involves structuring how your day unfolds to support your well-being as much as possible.

Let's start by considering how you structure your days now. Are you letting the needs of others determine how your day unfolds? Are you structuring your time—your days—simply out of habit, rather than out of conscious choice? For example, as a young mother, you might have rushed in the morning to get ready for work and to get your children ready for school. You might have said to yourself: "I have no time for myself in the morning." However, things might be different now.

Your children may be grown and out of the house; you may be working only part-time, but still you are following the same patterns. Now you can do something nourishing for yourself in the morning to help you feel better throughout the day. Don't deny yourself that pleasure!

In catching up with an old friend whom I hadn't talk to in years, I asked what changes she had made in the past year to help her to enjoy her life more. Her answer was illuminating. Two of the three things she did were about scheduling more of her time around her own needs:

> *The biggest change was adding a long break in my workday. Even though my daughter had left for college two years before, I had continued to structure my workday around her. I worked straight through from 8:30 in the morning to 3:00, with 15 minutes for lunch, so that I would be free to drive my daughter to her activities or to attend her athletic events. Finally, I realized I didn't have to do that anymore. I decided to take a two-hour break during which I eat a leisurely lunch, walk or swim, and then work till 5:00 pm. I like my work more. I have time to enjoy exercising. I am less tired at the end of the day. It's great!*

It's true that there is a serenity in accepting what we cannot change, but many times there are things we can do, if we just look at our circumstances or situations creatively, with imagination and curiosity: *Is this situation really set in stone, is there any wiggle room? How might I shift things so they work better for me—and maybe everyone else, too?*

Here's a story as an example:

A client, Jennifer, is a single Mom who has a demanding teaching job. Jennifer loved both her son and her job very much. However, her situation was stressful because she was always "on." All day long, someone always needed her attention. She really needed some quiet time in order to regroup and renew. After talking about it, she came up with a creative solution. She worked it out to have a classroom aide take the kids out to another part of the building at lunchtime. She was then able to have time in her classroom alone, where she could think about what would work best for the kids for the afternoon, or just putter around and enjoy the quiet.

While we were talking about lunchtime and food, Jennifer came up with another great idea. She would ask a colleague and friend, also a single Mom, to alternate bringing in lunches for each other. They would take turns stocking the fridge at work with sandwich fillings, and other lunchtime foods. Then, if one of them had a chance to make extra dinner they would bring that in, too. Soon it worked out that they each got a day off from making dinner every week. The whole arrangement helped each of them to feel deeply supported.

Anticipate Your Needs – Be Ready for Your Day

Anticipating your needs is an important way of looking out for yourself. It's part of knowing how you operate the best, what's the best fuel for you, what works for you. It involves thinking ahead about what you will need throughout the day, and organizing your day so that it works best for you. In all areas of your life from the time you get up in the morning to the time you fall asleep, anticipating your needs will contribute greatly to the quality of each day and your life. Whether you want to exercise or move more, sleep better, etc., anticipating your needs will make any activity more fun, easier, more satisfying. The extra thinking or additional few minutes organizing what you need will more than pay off when you are well prepared for that activity.

Here's a simple example:

> *When I expect to walk any distance like when I go to New York City, I wear my sneakers. If I want to be a bit more dressed up, I take my most comfortable dress shoes with me. Of course, I wish I could wear sexy, attractive shoes. However, I know that cringing from pain as I walk isn't all that sexy anyway! Maybe my dress shoes are not stylish but I know I won't enjoy whatever I'm doing if my feet hurt!*

What happens if we don't anticipate our needs? Here's an example, also foot-related:

> *A friend with terrible bunions wouldn't give up her too-tight high heels because she felt the need to look taller, even when her feet had really started to hurt. Unfortunately, she is now experiencing more and more pain as she walks, and is hardly able to walk at all. Recently, on a vacation, she felt very limited, as she was unable to see any of the sights that required walking. Since she no longer can walk as exercise, she is feeling more joint stiffness, pain and lack of energy.*

Of course, many times we can get away without considering or anticipating our future needs, whether it is in a day or years from now. But as we get older or sustain injuries or develop serious medical issues, the price of not anticipating our needs becomes more serious.

Some women find that anticipating their needs is just second nature to them. Others have trouble even grasping the concept. We may have been able to do this for our children or for someone else who needed our support—but when it comes to tuning into and anticipating our own needs, we are at sea. If that's you, a good place to begin is by asking the question: *How can I best prepare for whatever I need to do today?*

Resources Page for Anticipating Your Needs

1. Plan ahead to gather the things you need for the day such as lunch, snacks, papers etc. *What time of day works best for you to gather what you need to take with you?*

2. Make a checklist of the things you need to help you remember to take them. Here are some things to add to a checklist, whether you are going out for fun or recreation, or to work:

   - Food/nourishing snacks

   - Water or other drinks

   - Clothing appropriate for different temperatures; layers and sun protection, if needed.

   - Comfortable footwear

   - Important papers

Obviously, there's much more to the idea of making your day work for you—and it's very connected to our relationship with time. Since this is a big topic, there's a whole section on looking at your day from morning to night so you can make it as smooth as possible. (See *Smoothing Out Your Day* in the chapter *Your Relationship with Time* for more.)

Appreciate All Your Efforts

This guideline speaks to all the times when you've felt lazy or guilty or inadequate for not doing more. Let's stop that! It's time to celebrate all the things you do manage to do!

Appreciate All Your Efforts—no matter how small. Appreciating whatever you have done is critical to sustaining self-care. Accomplishing each small goal leads you to what you want. Over time, as those small steps add up, you'll be even more motivated to keep doing them. You'll have less stress too.

Remember: if you *Keep It Small*, it will be easier to accomplish something you can appreciate yourself for doing! For example, some of my clients find that setting a timer for 10-30 minutes for the tasks, or self-care activities that they have difficulty starting really works for them. When they do this, something magical happens. Most of the time they find that, after the timer goes off, they actually want to continue doing the activity a bit longer.

If you accomplished only part of a task, appreciate that. Our lives are so busy, and tasks often so large, that it's only possible to complete a part of a task or goal—and that's okay. For example, maybe you wanted to have more nutritious snacks around the house, and yesterday you purchased one item.

That's a good beginning—appreciate it! We often expect too much to happen all at once; like organizing the whole messy desk, or getting the entire garden ready for spring in one fell swoop. Remember: It's all too easy to focus on how much you think you *should* have accomplished, or even what you *failed* to accomplish. Forget that! Instead, take a moment to notice and appreciate what you have done.

When you notice *all* your efforts it is easier to feel a sense of accomplishment: the 20 minutes spent pulling weeds that created a beautiful patch of garden, the 10 minutes sorting mail to organize a part of a desk, the hour working on your craft project, the 15 minutes moving gently to loosen up your stiff joints.

Celebrate!

At the end of any accomplishment, celebrate. Give yourself a cheer (out loud) or an imaginary pat on the back, whatever works to make you feel appreciated. Appreciate yourself especially when you find a way to do something that's important but hard for you to do! Share your accomplishment with a friend that you know will be happy for you.

Another powerful way to reward and motivate yourself is by using encouraging self-talk. So, say "Hooray!" if you just started exercising by walking 5 minutes. Think of a boosting statement like, "I walked once this week. That's more than I ever did before." Say this to yourself, especially if you hoped you would walk every day.

I invite you to take a *Touchstone* moment now. Place your hand on your heart area. Enjoy a deep breath. Allow yourself to breathe in anything you found helpful in the Guidelines.

Now, appreciate yourself for reading this chapter. *How does this feel in your body?*

Part Two:

Exploring the Many Wonderful Dimensions of Self-Care

This next part of the book introduces you to the many dimensions of Self-Care. While many of these topics, such as Movement and Food, you would expect to see, I believe my approach to them is unique—and refreshing. Some of the others I've included, such as managing your relationship to time, smoothing the many transitions you go through each and every day, taking time for yourself, returning to balance, growing older and sexuality may surprise you. But while these may be less obvious, they are also essential to true self-care.

As you read through each of these dimensions, and consider including them in your life, my five *Guidelines* can help you do so in a way that is sustainable, easy and yes, even fun. Based on the *Guidelines*, here are five key questions to ask yourself:

1. When I choose to do a new self-care activity, how do I keep it small so that it fits into my life with ease?

2. How can I make my self-care as enjoyable as possible so I feel motivated to keep doing it?

3. How can I find my own way by changing or adapting a self-care activity so that it works better for me?

4. How can I make each day work for me so that it brings me as much joy, ease and well-being as possible?

5. How can I appreciate all of my efforts to care for myself?

3

Movement, Exercise &
Physical Activity

There's no question that movement is essential to our well-being. It is critical for maintaining our vitality, flexibility, mobility, strength, mental functioning and overall quality of life.

We need to move in order to feel good now and to prevent problems later. Movement is necessary for your body to function well. It aids the circulation of blood and the removal of toxins, promotes healing and deeper breathing, and so much more. Furthermore, our minds benefit from movement. There is much new research about the importance of exercise to maintain and enhance one's mental functioning.[7]

Yet, despite the many benefits of movement, finding a good way to incorporate it into our lives is a challenge for many. Therefore, in this chapter, we will provide important groundwork, review foundational ideas, and apply the *Guidelines* to help you incorporate movement into your life in a sustainable way. We will look at how you can motivate yourself to move, how to overcome obstacles, and how to find an approach to exercise and movement that not only works for you, but is also enjoyable.

Motivate Yourself to Move

First of all, most of us need to forgive ourselves for having a hard time with this aspect of self-care. The truth is that making sure we get adequate exercise is a relatively new human need. Our ancestors carried their clothing to a water source, beat them on rocks to get them clean, and hung them out to dry. They churned butter; they hunted, foraged for or grew their own food. They chopped wood for warmth, carried children on their backs, and walked long distances to get anywhere. They performed so many physical activities in the course of a day that they didn't need to set aside time to exercise. They had plenty! Even many of our more recent ancestors needed to walk 7-10 miles a day just to get food and water, or to meet other basic needs. Not so long ago, most children had to walk miles to get to school.

But in just the last hundred years, the lifestyles of many have changed radically. My mother was born in 1912 on a small island off the coast of Sicily, and at the time, my grandmother grew most of her family's food, made their clothes, baked their bread (without a bread machine!), worked as a midwife and healer, and did odd jobs, all while raising five children. She certainly did not need to think about getting enough exercise! Things have changed greatly in that regard.

In addition, the allure of sitting still while being sucked into our smart phones or computers makes it even more difficult to get up and move.

Our lives may be very different now, but our bodies' need for movement is not. And here's the good news: our bodies are *designed* to move. Our bodies are wonderful constructions; we're built of many bones, joints and muscles, all ready to spring into action. In addition, movement actually *creates* energy. It lifts your mood and spirits as well. Movement is joyful for infants and children. You, too, once loved to move, and you can reclaim that joyful sense of moving at any age. It's not too late! Let's look at how you can motivate yourself to embrace more movement in your life.

If you need to bring more physical activity into your life, but don't know how...

Let's say that you are experiencing a pressing health issue, such as high blood pressure, or you're finding that your joints are getting stiff or you just know that you need to start moving more, but you don't know how to begin. When you find yourself in that place, here's what often happens. You might feel pressure to join a gym, buy the "correct" walking shoes, spend a bundle on a treadmill, read lots of books on exercise, or find a personal trainer, but meanwhile just the idea of beginning "an exercise program" might feel overwhelming. Some of these options involve expenses, so money might be an obstacle. In the midst of all these considerations, you might find yourself in a muddle and have trouble doing anything at all.

Still, many of us go ahead and buy that exercise machine or join that gym. We do so with the best of intentions and we might even feel excited to begin—but it doesn't last. At many tag sales, you can observe the evidence of failed attempts, as sellers eagerly try to rid themselves of the practically brand-new rowers or stationary bikes that are collecting dust and wasting space in their homes. But that's not the only thing that's been wasted. What about all that initial excitement and all those good intentions? They took a hit, too.

To avoid unnecessary setbacks on your way to getting more physical activity, ask yourself these questions now:

- *Have I tried to bring more exercise into my life before? Did it work?*

- *If it didn't, did I feel disappointed in myself? Did I feel self-critical about not meeting my expectations?*

- *And what about my expectations? Were they unrealistic?*

So, what can we learn from this phenomenon that can help us succeed in bringing more movement into our lives? In the next pages, I would like to offer you a different approach to movement and exercise—one that works for you. Right now.

This is not a one-size-fits-all routine or program of exercises created by a know-it-all expert, but rather an inside-out approach—because that's where it has to start: with you. Not with the gym or the machine or the routine. With you.

In my approach, your background, your current situation and your likes and dislikes are all considered. I do not suggest setting big goals. When our goals are too great, too unrealistic, and we find no way to meet them, we are left with the sense that "I can't do it," "It's too hard," or "Something is wrong with me." Nor do I favor the "push yourself to do more boring exercises" method. The "No pain – no gain" style has no place here either!

No matter your age or whether or not you've moved much before, it's never too late to start including more physical activity in your life. The key is discovering a way to move and exercise that meets *your needs,* respects *your* body and makes *you* feel good. That's what will inspire you to move today, and to continue exercising throughout your life. It's important to ask yourself: what will really work for you, right now?

Begin on the Inside

The way we think about things on the inside, including the language we use, can make a huge difference in what we do on the outside. When we think of the word "exercise," for example, we tend to put it into a category all by itself. Having a special word for it makes it feel separate, different from our everyday lives. When we think about it that way, it can seem harder to fit in. So instead of thinking in terms of exercise, I find it helps to think of physical activity. We all do some physical activity as a part of our normal, daily lives. We all have to move to get places, whether we drive or take public transportation. We have to engage in physical activity to do our laundry, shop, cook, etc. So, since we already do some physical activity, we just need to think about how we might *increase* our physical activity to become more flexible and vital. Can you feel the difference? Now let's talk about *how* to do that.

1) Focus on taking care of you to feel better. As I discussed earlier, most exercise programs focus on self-improvement with an emphasis on the external, i.e., how you will look as a result. Remember the story of the carrot and the stick? If you equate exercising with "improving" or "fixing" yourself, then what happens when you don't exercise? Does that mean you are a bad person? Of course not! So, instead of focusing on the end result as a source of motivation, I suggest tapping into how you *feel when you move.* Luxuriate in that. Draw upon that feeling when you need to motivate yourself.

2) Connect with your body's inner desire to move. We are all born ready to move. Inspired by our reflexes, our little infant bodies practice all the movements needed to crawl, walk, reach for objects and so much more. Unfortunately, we then go to school where we have to learn to sit still. As a kid, I hated sitting still in school and used to get in trouble all the time for moving around too much. Then, ironically, as a young adult I had to work at getting myself to move more!

At this moment, it might be difficult for you to imagine that you have an inner desire to move, but it's there—you just have to re-find it.

It was dance that finally helped me to connect to my body's inner desire to move. For me, there's nothing like good music to get my feet tapping and my body swaying. So many adults I know really love to dance, but they suppress the desire, only letting go at the occasional wedding, bar mitzvah or party. What a shame! How about you? Can you put on a favorite dance song and just experience your body wanting to move? Can you let yourself dance around your living room?

If dance or music isn't your thing, and you're having trouble connecting with your inner desire to move, you can use *Touchstone* to help you re-discover your innate love of movement:

♥

Place your hand on your sternum and inhale deeply, several times. Can you remember times in your life when it felt really good to move? How old were you? Were you a kid, or was it more recently? Take a moment to re-experience that feeling. What were you doing? Were you walking in a beautiful place or swimming at the beach, taking a fun exercise class or stretching luxuriously in the early morning?

That feeling is the key. Once you've connected with that memory, imagine how you might re-create that feeling of enjoyment through some form of physical activity today. This brings us to my second guideline: *Make it Enjoyable.*

3) Make it enjoyable. This Guideline reminds us to find fun, enjoyable ways to move/exercise. This needs to be underscored! So many of our attempts to bring more exercise into our lives don't work because we forget about cultivating joy. We assume that physical activity has to be boring or tedious in order to be good for us. Either that, or we choose exercises based on how we imagine they will make us look or feel, rather than on how they actually feel.

If we don't tune into ourselves, we might choose exercises that don't really work for us. We may force ourselves to do things that are too structured—or not structured enough—for our wants and needs. We'll sign up for a class when we really prefer to work out by ourselves, or we'll be unrealistic and try to jam movement activities into the day at times that don't work. These things are more likely to happen if we don't know what our needs and inclinations are. That's why it's so important to tune into ourselves.

No matter what our circumstances, we can find a way to move. There are so many different kinds of physical activities! Here are a few you might consider: walking, biking, dancing by yourself or to a DVD, swimming, yoga, aerobic classes at a gym, rowing, kayaking.

Again, use *Touchstone* to ask yourself:

> • *What kinds of physical activity appeal to me? What do I really enjoy?*
>
> • *What are my needs in terms of physical activity?*
>
> • *What are my preferences? Do I prefer more or less structure?*
>
> • *Do I like to exercise alone or do I prefer being with others? If you like to exercise with others or go to classes, ask: Are there some classes that are convenient for me?*
>
> • *What kinds of physical activities will work for me now in terms of my lifestyle?*

First, imagine; then, experiment. Remember the guideline: *Find your Own Way.* Discover what really works and feels most enjoyable to you.

One way to make movement more enjoyable is by exploring different types of physical activities. Variation of these activities will help you to enjoy exercising more. Another reason to vary your movement/exercise choices is that different types have different benefits. Qigong, Tai Chi, and Yoga, are helpful for gaining flexibility and balance and inner calm. Consider a dance, exercise, or Pilates class at your local Y to gain strength, connectivity, or balance. Enjoy a night out dancing! Want to dance at home? Dance with a wonderful *Moving for Life Dance Exercise for Health* DVD. The movements offered in this DVD will increase flexibility, connectivity, strength, co-ordination and balance. The music is great and it is fun to do!

4) Accept your starting point. Many approaches to exercise assume a set of conditions that may not apply to you. Real lasting change begins when you accept and honor your starting place—whatever that is. Wherever you are with respect to movement and exercise is okay because that is where you are. You may say to yourself: "I want to be totally healthy, strong, fit, and relaxed now." Me too! But if that's not currently the case, thinking that you should already be in a perfect state will only discourage you from doing anything at all.

Pay attention to the way you talk to yourself. Self-talk such as: "Shouldn't I be stronger or more flexible than I am? Why didn't I exercise more before? How can I catch up now? It's too late!" are unhelpful. These thoughts and words may discourage you completely. Instead, focus on your desire to feel better now, and say encouraging words to yourself like "I am glad that I want to exercise more. I wish I had done it before, but I can start now. It is not too late."

5) Start Small. Remember my guideline: *Keep It Small?* It will set you up for success. Begin with bite-size, do-able activities that are *not dependent upon anyone or anything else.* Success with small steps will then lead you naturally to continue to move and exercise over time.

Here's an example of what I mean: Instead of making things complicated . . . just go for a walk. Put on your most comfortable shoes, open the door, go out and walk for just five minutes. That is all! Later, you can find the nicest walking places, the best walking shoes or the best time of day for your walk. What's most important is to just start moving now.

Do you see how beginning with a short daily walk is more of a sure bet than planning to do a long hike once a week? A hike could involve 3-4 hours depending on the difficulty, plus the time it takes to get to the trail, or to perhaps find a hiking companion. Any one of these conditions might be time-consuming and/or prove to become an obstacle. In addition, if you have not hiked much for a while, you may end up with painful muscles, strained joints or other injuries, which could make future exercise difficult, if not impossible. But starting small, with a short walk, sets you up for long-term success.

> *A friend reminded me that when she first told her friends that she had decided to start exercising by walking 10 minutes a day, they seemed puzzled. She received blank stares and a few mumbled questions about it not being enough. Her friends did not relate to the concept of starting small. Today, however, some 20 years later, she walks for 45 minutes 5-7 times a week, and when she doesn't get a chance to walk, she misses it. Meanwhile, those friends who stared at her blankly sold their dusty exercise machines long ago.*

So, try it! Play with setting mini-goals along the way, such as just going as far as your neighbor's garden to look at the flowers, walking to the mailbox to drop off a letter, or dropping by a café for a cup of coffee. Once you have begun, you can focus on motivating yourself to walk more often, for longer periods of time. (See the next chapter on *Walking* for more ideas about how to successfully add walking to your day.)

6) Set realistic goals. We often expect too much of ourselves. For example, you may decide to exercise more in order to become healthier or to lose weight or because your doctor strongly recommends it. Once you make that decision, you might then expect yourself to exercise "religiously" every day.

But then you don't, and that makes you feel self-critical.

You might also—unrealistically—expect "miraculous" results. You may say things to yourself like: "I'll lose 20 pounds, look wonderful in a bathing suit, and be pain-free. This particular exercise will transform my life—after all, it worked for the celebrity on the DVD!" You may expect that doing a certain movement or exercise just a few times will have a profound, instantaneous effect, but this, too, is unrealistic. Even though some exercises can be helpful immediately, repetition is necessary for lasting effects, especially when dealing with chronic or difficult physical conditions.

In short, having unrealistic expectations could sabotage your efforts. When you are realistic about what you can accomplish, you will not only be inspired to continue doing the activities you've chosen, but also to try new things. You will also reduce your stress: a positive spiral!

> *My former daily to-do lists were so unrealistic that they could have taken up every hour of the day. By the evening, I was exhausted—and still not done. Finally, I realized I needed to do something different, so I tried an experiment: I set more manageable goals for myself. When I did so, I discovered that, at the end of the day, I felt a sense of accomplishment, not frustration. This is how the Guideline, Keep It Small, was born.*

7) Assume you can do what you choose. Too often, because of past experiences, we begin something new with the underlying assumption that it won't work. Yes, you may have experienced setbacks, or even injuries, when you tried to bring more exercise into your life before, but don't let those memories stop you! The tools in this book can help to find a way to include more physical activity into your life in a way that actually works.

8) Expect that some days will be harder than others. We expect ourselves to be the same every day, and we expect our bodies to be the same every day, too. But the truth is, on some days you will wake up with a lot of energy, eager to exercise, stretch or do other forms of self-care. On other days, your joints may ache or you may just feel exhausted with very little inclination to move/exercise. Here are strategies to help you get active when you just "don't feel like it."

- Start by doing just *one* stretch or gentle movement. Choose one you enjoy doing and that you think will help you feel a bit better, such as one of the "oiling" movements from my chapter on Joints.

- Use encouraging self-talk statements, such as: *"Let's stretch just for a few minutes,"* or *"How about moving to music, or bouncing on the large ball, or trying that new exercise now?"*

- If you liked how that movement felt, then use encouraging self-talk to inspire yourself to do one more.

9) Expect to get sidetracked…and to begin again. Life happens; interruptions occur. Whether it's because of a bad cold, a family concern, or a trip out of town, you'll find yourself getting sidetracked. When that happens, accept it. Breathe out your disappointment, and find your way back—again and again. And remember, it is easier to get moving again if you are gentle with yourself. Encouraging self-talk such as, "Today, I am walking again," or "Today, I am stretching and moving to ease my tight back" will help you begin anew.

10) Find your own way: Modify exercises to fit your current conditions and abilities. Earlier, we talked about another of my Guidelines: *Find Your Own Way.* This is so important because WE ARE ALL VERY DIFFERENT! We have different physical constitutions and life histories, which means that a way of moving that works for one woman may not be helpful for another. At the suggestion of others, you may exercise too much or do exercises that are not suited to your body that could even lead to pain or injury. That's why it's so important to listen to your body and find your own way. Here's a story to illustrate:

> *One client pushed herself to lift heavy weights and use exercise machines at the gym for years, but never reached her goal of having muscles that looked good enough to her. She came to see me because she had repeatedly injured herself trying to attain that goal. Through our work together, she finally came to accept that her body would not have the shape she wanted. She also accepted that lifting weights and using exercise machines didn't work for her body; in fact, she hadn't enjoyed doing those things for years. Instead, she returned to swimming and biking, activities she had always loved. In giving up on that external goal, she reclaimed the enjoyment of feeling her muscles from the inside. Not only did she truly enjoy these activities, but she stopped injuring herself and got stronger too!*

11) Listen to your body. Your body knows what works for you, and it will tell you, if you listen. So, if you find an exercise that you feel good doing and that you enjoy, consider increasing it. For example, if you stretch once a week and that feels good, add one or two more stretching times, rather than trying to learn a whole new way of releasing tight muscles. If you already enjoy walking, then gradually increase the time that you walk.

12) Add new activities when it is easy to do so. Instead of trying to get clients to force something into their full schedules, I always ask clients for their ideas about how they might add more movement activities *easily* into their day. Most clients come up with some pretty ingenious ideas! Here's a story to illustrate:

> *Gail wanted to find a way to move more. When I asked what movements she did already, she told me that she often stretches while watching TV. I have found that many of my clients enjoy moving on a large ball, so I suggested that she try this in addition to stretching. She agreed, saying that she would like to move 5-10 minutes a day on the ball for the next week. Because she often beat herself up when she didn't exercise on a given day, I made sure to suggest an alternative. On those days, she could gently ask herself: "Why didn't I exercise?" Here's the key: She did so with a sense of genuine curiosity—not with any heavy self-criticism.*

> *After she had integrated moving on the large ball with stretching, I asked her if she could move on the ball at any other time during the day, such as in the morning, or while talking on the phone. I also asked her to check in with her body after she moved on the ball or stretched to notice how she felt. After just a week or two she noticed that she had more energy. Because of this, she began to consider also taking a short walk or a bike ride on the weekend. These things now seemed not only possible, but also enjoyable!*

13) Appreciate all your efforts – always. Remember this *guide-line?* Self-encouragement is critical to progress towards any goal you've set for yourself. It's also critical to bringing more self-care into your life in a sustainable way.

As you know, it is all too easy to focus on what you think you *should have* accomplished, but didn't. But instead, I am inviting you to put the focus on what you *have* accomplished, no matter how small. Cheering yourself on with statements such as "I walked once this week"—even if you had hoped you would walk every day—can make the difference between whether or not you continue to walk next week, and the weeks after that.

Remember: the best exercise for you is the one you actually do!

4

Walking as a Lifetime Activity

In this chapter, I hope to inspire you to consider walking as a way to bring more physical activity into your life. I will show you how to increase the benefits you derive from walking, and to help you to discover the sheer joy of it.

Walking is one of the easiest, most natural, effective and complete ways to move. When you walk, your whole body moves, from your head down to your toes. Walking helps you feel vital and strong, to stand tall and to feel deeply connected—to your body and self, and to your surroundings.

More and more, walking is seen as the ultimate exercise. Andrew Weil promotes the advantages of walking in *8 Weeks to Optimal Health*. Walking, he says, "carries the least risk of injury of any form of exercise. It can provide a complete workout, equal to or better than any other activity. It will satisfy all your exercise requirements throughout your life, even into old age."[8] Contrast this with your making one more attempt at an unrealistic exercise program, or buying an exercise machine that you then avoid like the plague!

The many physical and emotional benefits of walking

Walking is an easy, healthy, and inexpensive way to elevate your mood, deepen your breathing and clear your mind. Here are some more benefits:

- **Walking improves balance,** and that's good, because balance is an essential skill that we need to cultivate, especially as we get older.

- **Walking helps to build bone.** As a weight-bearing activity, walking is important in preventing or rebuilding bone lost from osteoporosis.

- **Walking is a helpful and healthful break** at lunchtime or during energy slumps. Fresh air, a sunny sky or a lovely tree can get us out of a bad mood. The movement of walking can help break the grip of negative thoughts or unhelpful self-talk, such as "I can't take a moment for myself" or "So-and-so is driving me crazy" or "I made a terrible mistake."

- **Fresh solutions to problems often arise when walking alone or with others.** The rhythm of walking is calming to the nervous system. It can free the mind and inspire clear thinking. This is useful when you're alone, and also when you want to talk about a touchy issue with friends, family or co-workers. The rhythm of moving together supports give-and-take, and may prevent both of you from getting locked up in rigid thinking.

- **Walking is a pathway to serenity.** The very act of walking can promote peacefulness. Some spiritual practices include walking slowly and mindfully as a form of meditation.

- **You can walk anywhere. That's the beauty of walking.** You can walk around the block, your apartment, or a mall. You can hike along a nature trail or up the tallest mountain, or to the grocery store. You can walk at a snail's pace or rapidly and vigorously, using walking sticks. You can walk alone, or stroll arm-in-arm with a friend. You can choose which type of walking fits your needs on a specific day, or during a certain period of time. You can walk to music, traffic noise, or to the sounds of birds singing. You can focus on feeling HOW you are walking, or walk without thinking about it at all. Walking is a great way to see the sights, whether fun urban settings or special nature environments.

By the way, did you know that walking for 10 minutes a day, 6 times a week, equals *50 hours* a year? That is a lot more than 0 hours a year! If you build up to 20 minutes a day, 5 times a week, then you are up to 100 minutes a week, or 5200 minutes a year! A short, manageable walk each day adds up to significant benefits over time.

Walking: Suggestions and Tips

1) Dress for safety and comfort. Comfortable shoes are essential if you want to keep walking and protect your feet from injury. Thick socks add cushioning. For more about this topic, see my discussion about feet in the next chapter, *Joints*.

Dress in any clothes that are comfortable and appropriate for the weather and for your particular body. Layers are helpful, especially if you are going through menopause or tend to be sensitive to extremes in temperatures. You can always remove excess clothing.

"You're so bundled up!" I have learned to ignore these comments from people I bump into on my walks. After years of having to shorten my cold weather walks because I felt

121

miserable, I finally figured out what I need to wear to be comfortable walking in a New England winter. In addition to my bulky coat, a friend suggested that I try wearing ski pants. To my surprise, my whole body felt warmer. I even found an inexpensive pair at a thrift shop!

2) Moving your arms doubles the benefits of walking, so keep your hands free. Moving your arms actively makes walking a more aerobic, full body activity. Why miss out on one of the benefits of walking by carrying a water bottle or smartphone in your hand? Instead wear clothes with secure pockets, or strap on a fanny pack for water, keys, cell phone or other items. Swing your arms to expand your lungs and deepen your breathing. Try other ways to move your arms like pumping, flowing, or punching. I do these movements in cold weather to warm myself up.

3) Establish an easy walking rhythm to make walking more automatic and enjoyable. To encourage the ease of automatic moving, walk at the pace of one step per second. Try counting 1-60 to begin, one step at each count.

4) Walk to music: Listening to music will increase the "bounce" in your walk and make it feel more like dancing. It can also help to vary the rhythm and pace of your walking. Experiment to find the pace you enjoy the most.

5) Walking is a perfect time to tune into your body. You can become aware of such things as how your feet feel as they meet the ground; whether your hips sway as you walk or feel stiff; your breathing; and whether or not you look down at the ground or keep your gaze at eye level. You can use this awareness to move more freely. Free your breathing, stand tall and vary your gaze. Dip into this awareness from time to time, and then return to easy, automatic walking.

6) Count your steps: Use an app on your smartphone or a pedometer to motivate you to keep walking. Choose a reasonable goal to start.

7) Choose a destination: Often, people find they walk more when they have a specific goal. Research has shown that city dwellers, who regularly walk to stores, subways, etc., tend to walk more than the rest of us. Here are some helpful questions to ask yourself: *Can I walk to do that errand? Are there places where a walk might be especially enjoyable for me? Would I like to walk in a park, near a river, or on a special street with interesting buildings or gardens? Would exploring a new park or area of town motivate me to walk more?*

8) Walk alone or with a companion: Consider a walking date with a friend or loved one once a week or from time to time. But remember that walking companions are not always available; so, don't make your walks dependent upon having a companion.

Walking and recuperation – a final note

When you are recuperating from an injury or have limitations in your movement, it's very important to remember the *guideline: Keep It Small.* Walk only 5 minutes in one direction, and then return. If that feels okay, then repeat. It's best not to overdo so you don't find yourself far from home and limping in pain. While you're recuperating, exercise caution and think about HOW you are walking to protect your body. Later you can let your walking become more automatic again.

Whatever your situation, please don't give up on walking! Even with an injury, there may be a way for you. For example, many people with knee injuries are able to walk with the support of a soft knee brace or walking sticks or a cane. Ask for advice from others who have sustained a similar injury or had a similar issue. It can be incredibly helpful to get help from a movement/ physical therapist. Just be persistent.

Walking uplifts my body, mind and spirit. I love to walk and I sincerely hope that you will too!

5

Your Joints: Your Key to Staying Flexible and Mobile

Joint flexibility is essential to your quality of life. This chapter specifically emphasizes safe, effective and enjoyable ways to help you maintain, increase—or even regain—the flexibility and freedom that come from optimal joint movement. In addition, I hope you will gain a greater understanding of, and appreciation for, your wonderful joints and how they contribute to joyful living by enabling you to do all the activities you want to do.

Why Joints?

You may find it curious that I'm choosing to focus on moving your joints rather than on strengthening your muscles. You're right; this is a different approach to healthy moving, one that is not commonly discussed. In fact, that's precisely why I am emphasizing your joints: they're vitally important, yet often neglected.

Most physical training methods do focus on strengthening muscles. Strength is, of course, very important. However, sometimes this approach to exercise can have an unintended consequence: you can end up *sacrificing flexibility for strength*. It's sad to see, but many people who exercise faithfully do not do so in ways that also promote flexibility. As a consequence, they lose essential joint mobility. This is not necessary. (I write more about this in the *Growing Older* chapter.)

Flexibility is essential to a good quality of life. Without it, our quality of life can lessen. Let me illustrate with an example that shows how inflexibility in a single area—your neck— can impact your life.

In many settings, such as crossing a street, walking on uneven surfaces, and especially in new situations, it is important to first visually scan the area in order to become oriented; this helps us feel safe. To scan effectively, we need to be able to turn our head from side to side, down, up and all around. This kind of neck mobility is also necessary for safe driving. If we can't move our neck in all these ways, we may feel insecure about our ability to navigate the world. This can, in turn, inhibit our willingness to try new experiences, limiting opportunities for learning and growth. This example clearly demonstrates how physical flexibility can affect our emotional and mental flexibility; if we are inflexible physically, we risk becoming rigid or restricted in our thinking as well.

When it comes to retaining our flexibility, there's a lot of truth to the phrase: "Use it or lose it." That's why I want to inspire you to cultivate flexibility.

With regard to how we move, we all have habits; we move certain areas more than others, either because of preference, or because of the usual physical activities that we generally engage in. Unfortunately, our habitual movements don't always add up to exercising all our joints; many get neglected. Even worse, our habits may prevent some joints from moving as they should. Our necks, in particular, often become tight because so many of us hold them in one position as we stare at screens. When we don't move a joint regularly and fully over time, we can lose mobility—not only in that joint, but also in whole areas of our body. That's because *everything really is connected*.

If you are still flexible, that's great, and you'll want to maintain that. It is far easier to maintain flexibility and prevent restricted movement than it is to regain it once it is lost. If, however, you have begun to lose some flexibility—if, for example, you relate to the story of lost neck flexibility —I want to emphasize that you can begin to regain your flexibility by working with your joints. In this chapter, I will show you how.

Getting to Know Your Beautiful Joints

It is easy to overlook the importance of joints, but here's a little-known fact: your body has *360 joints*! In the foot alone you have 33 joints. Your joints make it possible for you to move in all the many wonderful ways that you can, from your head down to your toes and everything in between. For example, right now, I can write this chapter on my computer because the joints in my fingers and hands allow for so many movement possibilities. Think of all the many things you can do with your fingers and hands, from playing an instrument to knitting a lovely sweater, to stroking a baby's face, and so much more.

So, what are joints? Simply put, a joint is an area where the two ends of separate, adjoining bones meet. The two bones are united and held together by strong bands of connective tissue called ligaments. Your ligaments guide the movement of your joints, as well as stabilize them. Your tendons then connect your muscles to bone and also help stabilize your joints. Your muscles power your movements, but you need flexible joints to move well.

Joints are the place where two bones meet. The ends of each of the two bones are shaped such that they fit together well, while also allowing for optimal movement. For example, in the hip joint, the long, large bone of the upper leg (the femur) ends in the shape of a ball. This meets, and fits inside the rounded socket of the pelvic bones.

The type of movement a joint is capable of is determined by the shape of the joint and by how the ligaments are attached. For instance, some joints are described as "hinge" joints; others are ball-and-socket joints. Hinge joints allow movement along one axis, whereas ball-and-socket joints allow for movement in all directions. The elbow is an example of a hinge joint; it allows you to flex or extend your hand along one axis. When you flex or bend your elbow, your hand moves close to the center of your body; when you extend it, your hand moves away from the center of your body. The ankle and knee are also hinge joints, but the hip is a ball-and-socket joint. Can you visualize why?

Here's a fun activity to learn more about how your joints help you to move.

Walk around the room as you usually do for a minute. Now walk, but don't bend your knees or your ankles. Keep your arms straight. You may feel like a toy soldier or a robot. Now take another turn, allowing your knees and ankles to bend while you walk, and relax your arms.

- Which kind of walking did you enjoy more? Which one felt more flexible?

Reconnect with Your Joints

Unfortunately, most of us neglect our joints until they either begin to hurt or become stiff and rigid, inhibiting our ability to move; then we *really* notice them. It might begin with a feeling of stiffness in the morning, or a discomfort that grows into pain when we engage in certain movements. For example, my ankles generally feel fine; it's only when I don't walk or move much in the course of a day that they feel stiff and need loosening.

How about you? Do you experience stiffness or pain in any of your joints, perhaps when you first get out of bed in the morning? Or when you get up to move after sitting for long stretches? If so, these pages contain hope.

Want to maintain or restore your joint mobility? Get out the oil can!

Have you ever wished that you could put some oil in your knee or another joint when it felt creaky, like a rusty hinge? Well, you can! You can regain or ease joint movement because of a wonderful substance called synovial fluid. Think of this fluid as a magic formula you can use. Synovial fluid is the "oil" that keeps joints mobile and flexible.

You can encourage your joints to produce more synovial fluid by doing specific slow, small movements. This is what I mean by "oiling" the joint. When you move a joint gently and slowly, synovial fluid is produced. This fluid literally helps the "rusty" areas to move with less friction. It also renews and nourishes the important cartilage that surrounds, and provides cushioning for, each joint. Yes, even your joints need nourishment.

For example, to keep my ankles from becoming too stiff to move freely, I move them in a circle in that slow, small way for 1-2 minutes in the morning and then again, right before bed. I also sprinkle this movement throughout the day. I do this when I sit and talk on the phone, or watch TV, or just before I go for a walk.

This simple ankle movement, which requires only a few moments, is a good investment of my time and attention. It will not only release my ankle stiffness, but its effects ripple positively throughout my body. Freer ankles help keep my knees, hip joints and back moving with greater ease. I see the benefits of oiling movements in both clients who are healing from injuries and for those who just want to move more freely.

Fortunately, simple and easy joint movements like this one can relieve the feeling of temporary stiffness and keep our joints flexible for the long-term, but remember: the results won't happen instantly. They only happen over time, with repetition. However, the good news is that the movements suggested here don't take a lot of time. A few minutes each day is helpful, whether first thing in the morning or sprinkled here and there throughout the day. Here's a story to inspire you:

> *A friend who is close to 90 became concerned because she was having difficulty turning her neck when driving. Never one to give up, she asked for my advice. I suggested she try the neck movements in this chapter. Slowly but surely, her neck began to free up. She regained her ability to drive with ease, and her confidence increased as well.*

Isn't it wonderful that your body produces substances like the synovial fluid so that you can keep moving? These kinds of movements feel good and are easy to do—what could be better? So, let's learn how to oil our joints.

What does oiling your joints feel like? Oiling has a quality of ease, leisureliness and sensuality. It has a sliding or gliding quality, and a sense of effortlessness. It is comfortable, neither straining nor difficult. Note: If you've done many strengthening exercises in the past, you may tend to approach these movements with a lot of effort. This is different. Easy does it. A little oiling movement goes a long way.

Mobility Exercises for Specific Joints

In this next section, I'm going to take you through exercises to increase the mobility in your joints. It's *how* these exercises are done that make them effective, so I've included some principles to guide how you approach these exercises:

Pick one area to start. I'm going to suggest that you start with your smaller joints—those in your hands, feet, wrists or ankles. Loosening up the smaller joints first makes it easier to move the bigger joints, which are closer to the middle of your body. For example, to free up your shoulder, it helps to first loosen your fingers, wrists and forearms. In a similar way, if you move your neck first, it helps to free your whole spine.

Apply these principles to all of the suggested movements:

- Focus on moving a specific joint or area.

- Start with s-m-a-l-l and s-l-o-w and gentle movements. Remember you're aiming for ease and effortlessness, so bigger is not necessarily better.

131

- Stay within your comfort range to ensure that you don't strain or tighten your muscles and joints. Stop if you feel pain in your joint, or if your joint feels stiff and is hard to move.

- After pausing, try an even smaller version of the same movement. This smaller version oils the joint even more.

- If a joint felt hard to move, switch to a nearby area that is easier to move, or move a joint closer to your fingers or feet. Then return to the area that felt hard to move, and move it just a little.

- Breathing freely always helps movement, so go ahead and sigh or blow out the air as you move!

Here's a reminder of two important Guidelines to apply to these joint movements:

1) *Make Your Day Work for You: Start your day out right.* You will get the maximum benefits of these joint movements when you do them in the morning.

2) *Find your own way.* Be Playful. Begin with any movement you chose. Put on music, and move in any way that feels good and is enjoyable.

Make these a part of your day! Joint movements become even more effective when you sprinkle them throughout your day. Try them waiting on line, on the phone, watching TV, wherever.

Your upper body

Hands, Fingers and Wrists:

- Slowly open and close your hands. Start small. Find a soothing rhythm to the movement.

- Gradually increase the opening and closing movements.

- Alternate closing your hands with your thumb out, or by making a fist with your thumb tucked in.

- Bend your wrists forward and back. Circle your wrists. Combine these wrist movements with opening and closing your hands.

Free up your shoulder joints:

It is vital to regularly encourage full movement in our shoulders to prevent limitations that can occur over time. Full range of movement in your shoulders is necessary for many daily tasks, such as washing your hair, cleaning your house, as well as many enjoyable activities like gardening, sports or dancing. Here are some activities you can do to prevent loss of shoulder mobility:

- **Figure 8's** - With your arms by your sides, start to make small figure 8 movements with your fingers as if you had ink on your finger tips and were drawing these shapes on paper on the ground. Then, gradually make the figure 8's larger and larger. Continue the figure 8's as you bring your arms up to waist level, and then above your head as high as is comfortable.

- **Elbow Circles** - Bend your elbow and place your hand on top of your shoulder, or as close to your shoulder as is comfortable. Make small circles in the air with your elbow in one direction, then the other. Start with circles the size of the palm of your hand. Gradually make the circle larger. Note: This exercise can be done standing or lying on each side with your knees bent and your head on a pillow.

- **Arm Circle Movements** - Lie on your side. Allow your knees to bend comfortably. Rest your head on a pillow. Lengthen your arm out, but allow your elbow to be softly bent. Imagine that you are drawing a large circle around your body with your hand and fingertips. Be sure to go in both directions. Start with a smaller circle and then make it larger. If you feel any stiffness or discomfort, make the movements smaller. Remember that you want the movement to feel smooth and enjoyable.

Please Note: The previous shoulder movements are not recommended for the condition known as "frozen shoulder," which is a serious problem. If you suspect this is happening to you, please find a good practitioner to help you. Don't wait. The sooner you get help, the sooner you can recover. This is an example of listening to your body.

Your Neck

The neck is an area where most of us hold tension, so restriction can easily develop. That's why it's so important to oil your neck joint. As you read earlier in this chapter, keeping your neck flexible helps you feel safe and open to new experiences;

it also frees your whole spine and prevents pain. Your neck moves in many directions, and we will address all of them. Your neck will really appreciate doing movements that are not forced in any way, movements that are slow and small, so take a moment to review the guiding principles at the beginning of this exercise section.

- Move your chin towards your chest by looking down and then back up again to look straight ahead. Do this as a small rocking movement, looking down just a little and then straight ahead. Then try a larger movement. Exhale as you bring your chin down and inhale as you bring it up.

- Now bring your head back to look up towards the ceiling, then back down to look straight ahead.

- Turn your head to the left and to the right, gradually increasing the amount of turn.

- Tilt your neck towards your right shoulder, then towards your left shoulder.

- Bring all the movements together and make a slow, small circle, while inhaling and exhaling deeply.

It's especially helpful to do neck movements when you are sitting at a computer or after driving, but you can do them just about any time, such as when standing over the stove or in a line. They really do make a difference!

Your spine

Here's a favorite movement of mine, one often done in yoga and other classes. Lie on you back with your knees bent, and your feet on the floor. Then:

- Slowly move your head from side to side

- Slowly move your knees just a little to one side, then the other

- Now bring your head to one side, while your legs go to the other.

- Continue and increase the movements in both directions

Your lower body

Your feet - Massage and Move to keep flexibility. One of the most effective ways to improve and maintain flexibility in your toes and feet, as well as the rest of your leg, is to massage them for 1-5 minutes a day. This can also relieve pain.

- Before you begin keep this in mind: there are 26 bones and 33 joints in your feet.

- Pay particular attention to the middle of your foot. Gently and slowly move as many of the joints in your foot as you can. I often imagine that I am "mushing around" my feet.

- Gently move and massage all parts of your toes.

Note: If it's hard to reach your feet, put your feet on a small stool while sitting. Experiment until you find a position that works.

I do this massage for one minute every morning to keep my feet flexible. It works! If ever I don't do this quick routine, I often develop pain in my feet. Luckily, this massage also helps to relieve pain, too. I've found that sometimes when I go for an especially long walk my feet will start to hurt. I sit or lean against something, take off my shoes, rub my feet for a minute or two, and then slowly circle my ankles in both directions. Then I'm ready to go enjoy walking again!

Rock and Roll your Feet - This is another way to oil your feet. Remove your shoes. Sit with your feet on the ground.

- Lift your heel up until only your toes are on the ground.

- Lift your toes up until only your heel is on the ground. Wiggle your toes up and down.

Your Ankle

Here's the easy ankle movement I referred to earlier in this chapter. I sprinkle this movement here and there throughout each day:

- While sitting, bring one foot up and down several times.

- Circle your foot in both directions.

Your hip joints: An exercise with the large ball

One of the most effective and enjoyable ways to encourage full and free movement of your hips is by moving on the large ball—especially by making circling movements while sitting.

- Sit on the ball with your feet only hip-width apart. Begin with a small circling movement.

- Increase the circling movement with your hips, until you find the largest circle that you can do easily without any discomfort in both directions.

The following Breath Wave movement is another option for hip mobility, and much more.

Oil Your Whole Body: The Breath Wave

Here is a wonderful whole body movement that feels delicious and has many benefits. It lubricates and warms up the joints of your spine and hips, activates the pelvic floor muscles and releases back tension, tightness and pain from sitting. What could be better! Try it when you wake up, or before bed. It also works wonders as a short break from sitting at the computer. Add some sexy music and it can be a sensual warm up! And don't worry about "getting it right"—having fun and being relaxed is much more important!

The Breath Wave – Sitting

- Sit with your feet flat on the floor. Sit forward in the chair. Don't lean on the back of the chair.

- Place your hands on the top of your hipbones.

- To warm up rock your pelvis forward and back in small movements. Let the movement become as easy and effortless as possible. Let your hands ride along with the forward and backward movement of your pelvis.

- On the exhale, tilt your pelvis back, blow out the air and curl up your body forward like a ball.

- On the inhale, tilt your pelvis forward. Open up and expand your chest, arms, and torso and bring your head up. Let your whole body expand in all directions and as you inhale.

Note: The Breath Wave can also be done standing. Please refer to chapter 12, *Turn to Your Breath*. There, you will also find the Move and Breathe Activity, another whole body movement.

Use Oiling Movements to Warm Up

Oiling movements make a great warm-up before you engage in other larger, faster or more strenuous moving activities. And while we're on the topic, I want to emphasize the importance of warm-ups, especially if you have any movement restrictions or injuries. Warm-ups often involve stretching. Stretching can be extremely helpful—but it can also be problematical.

A word about stretching

Many approaches to exercise/movement, including yoga, emphasize stretching your muscles. Stretching your muscles is a very important aspect of exercise, but its relationship to joint flexibility can be misunderstood. Stretching is common-ly thought of as a way to increase joint flexibility. However, stretching may or may not contribute to the flexibility of specific joints. Here's why: When we stretch our muscles, we stretch our joints as well. Most times, this is done in a very positive fashion, but other times, without realizing it, we *over-*

stretch our joints. This can overtax the ligaments that hold the bones together, causing strain—or even injury.

It is important to stretch in a way that cares for *both joints and muscles*. It's vital to stretch gently and slowly, starting small and not forcing more movement than is comfortable. And it's essential that you listen to your body. I, for example, have injured myself stretching in so-called "gentle" classes. You may need to modify the way you stretch to suit your body.

That's also good advice with respect to the movements offered here. Find what works for you in terms of keeping your joints flexible, supple and functional. It's also a good idea to take classes or work with a movement therapist if you are healing from an injury, or have a serious restriction of movement.

Now that we've come to the end of chapter, take a moment to tune into your body.

Stand up and walk around the room. Do you feel stiff anywhere, in your neck perhaps?

Does it feel hard or easy to walk? Can you choose one area to oil now?

Would you enjoy massaging your feet for a few minutes?

Remember, you can oil your joints anytime, wherever you are.

6

Rest and Renewal

Our bodies operate in accordance with a natural rhythm. Your heart, for example, pauses for a brief moment between each beat. There is also a natural pause in your breath, a space after each exhalation and before each new inhalation.

This is the wisdom of the body: a circle that moves from exertion to rest and renewal, and then begins again. Exertion, followed by rest and renewal. We embrace self-care when we replicate this natural rhythm in our lives. Unfortunately, our culture puts a high value on just one part of the cycle: exertion. The idea that we can be "on the go" all the time is a kind of society-wide false belief—one that is growing even stronger with the use of smartphones. This false belief exerts a very powerful influence. As a consequence, many women do not value the importance of rest and renewal.

Working, working, working – day and night

Whether you work outside the home, run a business from your home, or are retired, it's all too easy to work all the time. Even if you don't "work" *per se*, you may still feel the urge to keep busy. You may, for example, involve yourself in artistic projects or volunteering for community or religious organizations. You may plug away, making home improvements or helping out your parents, children, grandchildren or neighbors. All of these things are worthwhile, of course, but are you doing too much—without taking time to rest and renew? Most likely, the answer to this question was yes. If that's the case, read on, starting with this story:

> *One day, a friend confided in me that her husband was complaining that she was working all the time even though she had retired. As we spoke, she realized that whenever she had a few free moments, she would always try to squeeze in just one more task, such as writing an email on behalf of one of her community projects. The truth was that she did not pause at all, and her sense of feeling driven to work all the time was having a negative impact on both her marriage and her personal well-being. For example, she would often skip her daily walk because she "had no time."*
>
> *Through our conversation, my friend realized that she could find ways to relax. We discovered that it worked best for her to schedule specific times for her self-care activities, like walking, and also for fun dates with her husband.*

Given our cultural conditioning, the ability to rest and renew adequately is actually a skill to be learned. If acquired, it will serve your health and well-being throughout your life. In this chapter, I will remind you of a variety of fun ways to rest, renew, refresh and restore, including taking short breaks.

Take a break!

In our culture, it is all too easy for us to push beyond our reserves, and to do so habitually. When that's the case, life becomes like one big race; we just keep running without ever pausing to catch our breath. To make matters worse, many of us think we have to wait for weekends or vacations to take time for ourselves. This is not so! *Momentary pauses taken throughout each day can do wonders to rebuild our depleted stores of energy.* Not only is this approach much more natural, it's also more efficient, and it can be accomplished quickly and easily, as you will see.

Why are breaks so important?

You need them. You will actually accomplish more when you take a break. *You deserve them.* You will feel refreshed and be more efficient.

New ideas or solutions to a problem often come during a breather. If you've completed a task, even a moment's pause to mark that completion helps you shift gears and get ready for the next task or activity. A sense of completion is important to our well-being, but dashing from one task to another without a break makes it difficult to experience either the satisfying sense of accomplishment or the delicious feeling of relief that comes from finishing a task. (Note: A completion is a type of *transition.* I'll speak more about this important concept in a later chapter, *Your Relationship with Time.*)

In sum, breaks are very beneficial, and we need them. But do we take them? I've asked that question of clients many times over the years. Here are some typical responses:

- *Are you kidding? I don't have time for a break!*

- *What do you mean? If I stop even for a few minutes I'll never get going again. I'll just become a big lump!*

- *Are you suggesting that I lie down and gently stretch to*

143

relieve my painful back? Worse still – do you expect me to stop what I am doing and do nothing for a few minutes?

- *I would love to take a break but whenever I do, I just feel more tired.*

- *If I stop, I'll forget what I need to do.*

Do any of these responses seem familiar to you?

Our body and mind frequently issue calls for attention and care, but our constant busy-ness causes us to ignore these messages. That is a habit we can break. Here's how to begin:

Use Encouraging self-talk

Much of our resistance to taking breaks comes from our false beliefs, especially the belief that we do not deserve self-care. Encouraging self-talk is the antidote. Here are some examples:

- *It's okay to take a break. In fact, it's natural.*

- *I'll feel more energized and be able to think more clearly after I rest.*

- *Yes, this is important to think about, but not now. Right now, I need a break.*

- *I can call so-and-so this afternoon. The bills can wait— there is time.*

A quick pause—time to check in with yourself.

When we get caught up in doing, doing, doing without a

breather, it is difficult to notice how we are actually feeling. But tuning into what our bodies are signaling—and not ignoring or overriding those signals—is essential to self-care. Because of our conditioning, we may need to pay extra attention in order to learn this skill. To illustrate, here's a story from my own life:

One day, when I took a break from writing, I suddenly realized that I was very cold. However, I was writing easily, and so I didn't want to stop to get warmer clothes. Later, when I thought more about it, I realized that if someone I loved was feeling cold, I would have stopped whatever I was doing and brought them some warmer clothes immediately. I was puzzled by my reluctance to "bother" making myself more comfortable, even though I knew that when I feel cold I don't think as clearly.

Another time while writing, I stopped to make myself a favorite nourishing drink and quickly returned to my writing with the drink in hand. Then I remembered that I could take a little break to savor this delicious drink! Why not? I could enhance my break even further by playing an inspiring song. A few minutes later, I felt restored and ready to continue writing. This incident again reminded me how a good break can help me to accomplish more and with greater ease!

In the midst of it all, no matter how caught up you are in being productive, it is important to pause and connect with yourself and listen to your body. *Touchstone* is a good way to do that.

Place your hand on your heart, and exhale out a few times. Close your eyes and ask yourself some questions, such as these:

- *How am I feeling? Am I comfortable?*

- *Do I want to continue what I am doing now?*

- *Am I making progress on my task, or am I spinning my wheels because I am too tired?*

- *What do I need right now? Am I feeling hungry, cranky or about to have a low-blood-sugar crash? Is there anything else I need? A walk, a cup of tea, a warm sweater?*

- *Can I do this task or activity using less effort? Can I relax my tight shoulders and let myself breathe more fully?*

Sometimes just stop what you're doing—and rest.

I've learned over and over that even a short rest replenishes me and gives me more energy for the remainder of the day. I especially need to rest if I did not sleep well the night before. However, I did not always know this. In the past, I tended to push myself beyond my available energy and into a state I call "overdrive." When I was in that state, I'd ignore my body's signals and continue working, even though I felt tired. On those days, I often felt exhausted after dinner. If I was supposed to go out, I'd force myself, but I wouldn't really have the energy to truly enjoy the evening. Then, because I'd wound myself up to keep going all day, I found it hard to unwind at night, which often resulted in poor sleep. Before I knew it, I was in a downward spiral.

Does this downward spiral feel familiar to you? If so, it's time to break it. But even if we *do* stop to rest, we might not know quite how to derive the most benefit. Here are some tips and pointers for how to make the most of a rest break.

Double the benefit of your rest break: Breathe

Exhale a few times. Blow out any tension. Do so with an audible sigh or sound. It's okay! Feel your muscles let go and relax as you exhale. Then, inhale naturally. Imagine that each inhale deepens your relaxation. (We'll talk a lot more about the rejuvenating power of the breath in an upcoming chapter.)

Lie down and take a load off

I like the expression "take a load off." To me, it's an invitation to sit, or even better, to lie down, unwind, and put my feet up. *Just lying down is very valuable in and of itself; you don't have to fall asleep to enjoy the benefits.* When you lie down, you relieve your bones and muscles—especially those in your feet, back, and neck—of all the work they do to support you to stand upright. This is especially important if you have injuries or problem areas that hurt, or you have been sitting too long at a computer.

- *Take the time to make yourself as comfortable as possible.* Place a large pillow (or a few small ones) under your knees when you lie on your back.

- As you do so, *allow yourself to feel supported.* This feeling of support brings about deep relaxation, re-alignment and the release of stress. Healing modalities such as Constructive Rest and Restorative Yoga bear this out.

Now let's look at another type of rest break, one we may have forgotten: the nap.

Celebrate the Nap!

Can you recall a time on vacation or on a quiet day off when, if you felt tired, you simply allowed yourself to lie down and fall asleep? Can you remember the feeling of your body letting go, deliciously melting into the sand or the couch? Wasn't it satisfying? Remember dozing off, stretching lazily and then feeling good when you awoke? Could you allow yourself to enjoy more of these rest naps—maybe every day?

Naps do work. To inspire you, I'd like to share a success story about napping:

> One day, a client, a man in his late 60's, arrived at my office for a session. He was healthy, successful in his profession, and had a wonderful, easy demeanor. Clearly, he greatly enjoyed his life. Intrigued, I asked him what had helped him to be so accomplished and also so relaxed. He said that he had taught himself to fall asleep for short periods (10-20 minutes) during the day and to wake up refreshed! This enabled him to work effectively and to release stress during the day so that it didn't accumulate.

Here's another success story:

> A friend, who is in her 70's, recently experienced for the first time the deep value of lying down for 10-15 minutes. Up until then, whenever she tried to nap, she could never fall asleep, so she assumed it was pointless to rest at all. Instead, she tended to keep busy until she dropped, which was generally sometime after eating dinner. All the while, she frequently complained about feeling too exhausted to do anything at night but watch boring TV shows. Then one day, she let herself rest during the day. That evening, a friend

*invited her out for a spontaneous visit. To her amazement,
her rest had given her the energy to say yes to the invitation!
That night became a turning point. From then on, she began
to give herself the gift of rest.*

Despite the benefits of resting, many women resist doing it
just as they resist the idea of taking naps. Here are some reasons they give for this reluctance:

- *"I don't nap because I wake up grumpy."* I have heard
  this phrase uttered many times. These women report
  that if they lie down intending to rest for only a few
  minutes, they will sleep for an hour or more later, and
  wake up feeling grumpy. I suggest that they set an
  alarm to awaken them in 20-30 minutes. For most,
  this is the optimal length of time for a nap.

- *"I shouldn't need a nap. Only old folks take naps!"* I hear
  this phrase a lot as well, but it's a false belief, and it
  prevents us from listening to our bodies. We believe
  that needing a nap means we don't have the energy
  we used to, which can scare us. We can also associate
  naps with being sick. However, it seems foolish to let
  that belief prevent us from enjoying the big pay-off
  of having more energy to enjoy life! I have talked to
  many people in their 60s, 70s and 80s who say that,
  with the help of a short daily nap, they have as much
  energy as they always did. They don't care about what
  others may think—they like the energy!

Learn to nap—It's never too late! In some cultures, it is usual to nap or rest during the day. This is not so in American
culture, at least at the moment. Nonetheless, a nap can still
become part of your daily routine.

I am relearning how to nap. I try to plan my days so that I can have 15-30 minutes available for a post-lunch nap. Once, I could fall asleep easily; now, I fall asleep only rarely. However, I always feel better after lying down to rest— even if only for a few minutes. To encourage the possibility of sleep, I signal my body that it's time to rest: I lie on my back with a pillow under my knees, put on my eye mask and play soothing music or a guided relaxation. This adds to my feeling of renewal, whether or not I fall asleep. If I only have time for a 5- or 10-minute break, I'll still lie down and do some gentle joint oiling movements.

Give yourself the opportunity to rest and maybe nap, too. You might just like it!

Breaks Come in Many Different Shapes and Sizes

Sometimes, resting is the most recuperative thing we can do for ourselves. If you feel tired, lying down or gently stretching can feel wonderful, especially if your neck or back aches. Other times, you don't need a rest so much as a change of pace.

Sometimes we crave the balance that engaging in a different type of activity can bring, especially one that uses different muscles or different ways of thinking. When we feel that way, it's time to shift gears. Shift gears to lift your mood and refresh your energy. Stop what you're doing, for example, if you have been working at the computer for a long time, and switch to a completely different type of activity. You could rest or you may find it even more refreshing to putter around your home or office or in the garden. You might want to do something playful, like bouncing on the large ball, or dancing to an upbeat song. These kinds of activities offer a balance to sitting and focusing, both mentally and visually, on the computer. Here's a story to illustrate:

Whenever I have a deadline that requires my sitting at my desk and working on the computer for many hours, I find creative ways to break it up and change the pace. Frequently, I do little household tasks. For example, I might wash a few dishes, hang out laundry, go to the mailbox, or fold clothes. This helps in multiple ways: the household chores don't pile up, and doing them also gets me up and moving, a good change from sitting.

Because our lives are *so* busy, it's good to remember the Guideline: *Keep it Small.* Here are some other examples of breaks that take almost no time at all, but can have a big effect:

- **Let it go** – Release difficult physical and/or emotional feelings, such as tension, tiredness, or aggravation. (My 5-Minute Helpers, *Blow It out, Shake Out* and *Move!* are particularly helpful here. For a review of all the Helpers, see the chapter on *Return to Balance.*)

- **Revive & re-charge** - Get some fresh air, wash your face, light a scented candle, or do some self-massage such as body drumming. To relieve stiffness or aches, do movements to oil your joints. (See *Joints* chapter.)

- **Renew yourself through food or drink** - Choose foods or drinks that will boost your energy for an extended period of time, rather than only briefly, leaving you depleted shortly after.

Take a moment now to tune in and ask yourself: *Do I need a break now? If so, what would be most restful, renewing and replenishing for me at this time—a stretch, a walk, a cup of tea, or a change of pace?* Then give yourself permission to take the kind of break that best meets your needs at the moment.

In the next part of this chapter we will look at another important part of rest and renewal: planning a renewing and relaxing vacation, whether for just a day trip or a longer break.

Vacations – What kind do you like?

Vacations are all different. I have had many that were great, others that were miserable, and some that required a week of recovery! Some vacations were too costly, leaving me with a large credit card bill that drained away the benefits.

After a couple of less-than-ideal experiences, I began to ask people about their vacations, seeking to learn if my experience was unique. Many reported that their vacations, as well, were less than satisfying. Often, it seemed, what they had imagined didn't match the reality. Why? I began to conclude that there is a real art to planning a vacation that truly meets your needs.

Good planning might start by realizing that there are *many types of vacations, and each meets different kinds of needs.* At one end of the spectrum, there are quiet, stay-in-one-place vacations, including "staycations," where you take time off but stay at home. At the other end of that continuum are trips that involve a lot of moving around. These vacations are more demanding. Organized tours, for example, generally require adhering to a fixed schedule, adjusting to different situations and being in the company of lots of other people, along with all the accompanying packing and re-packing. And then there's everything in between.

Each type of vacation can be good, of course. But when planning a vacation, it's important to ask yourself: *What type of vacation would best meet my needs now?* If you're planning a vacation way into the future, take time to look ahead at your schedule, and imagine how you might feel at that time. Will you be exhausted from being very busy, or ready for an adventure after being cooped up all the winter? Then, if you are going with someone else, you need to talk about how to meet *both* sets of needs and desires. But the first step is determining what *you* need and want.

As we discussed in the chapter on The Five Practices, discovering what you need and want—let alone anticipating our future needs—is not always easy for many of us. One way to begin to attune to what kind of a vacation you want is to recall where you most love to be, the place or environment that continuously calls to you. As you bring it to mind, think also about how you most enjoy spending your time there.

My favorite vacation place is a beach. When I am there, I love being out-of-doors as much as possible, including eating meals outdoors. I enjoy swimming, biking, walking, and having lots of time to just sit and be: time for watching the waves on the beach and taking in the sunset; time for napping, stretching, daydreaming, journal writing. I also enjoy having the leisure to cook delicious meals inspired by fresh seafood and vegetables.

I invite you to do *Touchstone* now to envision the best kind of vacation for you. Place your hand on your sternum, breathe out any other thoughts, and take the time to ask yourself these questions:

- *What are my needs at this time? Do I need a restful vacation or a stimulating one?*

- *What kind of vacation would best meet those needs?*

- *How can I plan this vacation so that I meet my needs and really enjoy myself?*

For more support on this, refer back to the Practice of *Discovering What You Need and Want,* and the part of the Guideline *Make Your Day Work for You* called *Anticipate Your Needs.*

Don't Forget Day Trips! We all need periodic refreshers. If you feel that need, but can't take a longer vacation, consider a day trip to some special place near where you live. This is an economical way to bring newness and adventure into your life. To plan your excursion, look at guidebooks to discover special beautiful, natural places in your area. Check out local papers or search on-line for events, such as festivals, art fairs or outdoor concerts. Ask your friends about their secret day trip places. I'm often surprised to learn about new places I've never been to that are close by:

One year, rather than organizing a party for my birthday, I wanted to take a fun day trip. In researching where to go, I serendipitously discovered that my favorite artist was having an exhibit at a museum only an hour away. While there, I also discovered two new places to walk. These places were beautiful, with breathtaking views. The day was a celebration!

I want to add another idea here: the half-day trip:

For many years my husband and I regularly went to a park on Sundays. The park was a 30-minute drive from our home along a very scenic roadway. The park had lots of easy walking trails, and stunning lake views. Then, for some reason, we got out of that habit. When we finally started going again regularly, we realized how much this weekly jaunt renewed us.

In closing, I hope this chapter inspires you to rest and renew more. Remember, as stated in other parts of this book, it takes both time and practice to learn new habits and to incorporate more self-care into our daily lives. I still need to remind myself to pause and notice when I am tired and in need of renewal. And sometimes I have to convince myself to honor my need to rest or shift gears. So always be gentle with yourself. Remember the guideline, *Keep It Small*, and check out my 5-Minute Helpers for quick, effective ways to renew.

7

Sleep

Sleep is a wonderful and necessary part of life. It replenishes and renews us. While we sleep, our body makes needed repairs, all without our having to undertake the unpleasant job of searching for the right repair person! It seems as though all we need to do is to just lie down and fall asleep—and stay asleep. Unfortunately, in our fast-paced culture, that's not always so simple. Why?

Sleep is our most natural fortifier and source of replenishment and renewal, and yet many of us struggle with it. There have been countless books written about sleep and more appear each day. That's because the number of people who are having difficulty is growing by leaps and bounds. If you have sleep issues, you are certainly not alone.

Sleep is a complicated issue. It's something I too struggle with from time to time. Most nights, I sleep just fine. At other times, when I cannot sleep, I can figure out exactly what has interfered, and take steps to change it—although sometimes it's because the moon is full! Then there are times when I can't sleep and have no idea what the problem is. Difficulty with sleep is not always an easy problem to solve because there are numerous factors involved. However, you can learn how to invite a good night's sleep.

In this short chapter, I will share the wisdom I have gathered about sleep from my work with clients, my own experience, and the scientific research that makes sense to me. I've included a range of practical tools to help you prepare for sleep by relaxing your body and calming your nervous system, as well as ideas for how to problem-solve your own sleep issues. As you read this, keep in mind two of my Guidelines, *Find What Works for You* and *Anticipate your Needs* which will help you discover your best path to a good night's sleep.

Obstacles to a good night's sleep

"In the past 50 years, there has been a decline in average sleep duration and quality, with adverse consequences on general health," begins a paper entitled, *Evening use of light-emitting eReaders negatively affects sleep, circadian timing, and next-morning alertness.*[9] This paper, based on research from Harvard Medical School amongst other places, highlights the relationship between the ubiquitous blue light that emanates from our electronic devices—our computers, phones and TV screens—and sleep disruption.

Within the scientific community there is a general acceptance of the physiological effects of this light and its effect on sleep. This blue light suppresses melatonin, otherwise known as the sleep hormone. This, in turn, throws off the body's natural clock, or circadian rhythm, the biological mechanism responsible for a restful sleep.[10] Even our small electronic devices emit light sufficient to miscue the brain and promote wakefulness,[11] making it harder to fall and stay asleep, especially when we use these devices right before bedtime.

Ironically, many people use these electronics right before bedtime because they believe they will help them relax. Evidence suggests that these devices can have the opposite effect. Rather than calming your nervous system, watching TV, for example, can hype it up. Using the computer to surf or check email just before bedtime tends to stimulate the brain, rather than calm it. The fact that many of us get limited exposure to natural light during the day may compound this effect even further. Because the potential for sleep interference is so strong, many sleep experts advise turning off these devices 1-2 hours before bedtime. [12]

It is easy to get "hooked" on watching TV right before bed, especially when you are tired, but you may actually be trading away your sleep time. In addition, when you are watching TV or working (or surfing) on the computer, it is very easy to block out any signals your body might be trying to send you about what you need. For example, I have noticed many times that as soon as I turn off the TV or the computer, I'm suddenly aware of being deeply tired, very hungry, or that my back is stiff and achy. My body was sending these signals all along, but I was too "mesmerized" to notice!

It's important that we attend to these signals, and not override them. When you are tired, but ignore your exhaustion to push on, it can feel like you're getting a second wind. This is an illusion, and it can come at a big price. When you push beyond your natural energy and shift into an overdrive state, you're actually running on empty and draining your reserves. It's especially problematic if your second wind comes too close to bedtime because, when you finally stop, you will find that you're unable to relax and sleep. Doing this habitually can even affect your nervous system to induce a chronic state of overdrive. Another factor influencing your ability to sleep concerns personal habits effecting the transitions from a busy life to sleep.

Then, put this all in a box, real or imaginary. Shut the lid and store it away from your bedroom. Rest easy knowing that everything in the box will stay there until you choose to open it. (This is one of my 5-Minute Helpers.)

Move to promote sleep - It may seem counter-intuitive, but moving before bed can be very sleep inducing. Just as children often need to be physically active right before bedtime, you may, too. It can help you release tension, anxiety or difficult emotions, and help you slow down, especially if you didn't move much during the day. By the way, I'm not talking about ambitious exercising, but more relaxing forms of movement such as these:

- **Try some gentle, slow, luxurious stretching movements or oil your joints.** (For ideas, see my chapter on *Joints.*)

- **Release your neck muscles** (which are probably tight!). Close your eyes, and s-l-o-w-l-y move your neck side to side, and up and down, or around a few times. Just do small movements. You can also do this lying down: slowly turn your head side to side on your pillow. Remember: the s-l-o-w-e-r you do these movements the more effective they are.

- **Yawn** - Yes, yawning is a good movement to encourage. It releases your jaw, opens up your breathing, and inspires relaxation and sleepiness. Unfortunately, some of us are taught to stifle our yawns to be polite, so I always encourage my students and clients to yawn.

- **Give Yourself a Massage** - Were you lucky enough to have your mom or caretaker gently stroke your forehead before you went to bed, or to comfort you when you felt ill or scared? You can do this for yourself. It's a wonderful, tangible way to be kind to yourself. Here are a few ways to massage your head: If your head feels tight, use both hands and "mush your scalp around" to release the tightness. Alternatively, stroke your head from your forehead up to the very top of your head. Another calming technique is to put one hand on your forehead and the other on the back of your head, while you breathe deeply. You can do this either before you get into bed, or in bed.

- **The Soothing Ball Hug – a Real Winner!** One of my favorite uses of the large exercise ball is the soothing ball hug. A few minutes of this movement before bedtime relieves physical tightness and tension, and slows down your body and mind. (See my website for more on this.) Here's an example of a client who found movement helpful:

Mary was dealing with her husband's serious medical condition. She found it hard to let go of the anxieties of the day at bedtime, and she noticed that her legs felt fidgety when she was especially tense. To relieve this tension, she shook out her arms and legs and sighed loudly. Then she would do the soothing ball hug to encourage sleep.

- Doing a simple task slowly is another way to move. Here's an example:

One night, a friend who was very upset came over to talk and stayed until it was quite close to my bedtime. After she left I found it helpful to slowly sweep the floor for a short time to quiet down.

More Sleep-Inducing Tools

Ultimately, your ability to fall sleep depends upon your quieting your body, especially your nervous system. If sleep doesn't come easily you'll want to discover some new, powerful ways to signal your body and mind that it's time to sleep. Here's a wonderful (and slightly unusual) sleep-inducing idea:

- **Look out your window at the night sky, or step outside.** This is one of my favorite ways to wind down, especially in warm weather. I love to stand and look at the sky, inhale the fresh air, breathe out the day, or walk a bit down my driveway. It works best when I have brushed my teeth and completely closed up shop for the night. There is nothing more to think about or do—only to relax into sleep. (Obviously, your ability to do this depends on where you live and the weather!)

Make Friends with your bed. Getting into bed is a mini-transition - a prelude to the major transition of going from wakefulness to sleep. As you get into bed, here are some other ways to send sleep signals to your body and mind while also giving you a delicious feeling of safety and security:

- **Take a Hot Water Bag to bed with you:** Many of my clients and their children (who call the water bags "baby gushies"), have found hot water bags to be one of the most effective aids to sleep. Their warmth gives a clear signal that it is time to relax, and it feels comforting. I use mine almost every night.

- **Tuck yourself in.** Or better yet, ask someone else to!

One evening, I got chilled from a spell of damp, unseasonably cool weather. I took my hot water bottle to bed to help me warm up, but my back still felt cold and vulnerable, so I asked my husband if he could tuck the covers in around my back. He tucked me in quite tightly. It felt so good and gave me a delicious feeling of safety. I realized that this was something I could do for myself, but never did. How did I miss this? It amazes me how much we can do for ourselves that we never think of. Now I tuck myself in whenever I feel I need it.

- **Turn the lights down** - Give yourself some time to rest your eyes in low light before you go to sleep. When you are ready to sleep, use an eye mask if it's not dark enough in your bedroom.

- **Bring your attention inside.** Let go of focusing on your environment, other people or your to-dos. Bring your focus into your body.

- **Release tension in your eyes** - Place your hands gently on your eyes. Breathe out a few times. Allow your eyes to rest deep down into the cradling nest of your eye sockets. This calms your nervous system.

Yield into the bed. Allow your body to be fully supported on your bed. If you sleep on your side, first take a few moments to lie on your back. Breathe slowly. As you exhale let your muscles release, and feel that you are dropping your weight and the burdens of your day into the mattress.

- **Say goodbye to the outside world for now.** Say to yourself, "No more to do now" and "Pleasant dreams."

Ways to Empty your Mind of Tense, Fearful or Obsessive Thoughts

We've already discussed *Put it in a Box*. That's the 5-Minute Helper my clients have found to be most helpful with sleep. Now consider also:

- **Breathing activities** - including **Blow It Out** (as described in the previous part of this chapter and my chapter on the Breath.)

- **Music Changes the Channel, another 5-Minute Helper** - Instead of reading in bed, induce relaxation by listening to a story (not a murder mystery!), calming music or a guided relaxation to shift your focus from worrisome thoughts.

- **Engage in some supportive self-talk,** such as: *"My day is done. I can get back to this project tomorrow or the next day. I deserve to rest now."* Or, *"Things have a way of working out,"* if you are worried.

- **Create a feeling of safety** - If you feel a connection to a higher power or angels or spirit, ask them to protect you. Imagine that a mama bear or lion is watching over you.

I remember a time, years ago, when I was anemic and consequently so exhausted that I longed for my bed all day. I imagined my bed to be like a large loving being that held me in her arms.

Might an image like that help you?

- **Practice Gratitude** - Recall something that happened during the day for which you feel especially grateful. If you had a difficult or busy day, feel grateful for the opportunity to finally go to bed and lay your body down.

Staying Asleep

Here are some specific ideas to help:

- If you need to get up in the middle of the night (to use the bathroom, or for some other reason), don't turn on a bright light. Use a nightlight or keep a small flashlight by your bed. Keep your attention focused inward. Imagine a cord or blanket that connects you to sleep as you get up. The image of a wide elastic stretch band may work best.

- Keep a relaxing CD ready by your bedside. Often lecture tapes or meditation CD's help me go back to sleep. (Avoid using your smartphone, as you might be tempted to get too involved in it. Stay out of the blue light.)

If All Else Fails

Most sleep experts suggest that if you have trouble sleeping, especially after a while, get out of bed. I have trouble doing this especially if it's cold. However, sometimes getting up and reading something calming or doing a mindless task, like putting away dishes or folding laundry, helps me feel sleepy. A light snack might do the trick as well. I hope you'll first try some of the wonderful, nurturing suggestions here to smooth the transition to sleep. Then, if that doesn't work, try getting up.

Explore Your Obstacles to a Good Night's Sleep

Let's look at what gets in the way of your sleep. Discovering a specific cause (or causes) is empowering, because it gives you an opportunity to make changes. Whenever my clients bring up sleep issues, I start by asking them questions such as:

- How do you prepare yourself for sleep? What do you do right before bedtime? Do you create a transition from the busy-ness of the day?

- When you get in bed, does your body feel revved up or relaxed? Are thoughts or worries keeping you up?

- Do you have more trouble *falling* asleep or *staying* asleep?

The answers to these questions help me understand how they are handling the transition from waking and sleeping. Then, together, we look at ways to increase their ability to unwind, relax and let go of their day, such as the many suggestions in this chapter.

You, too, can use questions like these to help you find your own way to a restful night's sleep. How would you respond to these questions?

A myriad of physical factors can also affect our sleep, so I always ask my clients about these as well. These factors can hold important clues, revealing potential obstacles or personal habits that may be interfering—things that, if addressed, can make all the difference. As you read through this list, notice if any seem pertinent:

- Physical issues, including hormonal imbalances, such as those that may occur during menopause.

- Caffeine intake and the time of its consumption. A while back, I noticed that when I consumed caffeine any later than 1 PM, it affected my sleep. It seemed like it shouldn't, but it did. Then, after a recent bout of poor sleep, I realized that 1 PM had changed to noon without asking me!

- Alcohol intake too close to bedtime, or too much.

- Inadequate physical activity or movement during the day.

- No time for rest and relaxation during the day.

- Inadequate exposure to natural light during the day. Exposure to natural light helps synchronize your brain and body's circadian rhythms.[13]

- Lack of time in low light in the evening, or not sleeping in a dark room. Your body produces melatonin in darkness, which helps you sleep.

- Eating before bed. Some experts advise not to eat within two hours of sleep. However, I find that I sleep better if I have a small snack before bedtime. Experiment to discover whether a bedtime snack helps you sleep or keeps you awake.

- Intake of fluids at night. When I drink sodas or any kind of tea, even herbal, in the evening, I usually wake up at least twice to urinate. So instead, I drink hot water with lemon or juice, or simply water.

- Staying awake to respond to others' needs. Some of us may dismiss our own needs at times in order to be responsive to others. Here's an example of how I became more conscious of this habit:

I find there's a critical window of time from when I begin to feel sleepy to when I fall asleep. If I get interrupted or if I push myself to do more during that time, that window closes, and I will not be able to fall asleep. This can happen if I answer the phone during this critical time, and especially if the conversation involves figuring out something more complex than my sleepy brain can handle. However, to respond to the other person's needs, I often override my sleepiness and push myself into overdrive. Then I'm fully awake and may not be able to get to sleep for hours.

Just recently, I successfully avoided this unnecessary scenario. After teaching one evening, I planned to go right to bed, since I had trouble sleeping the night before. But then, I discovered a phone message from a new acquaintance. She was going to be in my area the next day, and seemed anxious to make arrangements to get together. I knew that if I attended to this immediately—by calling her back and figuring out where and when to meet, etc.—I wouldn't be able to sleep for hours. In fact, this same thing had happened only a week ago. So, this time, I didn't call back. I felt bad, but I knew that the price I would have to pay was too high. Instead, I called her in the morning after a much needed, good night's sleep.

A Word about Sleep Medications

Sleep medication is a big topic, and I'm not qualified to write about it authoritatively. I can share personal experiences and draw upon those of my clients, with the caveat that we are all different. So as with all the suggestions in this book, I advise you to *find your own way*. I have not taken sleep remedies or medications on a regular basis.   I have used them at times to prevent the downward spiral that can occur when a few sleepless nights lead to worrying about sleeplessness, which leads to even more sleeplessness. Even one good night of sleep breaks that cycle for me. At those times, I may ingest a remedy or medication, but I also do everything else that I can to inspire sleep—including insuring I get enough physical activity and fresh air, and doing many of the relaxing suggestions in this chapter.

If you're considering prescription sleep medication, or planning to see a doctor or a therapist, it is helpful to track your sleep for a week or two beforehand and bring that data to your appointment. It will be easier to find solutions if you have detailed information about your difficulties.

Some women find help with over-the-counter solutions. There are both herbal and homeopathic sleep formulas, and other items like melatonin. You might experiment to see what, if anything, works for you. As I said before, everyone is different.

I've tried some remedies and medications that others swear by, but that didn't do anything for me. Some helped a little, some kept me awake, and some gave me a hangover! I have also had success addressing my sleep issues with a homeopathic physician, while other people I knew were not successful.

If none of these suggestions in this chapter seem to help, or if you have had sleep issues for a long time, you may want to consider getting some professional advice and support. Please remember that sleep is one of our most important needs; it's okay to ask for help. I work with many clients around sleep issues, and have received support myself. If one type of intervention or practitioner doesn't work keep trying until you find the help you need.

In closing, I've provided a variety of suggestions. I hope you will find one or several helpful in bringing you the restorative sleep you both need and deserve. The last thing I want is for you to feel overwhelmed, so please remember to *Keep It Small*. Begin by trying just one or two ideas that attract you. And, as always, *Find your Own Way*.

Check out my website for the Soothing Ball Hug.

8

Your Relationship with Time

There is actual time—24 hours in a day, 7 days in a week—and then there is how we relate to time. If you have ever waited to hear the results of a medical test, or to hear a report about a loved one's surgery, an hour can seem like a lifetime. On the other hand, when you are having fun, that same hour can seem to go by in an instant.

In this chapter, I want to talk about your relationship with time, and to do so in a way that helps you cultivate more joy. Usually when you read a book or article about time, the focus is on how to manage time better. Those writings often make time seem a kind of a monster that we need to control, organize, and direct. That's not the intention here. In this chapter I want to help you *befriend* time, to form a relationship with it that works for you. I want to help you structure your days so that you feel supported by time.

I also want to help sensitize you to the flow of time in your life. Our lives involve many transitions, moments when we shift from one type of activity, one type of energy, to another. We tend not to notice, let alone honor these many transitions. This can lead to a feeling of fragmentation, a feeling that nothing is ever accomplished or completed. We may not be consciously aware of these feelings, but they can undermine our joy. Rarely do you read about the many transitions in your day in as much detail as you will find here. You may wonder why it's needed. It's needed because how you live each day is how you live your life. You can bring more joy into your life by smoothing out the many transitions in your day so that you can flow from activity to activity with ease. So, let's begin!

The Time of Your Life

We each have our own sense of time, an internal clock that arouses us to wakefulness, and tells us when we need to rest. We also have unique attitudes and beliefs about time. These beliefs and attitudes—habitual ways of thinking about which we are largely unconscious—dictate how we relate to time. Many of us, for example, hold the unconscious belief that there is never enough time. If that's the case, we feel a constant sense of urgency; we hurry through life, missing out on being fully present because we're so fearful that we'll run out of time. This belief is very strong in our culture. On the other hand, some people have a very fluid relationship with time. They tend to believe they have all the time in the world, and act accordingly. Others of us may believe something in between.

We rarely notice these habits unless something brings them to our attention. I was fortunate that the time I spent alone writing this book helped me discover how I tended to relate to time. I became acutely aware that I constantly felt rushed, even when I had absolutely no place to be! As I explored this pattern, I saw how it added a great deal of stress to my life, and kept me from fully enjoying many activities and prevented me from being fully present. It was as if I was telling myself "Hurry up!" all the time. As a consequence, it was hard to settle into anything I was doing. Becoming aware of my tendency to rush gave me an opportunity to free myself from this unhelpful pattern.

Live Each Precious Day

Time is a precious and non-renewable resource. Time, we frequently hear, is all we have. What you do with your time is what you do with your life. It's a reminder to ask yourself: *What is the most fulfilling way for me to spend my time?*

A beautiful day. I imagine that you have experienced days where everything seemed to fall into place. In those days lie clues to a more joyful life. Think about a day or an activity that went fluidly and without a hitch. What made it work well? Was it because you gave yourself time to stretch for a few minutes the first thing in the morning to *start your day out right?* Did the activity go well because you were able to *anticipate your needs* so you had all that you needed for each activity?

Your needs do change. With this in mind, consider how you structure your days. In our discussion of the Guideline, *Make Your Day Work for You*, we talked about how you may be structuring your time—your days—simply out of habit, rather than out of conscious choice. It is particularly useful to reflect on whether long-standing routines and habits are working for you now. I have experienced how my needs have changed. For years, I preferred to teach and see clients as early in the morning as possible. I kept up that routine, thinking it still worked for me—but I felt myself losing energy. It wasn't until I re-evaluated how I scheduled my day, that I realized that it was better for my current body clock to begin working later in the day. *Can you adjust your schedule to better meet your current needs?*

Create Balance. As we discussed in the previous chapter, Rest and Renewal, a good and productive life is one that includes time for relaxation; a life that balances *doing* and *being*. In fact, this topic is so important, that the next chapter is devoted to it. For now, consider: What is the rhythm of work and play, rest and movement in your life? Look to balance boring or stressful tasks with nourishing, pleasant activities. Remember: it takes a lot less effort to *prevent* exhaustion and burnout than it does to recover from them.

Another very important way to make each day more flowing and enjoyable is by attending to transitions. In the next part of this chapter we will look at ways to move more smoothly through your day.

Smooth Out Your Daily Transitions

What, exactly, do I mean by a transition? A transition is change from one activity or state to another. We make these transitions constantly. Here's a list of just *some* of the transitions you may experience in the course of a single day:

- Waking up—a transition from sleep

- Getting ready for work and/or getting children ready for school

- Leaving home and entering the work world (Note: I include work of all kinds here, whether it's paid, volunteer or activities related to housework.)

- Arriving back home

- Shifting from work to relaxation or recreation

- Transitioning from being alone to being with others, and vice versa

- Preparing and eating meals

- Preparing for bed and falling sleep

It's actually quite astonishing to notice how many changes we go through in a single day, mostly unconsciously!

You may still wonder...

> *Why is it so important to focus on daily transitions?*
> *What does this have to do with self-care?*

Becoming more aware of these transitions offers us an opportunity to manage them more skillfully, which will make each day smoother and easier. Many of us deal with transitions by trying to push through them as if they didn't exist at all. When we do that, life becomes like a run-on sentence: we jump from activity to activity, with barely a breath in between, until we finally collapse into bed at nigh*t*. *Does this feel familiar to you?*

From a self-care perspective, when you attend to—and smooth out—your daily transitions you bring more ease and joy into your life. Here are just some of the concrete benefits:

- You experience less stress.

- Time feels abundant rather than scarce.

- You flow more easily and enjoyably through each day.

- You're better able to prioritize what is important.

- You're better able to structure each day and craft each week, month and year to support your needs.

Many of my clients have asked for tools to help them move more smoothly through their daily transitions: how to start the day on the right foot, how to leave work behind at the end of the day, and how to get to sleep after a too stimulating day are subjects that come up frequently. In this section, I provide ideas and tools to help you navigate these daily transitions with ease, grace, and joy. As you develop more skills to better manage life's daily transitions, you simultaneously improve your ability to handle life's larger changes more effectively, especially those that you have not chosen. During stressful times, having skills to help you cope with transitions is especially important.

Once again, there's no one-size-fits-all; we all respond to situations differently. Transitions that are a snap for some women may be very difficult for others, and vice versa. A transition we barely noticed can suddenly throw us for a loop, especially if we are already stressed. Some women, for example, never think about the transition from sleeping to waking. They wake up cheery and alert, while others (like me!) need extra time and helpful tools to start the day on the right foot. As you read this section, ask yourself: What daily transitions are difficult for me? Then, in keeping with the *Keep It Small* and the *Find Your Own Way* Guidelines, choose the tools you feel will be most helpful to you. As you read through the chapter ask yourself: What small things might I do today or tomorrow to navigate my daily transitions with ease?

1. Wake Up!

Some women wake up easily, cheerily and with barely an ache. If you are one of these people, you needn't read this section — unless you want to understand someone who is not like you! For many the morning can be the most difficult time of the day. Have you ever felt like you got up on the "wrong side of the bed?" Have you ever awakened and felt lousy in general, had trouble thinking clearly or felt your joints ache? In this foggy state of mind did you stub your toe as you dressed or spill your morning coffee everywhere? If so, paying more attention to this transition can help redirect the course of your day.

Being prone for hours during sleep can aggravate back and joint problems. When you awaken your joints may feel stiff. You may experience physical tension or pain or have difficulty waking and thinking clearly. If this is the case, moving for only 5 minutes in the morning can really make a big difference in your overall well-being. I have found that doing specific movements or breathing activities in the morning enables me to start my day on the right foot. These quick and effective activities can loosen your joints and ease stiffness and pain—a good way to start the day!

- **Body drumming** will wake up your body and mind in just a few minutes. It's fun, especially if you let yourself make silly sounds or sigh as you do it. Here's how to do it: Use the palm or your whole hand to tap or drum all over your body. Start at your feet or your shoulders. Adjust the force of your tapping so this feels good, and invigorating too, but not painful! Use only your fingertips to delicately tap your head and your face.

- **Joint oiling movements** (from the chapter on Joints) are great for relieving morning stiffness and pain.

- **Moving on the large ball.** The ball has been a gift from the gods to help me shift pleasantly from sleep to waking. Just 5 minutes of rolling around and bouncing gently to music helps wake my foggy brain, lift my sleepy mood and loosen my joints all at once! Many clients have found it helpful as well.

Of course, the other side of waking up is going to sleep. It's such a major transition that I devoted an entire chapter to it!

2. S-l-o-w down and eat

Just as with the transition from sleep to wakefulness, eating also involves a major transition from being active to being quiet and receptive. Like sleep, eating is also about replenishment. Our relationship to food and eating is such a major issue for many women that I have devoted a whole chapter to this as well. For now, I just want to emphasize the importance of pausing before eating to shift gears. This signals your body that you're no longer in active mode, and that it's time to relax and receive nourishment. This is especially important if you tend to rush when you prepare food. My chapter on food offers simple ways to pause and to s-l-o-w down before eating.

3. Leaving home – on time

This, too, is a major transition—or perhaps it is more appropriate to think of it as a series of mini-transitions, each needing our attention. If you work out of your home, this section is very important. Getting out of the house on time each morning is a nightmare for many! I have been struggling with this for years, but it is getting easier. A friend likened the furious morning rush to get her son and herself out of the house on time to "being shot out of a canon." Another friend gets up only a half-hour before leaving for work because the extra sleep is so important to her. That works for her, but when I have done this I've felt as if I had been thrown off a cliff into ice-cold water—hardly my idea of fun! For some of you, the time you wake up is the most critical aspect of getting out of your house on time. For others, these ideas may be helpful:

- **Not now!** In order to leave your home in a relaxed manner it is essential to focus on preparing to leave. To do that, you need to STOP doing other tasks: resist the impulse to answer a call or text, check just one email, do the dishes or whatever else might suddenly seem vital to you before you leave. Ask: What can wait until I get home? What has to be done before I leave? This is a good time for encouraging self-talk, such as: *"You don't have time for that now—let it go until later. Remember it's no fun to rush or forget your lunch like you did yesterday."*

- **Anticipate delays and leave time for them.** Remember the unexpected often happens.

- **Where are my keys?** Have you had a sinking feeling in your gut when you need to leave the house immediately and you can't find your keys? I hate that! I avoid that scenario by keeping my keys in the same drawer at home, or in a specific place when I travel. I still misplace my reading glasses, or other important items that seem to disappear right before I need to leave. However, I keep plugging away at organizing my things, and day-by-day, and little by little, I leave my house with greater ease.

- **Don't leave home without…** Make a list of the things you need to take with you each day so that in a flurry of activity you don't forget your lunch, snacks or important papers. Consider what time works best for you to gather the things you need for the day. Is it the night before or in the morning? Do you need to do this each day or a few times a week?

- **Leave yourself Reminder Notes.** Another time that I had a terrible sinking feeling in my stomach was when I drove off from my home wondering: "Did I turn off the burner after I just made tea?" At times, the feeling was so strong that I needed to turn around and check. I have thought about posting a "things to check" list before leaving the house, to remind myself to turn down the heat or to check the burner on the stove. I have started to do it some days. I hope to make checking a reminder list a daily habit. *Would a reminder list help you?*

- **Plan to leave earlier than necessary.** I have noticed that whenever I plan to get to my office 15 minutes early in order to sit quietly or stretch, I leave the house without rushing and arrive feeling relaxed and on time (though not 15 minutes early; I'm still working on that!). When a friend enters appointments into her planner, she often enters the time as 15 minutes earlier. *Would something like this help you?*

Arriving at work. Across the board, successful people say that one of the most important secrets to their success is setting aside quiet time when they first arrive at work: no phones, no talk, and no e-mails. This system allows space to look at the day ahead, figure out priorities, clarify their thinking and ease into the day's schedule. Your co-workers will easily support your quiet time when they discover that not only do you work well that way, but you are also in a better mood around them. Everybody wins!

Leave work behind. You may leave the workplace physically, but it is often difficult to set aside all that didn't get done today, and whatever needs to get done tomorrow. The inability to leave work behind is a big issue for many. It can make it difficult to enjoy family and friends, or renewing activities after work, and it can lead to sleepless nights. Following are some suggestions for those who work outside the home. They apply whether your work is paid or volunteer, caring for relatives, or other complex tasks.

Here are some ways to create a sense of completion and closure around your workday and smooth the transition to home:

- To help mark the closure of whatever you have been doing, put away any papers, or other articles you used, or cover them with a cloth. If you can't do that, then imagine putting them in a box or container of some kind. Place your "to do" books, or lists in a folder or drawer. As you do so, use encouraging self-talk: *I am finished for today. I appreciate what I accomplished. Tomorrow is another opportunity to do more.*

- Alternatively, write "I leave all my work here until tomorrow" in large letters on a sheet of paper or index card. Leave it on your desk, in a folder or in your locker.

- To further mark the transition and shift your energy, try my 5-Minute Helpers, *Shake it Out* or *Blow it Out*. If you have privacy, do a quick imaginary "shower" to brush off the day. (See 5-Minute Helpers in the Coming into Balance chapter.)

- Take a moment to note the physical acts that signify leaving your workplace: closing the door, turning off the lights or shutting down your computer. You might even exaggerate how you do these to emphasize to yourself that you are leaving work behind.

- As you leave the building exhale and sigh. (This is the *Blow It Out* Helper.) With each sigh, send the stress of the day out. As you travel continue to sigh or breathe more deeply. If you are driving, sigh or even make loud sounds if you wish. Imagine the stress of the day flying out of the window with every mile you drive. Play music, sing if you like, and let the music dissolve your cares.

Explore these suggestions. Modify them so that they work for you. Experiment until you find what works best.

Getting Back Home. Give yourself at least 5 minutes to actually *arrive* home. To mark this transition, you can:

- Put your work papers or briefcase in a specific place, especially one that has a door you can close, like a closet. Or put them in a box with a lid.

- Wash your face or hands and shake out the water from your hands.

- Change into "home comfort clothes."

- Play helpful music.

- Sigh, exhale or shake out. Try a "quick shower" technique to wash away the day.

- Do the shoulder release movement with sighs (from the Joints chapter).

- Bounce on a large ball.

If you work from home. Many of the above suggestions for leaving work behind are not only applicable, but they are even more important if you work at home. One of the most difficult parts of being self-employed or working from home is making a clear distinction between working and not working. It can be especially hard to "say no" to calls, texts or emails. Encouraging self-talk can help here: "*I am not working now. This is my time to enjoy… I can turn off my smartphone or computer now.*"

4. Beginning and Ending Tasks or Activities

The completion of a task is a major transition. Don't ignore it!

I'm done for now…

Acknowledging the ending of a task or project is essential. When you do, you have the opportunity to release the energy or emotions attached to it, including any frustrations. It allows you to drop the weight of the task, especially if it felt burdensome. You can then begin the next part of your day feeling energized and fresh. Unfortunately, many of us live with the lingering fear or belief that we are not doing enough, that we should be doing more. When you acknowledge the completion of a task—or part of a task— you have a sense of accomplishment, countering that false belief. This is a good time to remember the guideline *Appreciate All Your Efforts*. Appreciate yourself with self-talk, such as: *"I am glad I completed this today. It feels good."*

Warm up to begin a new task

It's important to signal our bodies, minds and spirits that we are beginning a new task or activity, and to ramp up slowly rather than expecting to accelerate from 0 to 80 MPH. Warming up before beginning any physical activity is important, especially as you grow older, or if you have physical problems or muscle tension. When I feel stiff, I take a few minutes to "oil" my joints. Then I enjoy my walk more, and feel better afterwards too. (See Joints chapter.)

Warming up doesn't just pertain to sports activities. Many daily activities would also be easier and more enjoyable if we did a quick warm-up to prepare our mind and body first. I found this to be particularly true while writing this book. Whenever I'd been away from writing, I needed to get myself back in gear. I eased myself in by working on the easiest part first, or by reviewing what I had worked on last. I also listened to the same song each time I began to write. This was a signal to myself that it is time to focus. (My 5-Minute Helpers in *Coming into Balance* make good warm-ups.)

This type of transition isn't often acknowledged, but it's equally important. The transition between sleep and waking involves that change. You are in your own world in your dreams, even if you sleep in the same bed with another person. Then, when you wake up, you need to leave that quiet inner world and shift to the outer world. The opposite is true when you rest or sleep; you leave outer-focused activities and return to your inner world.

The transition from being alone to being with others can be challenging. However, giving yourself a few minutes to acknowledge this change helps you to shift gears to be more present with your loved one. This is especially crucial if you are making a major switch, such as going from working alone to being with a young grandchild, or caring for someone who is ill.

Some women rarely have any alone time. They may be with people constantly all day in their job and find it hard to then come home and be with their family immediately.

> One of my clients found herself in this situation. After work, she needed some quiet time before fully involving herself in family activities. I encouraged her to talk about this with her family. Sometimes they were able to give her some space; other times, she just didn't get that time. Through our work together she came up with a solution. On her way home, she would stop to walk or window-shop for 10 minutes. She reported that these brief stops always gave her energy and enabled her to connect more with her family.

Home Alone

A major transition we might face involves going from being with others to being alone for a lengthy duration. For example, your home situation might change when a grown child goes away to college or moves into their own place, or when a partner is away for a while. Here's how one client dealt with this type of transition:

When her daughter went away to school, Lisa found herself suddenly at loose ends. She was used to having someone at home to eat and talk with over dinner, and she missed the company. We problem-solved together and came up with a couple of ways to ease her transition to her empty nest. Sometimes she made brief stops at her neighbor's house to chat for a few minutes. Soon thereafter, she began to invite a friend over for dinner one night a week, and organized a group of friends to meet after work for coffee or a drink.

Pause, Check In, Listen, Shift

When you are busy and active, you may hardly notice any body sensations. But consciously attending to transitions between activities can provide invaluable opportunities to pause, check in and listen to your body. When you pause between activities, you may notice that you're feeling cold, tense or stiff, or yearning for a stretch or a snack. Once you notice your discomfort, you can get a nice warm drink, put on an extra sweater, or take a few minutes to relieve cramped muscles. But if you don't take the time to notice, you won't have the opportunity to do these simple activities to care for yourself. It only takes a few extra minutes to pause and tune in, and it can prevent dropping into the doldrums later. (See the chapter on *Rest and Renewal* for more on breaks and pauses.)

As we draw this section to a close, I would like to remind you that each transition presents an opportunity to make a new decision, to "change the channel" and begin anew. If, for example, a certain task or situation has left you feeling a bit agitated or drained, a pause can shift your inner state. A pause can allow you to *blow out* those unhelpful feelings, and choose an attitude that is not only more pleasant but also more effective for your next activity or task. Stopping to acknowledge transitions can be very positive and empowering!

In sum, the better you get at smoothing out your daily transitions, the more your life will feel like it's flowing easily. As you smooth out the smaller transitions, you will gain skills to help you navigate the major changes that occur in your life.

9

Time Just for You

For your self-care, it is vitally important to give yourself time to just *be*. The time you give yourself for being may span an afternoon or a day or two, but even just an hour that is *truly yours* is invaluable. This is one of the greatest gifts we can give ourselves—but it is something we rarely allow. Instead we say things to ourselves like: "I don't have the time. It is impossible! Maybe next month or next year after I finish . . ."

Unfortunately, we do this because we have an ingrained belief that our value is based on what we *do*, what we produce or accomplish, rather than on who we are. Because of this belief, we feel constant pressure to be productive. Doing nothing, being truly at leisure is seen as a waste of time. Either that, or we think that we are being just plain lazy. In addition, we may avoid taking time for ourselves because we are fearful of being labeled "SELFISH." As a consequence of all this conditioning, it may be hard for us to take even a 15-minute break in the day to rest or to enjoy a quiet cup of tea. Often, we barely stop at all, not until we drop into bed.

In *Getting Over Getting Older,* author Letty C. Pogrebin explores her own struggles with this internal programming: "Indeed, I spend much of my life producing *things*—magazine articles, vegetable soup, political petitions — things I can see, touch, read; things I can measure as the product of my waking hours."- Later, she contemplates her preoccupation with *doing* in light of the meaning of the Jewish Sabbath: "On that one day, we are supposed to enter time's realm . . . and to treasure it for its own sake. This I have never done. Forget about for a full day—I've never done it for an hour … I always viewed it (time) as something to be trapped and utilized. -14-

Pogrebin's lament doesn't just apply to her; it applies to many of us. That's why I invite you to consider taking time to just *be*.

What does taking time to just be look like? It looks like an open time on your calendar; you have nothing scheduled, nowhere to be and nothing to do. It looks like time just for you, away from commitments or the demands of others. It looks like time spent alone. It is time for just being, for experiencing the freedom of doing absolutely nothing or, if you choose, doing just about anything that gives you pleasure. You might watch the clouds go by, listen to music, nap, knit, breathe deeply or connect to your inner wisdom, the earth and to spirit. You can tune into your body to feel what parts of you need to stretch, relax or move.

Taking time to just *be* means letting go of whatever you think needs to be done right now. You needn't justify to anyone why you are taking the time, or how you are using it: it is *yours*.

The value of doing nothing

I can hear you protesting already: "How can I possibly do nothing? I need to be productive!" The truth is that unstructured time is actually very productive, just in a different way. Having time to be allows your mind to release the clutter of all the to-dos. Creative ideas or solutions to problems often arise when there is *space for them*. When you keep yourself busy all the time, there is *no space*.

Taking time to just *be* provides space and time to return to balance. That's why it's particularly necessary following a period of extra demands from work, family, visitors or travel. When we're busy responding to lots of external demands, we often forget to listen to ourselves. But when you give yourself time to just *be*, the noise created by all those external demands begins to empty out, and you can hear your inner voice once again.

This is a good time to reflect on how your life is going. Here are some questions to ask yourself: *Do I feel satisfied with how I am spending my precious time? What is working for me in my life now? What have I always wanted that I can give myself now?* Having the time to sit with deeper questions like those is essential to our well-being. The answers will guide you towards what you wish to bring into your life. By pausing to reflect, you will become aware that you have some habitual patterns that no longer serve you. For example, perhaps, like me, you realize you have a tendency to go through your daily tasks with more tension and urgency than is really necessary. Awakening your awareness of that habit now makes it possible for you to make more conscious choices. You can *choose* to experience less tension, and to enjoy more relaxation and ease during your daily activities. Check out The Guideline *Make It Enjoyable* for suggestions.

Even though it's clear that taking time to just *be* has many benefits, our conditioning is so strong that we can still find it hard to give it to ourselves. I know this from personal experience:

> One Friday afternoon after work, I felt the sudden need to do nothing. I wanted to ignore that feeling because I'd just taken a 20-minute nap. Normally, that's enough to be very

renewing, but this time, I wanted to stay in bed. I didn't, though. Instead, I dragged myself to a planned event. I didn't enjoy myself and came home totally exhausted. What a waste of my time! Later that night, I puzzled over what had happened. I didn't give myself Time to Be, but neither did I enjoy my event.

The next morning presented another challenge. I had planned to go to a special Saturday winter farmers' market, then come home and write. When the time came, however, I just could not move. I kept trying to motivate myself, but couldn't. Then I remembered what had happened the night before, forcing myself to go to an event when I really needed quiet time. I decided to tune into the deeper wisdom of my body to see what it was trying to tell me. I did the Touchstone exercise. I placed my hand over my breastbone, and asked myself what I really wanted. Then I listened for my response.

My inner voice gently told me that pushing myself to do anything was not productive right now and that what I needed was to give myself the gift of time to be. I remembered that I could practice encouraging self-talk to help quiet my mind. That's what I did. I just kept repeating over and over to myself: "I need this time for me. I deserve this time."

After struggling and trying to get up and go, I finally gave myself permission to really rest. I lay down on the couch, and for two hours I watched the birds outside the window, petted my cats and listened to relaxing music. It was wonderful! But still, I felt a little guilty that I was not writing, so I decided that I should at least read something related to my book. Even with a lot of effort, though, I managed to read only a few pages. Clearly, I still needed to do nothing.

I repeated my encouraging self-talk.

Then, after another hour of resting, I had a strong urge to go outside—but not for my usual long walk. Instead, I puttered around the yard a bit. I cut branches with berries as decorations for the house, and enjoyed making the winter yard a bit brighter.

Later, as I returned to the house, I noticed a delicious feeling of well-being surging through me, and I realized how renewed and nourished I felt! I was so grateful that I had moved through my resistance and listened to my need for time to just be. This feeling is now sense memory. It is stored within my body, and I can connect with this inner knowing to remember how valuable a few hours— just for me—can be and how I can make it happen despite my own resistance.

Taking Time to Just *Be*: Ways to Begin

Touchstone is a great way to get in touch with what you really want. Place your hand over your heart, breathe in calmness and listen to your heart. Then, ask yourself some questions like these:

How would I like to feel during my Being Time? What would feel revitalizing and renewing? Would I like to sit or lie down indoors or outside? Take a leisurely stroll? Listen to or dance to music? Breathe deeply? Do I want to muse about (not figure out) a particular issue in my life at this time? What space or place would really support me to just be?

Here are some other gems that I have gathered about taking time to just *be*:

A good place to just *be*.

I realize that you may not have space, quiet or privacy in your home. With all the reminders of to-dos, you may find it difficult to just *be* at home. If that's the case, here are some ideas. Can you go to a park, a coffee shop or café? Is there a bird sanctuary nearby, or a space that carries spiritual energy? Or, if you have a friend whose home feels particularly nurturing and peaceful to you, you might ask to spend a few hours in their home while she or he is out. If you live alone, can you trade homes with a friend for a day, or even a few hours?

Some places, spaces and environments encourage us to just *be*. Many women favor a site near water, such as a beach, because the setting, by its very nature, encourages one to just *be*. Imagine that you are at the beach now. Imagine that you can: Look at the water. Watch the clouds go by. Listen to the music of the surf. Feel the warmth of the sun. Drift in and out of a nap. Read a novel. Knit. Stretch. Walk. Swim. Doesn't that feel good? If you can't actually go to a water site: *What would help you create a similar feeling? Where is your special place?* Here is a story of how a client found her special place:

> *After a particularly stressful year, Joanna, a busy single mom who lived in a big city, really needed a quiet vacation, but she couldn't get away. She didn't let that discourage her, though, and she kept looking for solutions. One day she went to a public beach in the late afternoon. While the beach was usually crowded and noisy during the height of the day, it wasn't then. As the sun lowered in the sky, people began*

leaving, and then it got even quieter as the sun started to set. That day, she stayed until, she said, she felt nature "seep into and renew me." Joanna had found her special place.

Once you find that special place, here are some ideas for how to make it even better:

- **Prepare a comfortable "nest."** Once you discover where you want to be, make it as nurturing as possible. For example, in warm weather my favorite nest is my back porch. I bring extra pillows and, if it's cool, blankets so that I can sit comfortably and enjoy the view. I also bring water and snacks, a writing pad and magazines or books. Then I settle in. If you want to spend time away from home, make your nest portable, as if you were packing things to take to the beach or a picnic.

- **Anticipate your needs and wants.** Taking time to *be* means exactly that: being, not doing. To enhance the experience, plan ahead to insure that you have everything you need nearby, especially if you plan to spend it away from home. Here are some of the things I gather for a being day: a favorite blanket, my special travel mug, a notebook and delicious, nurturing food. I either buy some special things ahead of time or I prepare extra food the day before so that it feels as though somebody else cooked something special just for me! On a being day, I usually don't eat 3 meals, but flow from different snacks to meals to hot drinks. I thoroughly enjoy everything I eat because I have all the time to truly savor my food.

Discover Your Special Time of Day

Now that you have ideas for a place, let's look at the best times in the day for you to take time to just *be*, especially if you are only taking a few hours or part of a day. Like the single mom who found that going to the beach in the late afternoon was renewing for her, I find that watching the sunset is a wonderful way for me to relax and let go. No matter how many times I have observed it, it is always unique and often surprising. On the other hand, if I need replenishing and energy, rising to watch the sunrise enlivens me. Ask yourself: *What time of day best supports my just being?*

Now that you have some ideas about place and time, let's look at how you can further support yourself to truly embrace taking time just to be:

- **Protect your precious time.** It is all too easy to give away any time that is not slotted for work or appointments. You may find yourself helping out a friend or working just a little. Write your time to just be in your calendar. Let people know ahead of time when you will be unavailable. If someone asks you to do something during that time, tell him or her that your calendar says you are not free then, and if you wish, suggest another time. As I suggested in Smoothing Daily Transitions, a helpful way to talk to them about this might be to say, *"When I am nice to me, I can be nice to you too."*

- **Get completely unplugged.** I turn off the phone. I know this is hard, but it is so essential. (I would bet good money that a promotional call would come just at the moment when I am sliding into a nap or a delicious dreamy state!) Or a friend with free time might call and tempt me with a fun suggestion. I don't check my email even "for a few minutes," because I know how easy it is to let my time get gobbled up in that way.

- **Empty the clutter from your mind: Put it in the Box.** This brief exercise helps to transition you from the world of doing, to the world of being. I imagine putting my list of to-dos in a box to be done later. I send any concerns, worries or thoughts about others to the box as well. Sometimes I feel the need to do "urgent" chores, or respond to last-minute requests from others, but making just one phone call or even worse, sending just one email, clutters my mind. So, I say no to these urges and put them in the box too. Sometimes I do this literally as well: I put my to-do list in my desk drawer or file, close my desk drawers and shut my study door. Then I do a few releasing breaths to send out tension. One time after I completed a huge project, I drew a picture and put up a big sign on my study door reading Time to Play! Most things can wait; really, they can.

- **Encouraging self-talk helps.** Even after I set aside time to just *be*, I still need to remind myself that it is really okay to have this time; that's how strong my conditioning is. I have to quiet the inner voices that tell me to get up and do something "productive." Whenever I feel this way, I repeat to myself, "It's my time. I need this time. I deserve this time." or "It's okay if I don't want to do anything—even fun activities."

Time to Putter

Puttering is a good bridge between doing/working and being. I write about puttering here because, although many women enjoy it a great deal, they rarely allow themselves this pleasure. For me, puttering is time *to play*, whether in my house or my garden. It has quite a different feel from *working* on a project. When I putter with my houseplants, I look at them and then perhaps cut dead leaves or wash the plant; I don't repot them, because repotting can become a big project that makes a mess. That's *work*, not puttering! Vacuuming or heavy cleaning is not puttering either. Puttering is more likely to involve straightening or re-arranging, moving this and that to here or from there. It can also be about beautifying. For example, I might muse about the colors, patterns or decorations I would like to bring into a room to make it more welcoming or cozy or dramatic. I might fantasize about choosing a new couch pillow, or look around to see if I already have something that might fill the bill. I might take out some candles I had stored away, or liven up a table with a decorative cloth. I do small, simple things like these and then sit back and enjoy the results.

Why is puttering so rewarding? Why does it nurture us? Here's what a client said to me about her need to putter at home:

> *All of my time during the week is highly structured, so I need the openness of going from one thing to another without demands or requirements. Puttering, for me, is a day off, well spent. It is relaxing, and my house benefits from it.*

Sometimes we have obstacles in our lives that get in the way of our giving time to putter. For example, my client's partner preferred that they do all household tasks together, in a linear fashion, whereas my client wanted to do many of those tasks in her own flow and time. In situations like this, it's so tempting to give up on our needs to please someone we care about—but don't give up! My client and I brainstormed about how she could help her partner understand her needs, and she came up with a compromise that worked for both of them.

What do you think? Can you let yourself putter more? Can you take some time that is truly for you … a day, a weekend, a few hours?

Taking Even More Time for You: Special Retreats

If you have a longer time available, can you design a personal retreat, perhaps by asking to housesit for a friend or acquaintance? Here, I will share a little about my own experiences with creating special retreat times:

Writing gave me permission to have more time alone than ever before in my life. I needed this time to know what was important for me to share with readers. Also, I wanted to embody the practices and principles in this book, to have the space to be nurturing and caring to myself. During these retreat times, I found ways to enjoy my daily tasks. In fact, being and doing began to feel the same.

Whenever I thought about the future, I realized that I wanted to continue taking time for a retreat even after the book was completed.

Only I can give myself this gift of Time for Me. I love my husband and my home. I love my work with clients. However, I need time to be alone to feel myself, to renew, and to discover what I want and need, now and in the next chapter of my life.

For me, even though each and every experience is unique and different, there's always a common thread. There's always a delicious feeling of flow that takes me from one activity to another. Ideally, it includes time spent outdoors. It might include some moving or walking, but there is always lots of "just sitting." My thoughts and breathing both slow down when I sit under a tree, listen to birds, feel a breeze caress my skin or watch a sunset. When I do these things, I feel deeply connected to myself, nature and to spirit. During the winter, when it's cold outside, I might gaze out the window while I play some relaxing background music. On a warm spring day, I sit next to an open window where I may smell the first sweet air of spring.

As you begin to think about taking time to just *be* for yourself, remember you can *start small.* Just as with adding more movement into your life, even an hour of being time can make a huge difference—and an hour now is better than a day that never happens!

Can you take a few minutes to muse about having some special time for you?

Can you put an hour of time to just be on your calendar now?

10

Return to Balance / Change the Channel

In this chapter, we're going to talk about something that is a very important part of cultivating well-being and joy: balance.

First, let me define what I mean by balance. I'm referring here specifically to emotional balance. To me, this encompasses our feelings, moods, thoughts and perceptions. Synonyms for balance include *equilibrium, poise, stability, steadiness*. But don't be fooled by these terms! Emotional balance is not a static state; it's a dynamic process. To understand this more we need only look at physical balance. We rarely feel out of balance when we walk, yet each step requires us to go momentarily out of balance. We don't notice because we've learned how to return to balance, naturally and easily.

That's why, for this chapter, I am using the term *returning to* rather than *staying in* balance.

We need to be reminded because, too often, we have unrealistic expectations concerning balance. We think that if we meditate, exercise, or do other things of that nature, we can always be in balance. Then, when that doesn't happen—which it won't—we can be quite critical of ourselves. Ironically, that can throw us even more out of balance! The truth is, being human means you're likely to go out of balance, no matter what, a number of times every day. Having realistic expectations with respect to balance is important, just as it is in all parts of our lives. In fact, you can think of life as an ongoing effort to return to balance—again and again.

Returning to balance is a skill that can be learned. With respect to our physical balance, we can do things to enhance it. For example, if you stand on only one leg, you will likely quickly feel out of balance. Your body will then begin to shift from side to side and back and forth, all in an effort to come back into balance. If, however, you practice standing on one leg a little every day, your balance will improve; you will more easily stand there with less moving around or without having to bring your foot down to keep from tipping over. If you should lose your balance momentarily, you will regain it more easily. Once learned, you can then call on this ability if, say, you're out walking and trip over a root or an uneven sidewalk. The same principle applies to emotional balance. We can't avoid going out of emotional balance altogether, but there are things we can do and practice to help us cope with this deeply human tendency.

Being in the Moment

The more resilient we are, the better able we are to we return to balance, quickly. Some people seem more naturally resilient than others, for whatever reason, but we can all develop more resilience. So how do we become more resilient? By learning to be fully present in each moment. The opposite of being present is being stuck in memories of the past, or worries about the future. Being present is also *not* about being mired in our emotions, especially fear. When we are fully present, our thoughts and emotions are not running amok; nor are they running the show. Instead, we are able to calmly choose where to put our focus.

This sense of being fully present is often referred to as mindfulness, though I would prefer to call it *body-mindfulness*. We develop this capacity by cultivating *connection*, by going within to connect with ourselves and with our spirit (*i.e.,* the source of well-being that exists both inside and outside of ourselves), and/or by connecting with nature. This sense of connection helps us to be more fully present in our lives, more integrated and whole. One of the best tools we have for going within is always with us: our breath. I will talk much more about the breath in the following chapter.

When we cultivate being present, our whole being knows what emotional balance feels like; it's that feeling of equilibrium, poise and calm I spoke of earlier, and it feels good. When we cultivate being present, we are preparing ourselves to deal with challenging times as they come. We are storing up energy and abilities to deal with the one constant in life—change— that seems to come around even more frequently as we grow older. When we cultivate being present, we learn to trust in that source deep within ourselves. This makes us more resilient and resourceful. Then, when we go out of balance, as we will, we'll know how to recover. When stress or difficulties hit, we'll bounce back.

Being present and living life as joyfully as possible go hand-in-hand. The more present we are, the more opportunities we have to notice and savor the joyful moments in our lives.

In sum, one way we can cultivate greater resiliency is by learning how to be fully present in the moment. Now let's look at another important part of returning to balance.

Choose the Channel, Change the Channel

On TV, there are many channels, some very specialized. There are stations that carry only news programs; others sell products endlessly or feature sports or scary movies. Having all these options means we have choice. We can select the channels and programs we want to watch, and switch away from those that irritate or bore us.

Like the TV, we have *internal* channels where thoughts and feelings tend to all flow in a certain way, perhaps, for example, toward anger or fear. Fortunately, just as with TV, *we have the power to choose which we tune into or tune out*. I cannot emphasize this enough. We can learn to *choose the channel* we pay attention to.

Why is it important to know that we can choose our internal channel? The channel we listen to—that is, the thoughts and emotions we latch onto and focus on—make a crucial difference. They can make us feel good or miserable, or anything in between. They can raise our spirits and help us to care for ourselves every day, and especially during challenging times, or they can drain and disempower us. They can also make self-care activities, such as moving and exercising, easy and fun or downright impossible.

There are ways of thinking and feeling that are more supportive, that make our lives easier, that give us a sense of well-being and serenity in our lives. Cultivating optimistic thoughts and feelings fortifies us. It helps buffer our nervous system, which helps us grow our inner resourcefulness. As we develop these capacities, we become more resilient.

That's because it really is all connected. The attitudes and thoughts we bring to life affect how we experience it. Here's an illustration to help reinforce what I'm saying:

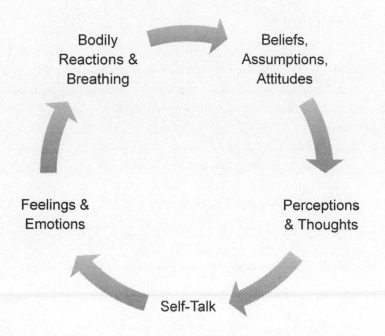

Our beliefs and assumptions affect how we perceive and think about what we are experiencing. Those thoughts and perceptions then affect how we talk to ourselves, what we tell ourselves about our experiences. In turn, our self-talk affects our feelings and emotions, and our emotions trigger bodily responses and reactions.

This cycle often operates as a kind of chain reaction, where each step builds on and amplifies what came before. Sometimes, the cycle becomes an upward spiral, lifting our thoughts and emotions and spirits such that our bodies and minds feel joyful and light. This is how we want to be. At other times, however, they can spiral downward, sending us into hopelessness or despair. Let's look at what happens when we slide out of balance, get very stressed and fall into what I call "the pit."

What is the pit?

A good friend and I independently started to use the words the pit to describe the sensation of sliding down the slippery slope from feeling upset or anxious to feeling much, much worse: panicked, desperate or impossibly stuck. Here's a story to illustrate:

Julia had been long anticipating a weekend visit from a friend who had promised to help her with a major home redecorating project. Unfortunately, her friend became ill and had to cancel at the last minute. Julia was quite upset because she had been having difficulty working on the project alone. She started to slip into a familiar unhelpful belief, which was that "No one ever helps me with anything." Soon, she noticed her self-talk shifting from "I'm so disappointed my friend can't come" to "I'll never get any help with this project. I'll have to live with this mess forever."

Julia's self-talk made her feel like sobbing, but she often had trouble just letting her feelings and tears flow, so instead she held her feelings in. Holding her feelings in created a lot of muscular tightness, especially in her neck and shoulders.

Do you see how Julia's self-talk deteriorated? It turned into discouraging, fatalistic self-talk, such as *"I'll never get out of this terrible situation."* This is the pit.

Fortunately, Julia recognized that she was in the pit and was able to climb out:

From our previous work, Julia knew she needed to change the channel as soon as possible. She felt it would be good to be around other people, and to move in any way to help free up her muscular tightness, so she went to a favorite store to do a small errand related to her project. While driving there, she listened to calming music. The music helped her relax and shift her thoughts, and soon she came up with a new plan for going forward with her project.

If this has ever happened to you—and if you're human, it probably has—remember that you, too, can always climb out of the pit. But even better, know that you can stop that downward spiral. It's possible to *change the channel*, to switch over to a more helpful one, at any point in the cycle. Let's talk about how.

1. Cultivate helpful beliefs and attitudes. Our deep-seated beliefs, assumptions and attitudes have a tremendous effect on how we experience life, as they tend to be self-fulfilling and self-reinforcing. Consider the timeless question: *Is the glass half empty or half full?* How we view the glass is a mirror; it reflects back to us our general attitude toward life. There is only one glass, but two very different attitudes toward life can affect how we perceive it. One is pessimistic; the other, optimistic.

So how about you? How do you see the glass? Do you tend to be more optimistic or pessimistic? Do you tend to see possibilities or only limitations? Do you tend to embrace life joyfully or live fearfully? Do you see life as a contest, a battle you always lose, or a celebration? Are you generally grateful or do you often feel disappointed and resentful? Now consider: which attitude is more likely to bring you joy?

Formed by early life experiences, these habitual ways of look-ing at things may have served you once, but they may no lon-ger. Unless you bring them out into the light and examine them, they'll continue to run the show. This means that if you want to change your experience of life, you need to consider changing your beliefs. Put another way, if your experience of life is proving less than you would like, look to your beliefs. *You always have the power to choose.* Can you cultivate that atti-tude to make your life easier, more joyful?

When we are committed to cultivating joy in our lives, we're inspired to choose the inner channel that maximizes our joy and pleasure. Just think of it as the Joy Channel. It's always there; you can turn to it any time, even right now. (You will find ideas about encouraging feel-good emotions in the prac-tice *Cultivating Joy*.) I can attest to this from personal experi-ence. I have slowly become more optimistic and hopeful over the years. I did this by changing the channel whenever I no-ticed myself becoming pessimistic and not seeing my options and choices. I also cultivated a more optimistic attitude by using the suggestions that come later in this chapter.

2. Shift your thoughts and perceptions: focus on what's working. Let's look at our thoughts and perceptions. How we perceive something affects how we think about it, what we tell ourselves about it, and how our bodies react. We can make mildly stressful situations far worse by believing our fearful thoughts. Our minds can cascade, causing us to experience a difficult—but contained—situation as if it were a major catastrophe.

Our initial perceptions can be shaped by false or unexamined beliefs, assumptions and attitudes. But again, we always have the power to choose. If a situation or occurrence is causing us stress, we have the power to choose to view it from a different perspective, one that is more positive and empowering. Psychotherapists call this process "reframing." To re-frame, take a step back and ask: How am I looking at this situation? Is that perspective helpful or hurtful? Does it make me feel empowered or powerless?

It is especially important to step back and re-frame if we notice that we are having a strong emotional reaction. That's a signal that something's amiss, that we may actually be reacting to something that happened in our past. Here's an example of how a client was able to re-frame an important issue:

Amy was disappointed because she was not offered a new job she wanted. She kept asking herself the same question repeatedly: "What did I do wrong?" As we talked, she realized this was an old pattern. This freed her up to have a new thought. "Perhaps the other candidate was chosen because of departmental politics. It was not about me." As she shifted her perception, more realizations came. The job would have required her to move far away, but she was in the midst of cleaning out her old house and caring for her frail mother, so that would have been nearly impossible. In addition, moving at that time might have jeopardized a new relationship. Looking back, she came to the conclusion that, under the circumstances, it was best that she did not get that job. Later, when she did get a new job, it came at a time when she was ready to move, together with her new special person.

Dwelling upon what feels wrong will bring you down in the dumps. One way to switch that around is by asking what is going right, instead. This will raise your spirits. Not only that, but no matter how bleak a situation seems at first, there are always things you can find that are going right about it. As Frederickson writes in *Positivity*, "There is particular power in the questions you ask yourself. *What's going right for me now?* can unlock so much . . . If only we persist in asking ourselves questions like *What's right here? What can I celebrate?* and are patient enough in letting our answers surface."[15]

Asking questions like *What's going right here?* or *What can I celebrate?* is similar to seeing the glass as half-full. Each time you ask these questions you are shifting to a more optimistic attitude and way of perceiving, and this moves towards a more joyful life. Here's an example:

> *A friend or spouse offers to make a meal or to pick up something special at the store to cheer you up because you've been struggling with a challenging situation. Perhaps he or she forgot one ingredient for the recipe or bought the wrong flavor of your requested goodie. You might be thinking or saying to yourself "It's just like him. He never remembers to get the right flavor!"*

> *If you keep your focus on what is wrong or is not working, you may soon find yourself in the midst of a confrontation. In any case, it is difficult to enjoy and receive the gift of caring concern that you have been offered. If instead you shift your focus and ask yourself, "What is going right here?" you will appreciate that he or she made a special trip to the store to do something nice for you, so relax and enjoy the yummy treat!*

Remember to keep this question in mind for daily use. I use it often, especially to avoid potential arguments with my husband. It stops me from making something that he didn't get "right" into a big deal, and instead shifts my focus to appreciation for what he does. It really works!

3. Change your Self-Talk. Your self-talk is what you say to yourself about a situation. Your self-talk can help you cultivate more joy—or lead you down ever further down the spiral into the pit. Remember how that happened to Julia? To help you recognize when your self-talk might be steering you toward the pit, I've listed some examples. Note the use of absolutes. Words like *never, forever, always* and *should* are a good clue. If you notice any of these, it's time to shift your self-talk.

- This will go on forever.

- I'll never get better.

- It's all my fault.

- I should never have done that.

- I always mess up.

Here are some examples of self-talk that can help you feel better:

- *I am feeling a bit better each day.*

- *Time heals.*

- *Things have a way of working out for me.*

- *Step by step, I am moving towards my goals.*

Here's an example showing how a clients' scary thoughts led to panicky self-talk, which triggered difficult bodily responses and reactions and led her into the pit.

A client was recovering well from a recent hip replacement. However, suddenly she felt intense knee pain. This triggered frightening thoughts about what that might lead to, which then ignited panicky self-talk: "Oh no! My knee is going to lock up. Then my back will go out and I won't be able to stand up, just like a long time ago. Today is Friday, so if that happens, I won't be able to get any help all weekend, and it's supposed to snow on Monday…" Down the spiral she went prior to our session. To help her feel calmer, I suggested she take a few minutes to breathe out the fear she was holding in her body. Then I gently explained that, during recovery from a hip or knee replacement, it's natural to experience some issues with your other leg, or your back since those areas have to compensate as one recuperates. I reminded her that now her body was naturally re-balancing after her surgery, and that was a big reason why we planned a number of sessions after her surgery.

I suggested that her knee was signaling that it needed some attention, so I began to gently move it. Her knee quickly loosened up, which was a big relief to her. Then the other muscles in her body began to relax, as did her breathing. This helped her knee move more easily, too. I then suggested she shift her thoughts about her knee pain. Rather than seeing it as a sign of impending catastrophe, she could reframe it as a stiff knee that needed extra attention to re-balance. I suggested some easy movements she could do to "oil" her knee joint, and also showed her a simple self-massage to do. I encouraged her to remind herself that any pain or discomfort was temporary, and not a sign of terrible things to come. I reminded her how much her body had already healed; she could barely walk a couple of weeks ago. Soon, not only had she climbed out of the pit, but she had also come up with a self-support statement: "My body is healing well. I know how to help myself re-balance."

How we talk to ourselves is so important! If you want to refresh your memory or learn more about self-talk, go back and review the *Inner Support* practice.

4. Change your thoughts, change your emotions. We can often feel at the mercy of our thoughts and feelings. But the truth is we actually have quite a lot of control. As Frederickson writes in *Positivity*, "Although it often seems that our emotions rain down on us as unpredictably as the weather, we have a surprising amount of control over them... especially positive emotions. We can turn them on whenever we choose. And nearly always, we can coax them to linger just a bit longer."[15]

Second, our thoughts and our emotions are deeply interconnected, which means we can affect our emotions by changing our thoughts. "Hundreds of scientific studies tell us that when people change the course of their thinking, they change the course of their emotions. This holds true both in the moment, if you want to zap an unwanted worry, and over the long haul."[16]

The more we can shift away from pessimistic thoughts into those that are more joyful and life-affirming, the more empowered we feel. This sense of empowerment becomes even more essential as we grow older, as we'll discuss in the chapter I've dedicated to that topic.

Let's say a situation is making you fearful. Here's how to break that cycle. First, just notice the fear. Don't judge it, just notice. Become present to it. Perhaps discouraging self-talk begins to arise. You might hear yourself saying something like: *It's all my fault. I never should have done that.* If so, just notice that too, without judgment. Now, pause and take a breath. Remember your breath is always there to help you to balance your body and mind. Replace that scary talk with some encouraging self-talk. Here's one that really helps me with fear: *Things have a way of working out for me.*

This example illustrates how we can shift our emotions by changing our self-talk and combining that with becoming more present. As you continue practicing this over time, that habitual fear response will change. Fear may still arise, but it will no longer control the situation. And the more you practice, the more the fear will diminish. (Note that a situation like this, when you are feeling fear, is a good time to use one of my 5-Minute Helpers, *Blow It Out/Let It Go,* which you will learn about later in this chapter.)

Now let's address the bodily reactions part of the circle, specifically the stress response and ways to deal with it.

The Body Under Stress

Let's look now at how your body/mind responds to stress. The dynamics are actually quite complex, but here is a simplified version.

Our Autonomic Nervous System (ANS) regulates the involuntary functions of the body, such as heart rate, respiration and digestion. The ANS has two major parts and functions. The first is called the sympathetic nervous system. Besides supporting us to be active and awake, part of its function is to respond to perceived danger. Feeling threatened triggers a cascade of chemicals to flood throughout bodies, raising our heart rate and otherwise preparing our bodies to respond. For example, our ANS sends more blood and oxygen to our legs and arms to help us get ready to run away or fight back, often called the "fight or flight response." It's important to note that when the blood and oxygen flows into our extremities, it is also flowing away from our internal organs and away from our brain, too! That's why it seems so difficult to think clearly when we are under stress.

The other part of our ANS is called the parasympathetic system. Besides helping with digestion, sleep and relaxation, part of its function is to slow us down after a stress response. It does so by sending the blood flow back to our internal organs and brain. The parasympathetic system also responds to stress, but in a very different way. This is known as a "freeze" response. Sometimes, when an animal (or human) is being threatened—perhaps being stalked by a predator—it cannot flee or fight, so instead, it holds its breath and plays dead, hoping that the predator will lose interest or get distracted. Think of a frightened rabbit you may have seen sitting stock still on your lawn, or the proverbial deer in the headlights of a car. Many times, this instinctive strategy works. You have probably seen a mouse freeze when captured by a cat. If the mouse stops moving, the cat loses interest. Then the mouse suddenly mobilizes and runs away as fast as it can.

The fight or flight and freeze responses, triggered by stress hormones, are *emergency responses,* to be used only as needed. They're also meant to be short-lived, meaning stress hormones are supposed to be *discharged.* They are not supposed to remain in the body.

Stress hormones are discharged through movement, by running away from or fighting a predator, or shaking fear off when the danger has passed. This worked for our ancestors. They probably ran away from most of their threats, which helped use up the stress responses in their bodies. But with modern-day stressors, running away (or fighting) is not usually an option. This means that, for us, those stress hormones may not be properly discharged. Instead, they linger in our bodies, taxing our nervous system and making us even more susceptible to stress. If this happens over and over, if we become stressed without discharging those stress hormones, this natural response can turn into chronic stress.

Everyday situations can trigger a heightened physiological response very similar to the response that was meant to help us only in life-threatening situations. Here's an example: Suppose you realize that you are going to be late for an important appointment. What happens in your body? Can you feel your heart rate go up, your breathing becoming restricted? Can you think clearly about how to handle the situation? This happens even though, in reality, being late is not life threatening. Here's another example. Say your boss becomes angry with you. Your body might respond to this in the same way that our ancestors responded to seeing a large predator, or being left alone in a dangerous situation: you might want to fight or flee—or freeze. Again, you experience it as if it were a life-or-death situation.

Responding in this way can lead to a chronic state of stress, especially if it goes on for an extended period. That is why it's so important to learn to manage and discharge stress.

The 5-Minute Helpers: Tools to Re-Balance and Manage Stress

As we've seen, stress can quickly take us out of balance. It can send us on a downward spiral to the pit—almost before we know it. Increasingly, we hear about the negative effects of excessive or chronic stress on our bodies, and more recently, our brains. Of course, we can try to reduce some of the things that cause stress in our lives, but stressful experiences are a part of life—they'll never go away completely. Our true power lies not in trying to eliminate stress entirely, but in changing how we *respond* to things that can cause us stress. As I've said, falling out of balance is just part of the human condition, but the sooner we can regroup, the better. That's what I mean by managing stress. If we want to stay healthy and have sharp minds, managing—and discharging—stress successfully is right up at the top of the list.

During any given day, things can happen that cause us to feel stressed. Say, for example, you get a difficult phone call or an email from an upset relative, a traffic ticket or a past-due notice for a bill you forgot about. I'm sure you won't have any trouble thinking of possibilities. Any one of those things might bring your stress level to a 5 before you even notice it. Then, if something else happens, you might skyrocket to totally stressed out: 10 or more. In that state, you're not thinking clearly. Your muscles are tight or painful and your breathing is shallow. You're having a miserable time. But what if you can catch the first wave of stress and bring down your level quickly? Then you can avoid getting to such high levels of stress.

To help with that, I've created ten *5-Minute Helpers*, quick, effective and easy tools that you can use wherever you are, day

219

or night. These tools help you to:

- Let go of unhelpful thoughts and emotions, and relieve tension

- Discharge stress hormones and re-balance body, mind and spirit

- Lift your mood, relax and re-charge your energy

To Let Go of Unhelpful Thoughts and Emotions and Release Tension

Let's look at how breathing can help us release unhelpful thoughts and emotions.

How we breathe both reflects and affects our emotional state. Breathing involves exhaling stale air and receiving life-sustaining oxygen through our inhalation. However, when we feel threatened or fearful, our body reacts. Our muscles tighten, and our breathing constricts. This is the ANS at work, but it can quickly turn into a vicious cycle. Constricted, shallow breathing lessens the amount of oxygen we receive, which leads to even more tension and fear, and more restricted breathing. It reduces the amount of oxygen we take in, which amplifies feelings of fear and makes it difficult to think clearly. This leads to more scary thoughts. That's why it's critical to release our breathing whenever we are stressed or anxious—yet that's hard to do.

The *Blow It Out/Let It Go* helper interrupts that cycle, and uses the natural power of your breath to expel those unhelpful thoughts and feelings from your body, mind and spirit. Exhaling more fully slows the heart rate, allows you to take in more oxygen, and slows the fear response.

Here's how to do it:

1. Blow it Out/Let it Go

- Exhale and blow out as much air as possible. Open your mouth and sigh or let out any sounds as you exhale. As you do so, picture all your unwanted feelings (fear, anger, tiredness, etc.) leaving your body.

- Open your mouth wide and yawn as you inhale. Imagine that this deep inhalation fills you with calmness and energy.

- Afterwards, breathe naturally, and enjoy this peaceful moment.

Blow It Out increases the amount of oxygen you take in, which helps you to think more clearly and feel calmer. It also brings feelings of ease and safety, as do the *Move and Breathe* activities, which you'll find in the next chapter, on the Breath.

The first sign of stress is a great time to use another Helper, *Push the Pause Button*. It gives you the opportunity to leave an unhelpful or hurtful situation, and to re-group. Use it also if you're feeling overwhelmed, angry and concerned that you "might lose it."

221

2. Push the Pause Button

- STOP whatever you are doing, even for just a minute or two. Imagine that you are pushing the pause button on your remote control.

- Walk away from the situation for a few moments. Get a drink of water, go to the bathroom, or step outside for a breath of fresh air.

- Invite easy breathing. Do *Blow It Out* to double the benefits.

Here are two other Helpers we can call on to release unhelpful thoughts or emotions: *Drop* It and *Put It in the Box.*

3. Drop It

Imagine that you are holding all your unhelpful thoughts, self-criticisms, worry etc. in your fists.

- Take a moment to tighten your fists and hold onto those thoughts even tighter.

- Open your hands and imagine everything inside your fists dropping to the ground. Repeat as needed. Experiment opening your fist slowly and then quickly to find which one works best for you. I do drop it by holding on to a pillow and then letting it fall to the ground.

4. Put it in the Box

Instead of carrying worries, problems, and unhelpful thoughts and feelings around all day, or taking them to bed with you, use this helper to get them out of your head and place them *in the Box*. It may feel similar to "turning it over" to a Higher Power. Here are two ways to do this.

- **Imagine a box** of any kind. It can be gigantic, or tiny with a large padlock. Have fun creating your own container! Imagine sending your worries and difficult thoughts to the box on a plane, train, magic carpet, in a cart – anything you want!

- **Use an actual box** - even a simple shoebox will do, so long as it has a lid or cover. Have fun decorating it! Write down your worrisome or difficult thoughts, draw them, or choose objects that represent them. Put them all in this box. You can revisit the contents anytime you chose.

A client used Put it in the box successfully to help her sleep after a difficult loss. She chose a large box and added rocks to it before bedtime that represented her loss. In that way she honored her loss, and gave herself permission to put it away for the night.

To discharge stress hormones and release challenging physical and/or emotional feelings:

Remember our discussing the dangers of stress hormones lingering in the body? If we have become stressed for whatever reason, it's very important to discharge those stress hormones. We can do this through movement. Physical movement helps release stress chemicals, such as adrenalin. Moving also gives you a sense of empowerment, which is especially helpful when you find yourself in a difficult and stressful situation. As you exert your muscles, you begin to sense your ability to change or leave a bad situation. If you feel "frozen" in fear or confusion, moving in any way helps get you going again. Here are two helpers that discharge stress, release tight muscles and tiredness, and increase your energy too: *Shake it Out* and *Just Move*!

5. Shake It Out

- Stand or sit, and shake your whole body. Shake gently or more vigorously—whatever feels right to you. Shake standing or sitting or even walking down a hall – anywhere!

- Shake different parts of your body individually: your hands and arms, your hips and lower back, your legs and feet—one leg at a time.

- Shake each for 30 seconds to 2 minutes.

NOTE: To double the benefits, combine *Shake It Out* with *Blow It Out/Let it Go!*

6. Just Move! and the Curse Dance

- First, move in any way that you can. Walk out of a room, down a hallway, in and out of a building, or around the block. Simple is good!

- Take it further - sway, swing, stretch, stomp—whatever feels good to you.

- Expand it even further and as you move, let out as many curses as you can, or say, over and over, NO, NO, NO! or whatever else helps get out your feelings.

- Alternatively, turn on music and have fun moving.

Here's an example of how I used *Just Move!* fresh from my life:

As I was writing this chapter my car mechanic called with a huge estimate for my repair. The best way for me to not go into despair, and unhelpful thinking of financial ruin, was to do the Curse dance. I stomped around the room and let out all the curses I could muster. It made me laugh, which opened up my breathing and helped me to Change the Channel. I switched from the "Poor Me" station to "I Got This." Then I could think more clearly. Yes, it would be tough to pay the bill but it was not going to lead to financial ruin. I didn't have to wreck my whole day (and maybe the next day, too, if I was still too upset to sleep well) and my well-being in the process: I could just pay the bill. And get back to writing.

To lift your mood, relax and regain energy:

Throughout this book I have suggested doing the Touchstone Helper with your hand on your heart area (the sternum bone) to connect deeply to yourself. This helper can also be expanded to include putting your hand on any of your bones. Our touch reminds us that our bones support and protect us. For example, your skull is a built-in protection for your brain. Holding your skull helps you to relax deeply and release fear.

7. Touchstone/Touch Bone

- Bring your hands to your head as if you were cradling all the different parts of your head—front, back and sides. Explore varying the pressure from a light touch to a stronger one to find the pressure that works best for you.

- Find two areas of your head that feel the best and hold for a minute or longer.

- Enjoy breathing deeply

Here's another version: Press down on the long bones in your upper legs from your hip joint to your knees. (This can be done easily while you are sitting at a table, even at a business meeting!)

Remember the illustration of a cycle from earlier in this chapter that demonstrates how we can spiral down into the pit, or lift ourselves out of it? Here is a personal example to show you how I used the helpers, changed the channel, and altered the way I experienced, perceived and thought about this stressful situation.

I came home from a nice trip visiting friends and family. Even though I travel quite a bit, I still find the transition back home difficult at times. This time, as I walked in the door I saw that one of my cats was walking only on three legs, holding her back paw up in the air. I was immediately catapulted back to a terrible experience I had years ago, coming home from a long idyllic vacation. When we walked into our home, we immediately saw that our beloved cat was horribly ill. He walked a few steps towards us and fell down. We jumped into the car and took the cat right to the vet.

This time, we had a different cat, but again we had a new house sitter. When I could not reach him, I could feel myself beginning to panic. My muscles were tightening and my breathing was constricted. My self-talk was also going awry: "Oh no, maybe my cat has a terrible disease."

By then, I knew I wasn't thinking clearly, so I turned to my 5-Minute Helpers, starting with Push the Pause Button. Then I tuned into my breath to calm down by using Blow It Out. After that, I used calming Self-Touch/Touchstone/ Touch Bone on my head.

At last, I was calm enough to realize that I could use some reassurance from someone who was objective, and not thinking in terms of the worst-case scenario. Since the vet was closed, I called a neighbor, a nurse, who has taken care of our cat and many animals over the years. Luckily, she was able to come right over, and we examined the cat together. She assured me that it was not an emergency, and that it would be best to observe the cat overnight to have more information for the vet. It was time for me to use the handy question: What's going right here? Plenty! I asked for help and advice and received it right away! I knew then that I could safely put my concerns about the cat "In the Box" until morning and get some sleep.

Can you see how I intervened and caught myself before I descended down into the pit? How the helpers, and the tools to change the channel altered my emotions, my self-talk and my body's responses?

8. Funny Faces

This might seem like a childish thing to do. That's what makes it fun! Do this when you feel frustrated, stuck, down-and-out, upset about a new wrinkle, or while you're washing your hands,

- Experiment with making all different faces, silly, scary, whatever you like.

- Stick out your tongue as far a possible

- Move your mouth in different directions

Bonus Idea: Take a photo of your funny face and text or email it to friends. Ask them to send you funny faces too especially at stressful times!

9. Music Changes the Channel

- Turn on music that you especially enjoy—or any that you can locate quickly

- Fully listen to the lyrics, especially when you need to change your self-talk

- Sing or dance along; clap or make sounds to the music to double the benefits.

- Play chants and sing along

Note: Look for music with cheery lyrics, and uplifting tunes to have on hand.

Here's a story of how I escaped how I shifted my self-talk with *Music Changes the Channel,* and used a helpful question to escape the pit.

I had to get my writing organized for an editor, and I was feeling under pressure, big-time. The hot, humid weather was fogging out my brain and making it difficult to focus at all. My self-talk became mean. It began with: "You'll never get this done," and soon progressed to: "What a waste of time to work on this book." I felt like crying. The pit was opening its wide jaws and was about to swallow me whole. I had to act fast.

Luckily, I had recently remembered that musicals were a great mood shifter and lifter. I played a favorite musical, and as if by magic, the song lyrics began to replace my mean self-talk. As I listened while preparing lunch, my mood lifted enough to ask myself: "What's going right here?" The answer followed. With the help of the music, I finally completed the huge project of organizing my material. That's a big accomplishment!

10. Revive

When we're under time constraints, we have a tendency to rush and work without breaks. Taking time to *Revive* in between tasks makes it easier to accomplish tasks effectively and reduces stress, allowing you to create new, positive energy. I developed Revive while teaching in a demanding training program. It helped me give my full attention when I felt worn out. I use Revive daily. It renews my energy and focus for writing, seeing clients and many tasks.

Here are some ways to *Revive*:

> *Revive through the Breath:* Enjoy a breath of fresh air. Open a window or door. Exhale out tiredness and stress. (See *Blow It Out*)
>
> *Revive through Water:* Drink water – A lack of fluids can cause tiredness. Splash water on your face, or wash your face. Wash your hands and shake them out.
>
> *Revive through Self-touch:* Give yourself a quick "energy shower." Start from your head and brush your hands lightly over as much of your body as you can reach, as if you were wiping off powder or flour that had spilled on your clothes. Imagine that you can wipe away tiredness and other feelings as you continue these strokes. Shake out your arms and hands and make sounds to help let go of what you have accumulated.
>
> *Revive through Scents:* Try aromatherapy sprays, hand lotion, and herbal teas. Experiment to find which scents work best for you

Can you imagine using some of these "Helpers" in this chapter? If you find one particularly useful, copy it and leave it in a strategic place. Also, check out my website for purse-size copies of the helpers to carry around with you.

In conclusion, do you remember what I've said regarding all the tools in this book? The more you repeat them, the better they will work. That's how we humans learn: through repetition. We also learn better when we are engaged and having fun (or just being silly; that's when we connect to the happy child within). That's why I made the helpers easy and enjoyable and do-able wherever you are. You can do them vigorously and let out loud sounds and sighs, or do them quietly and in a low-key way. No one ever seems to notice me doing a helper. I've done them in a parking lot, in my car, down a hallway, in the bathroom, on a bus or subway, or walking down a busy street. Create your own helper, and mix and match with the ones in this chapter. Remember that the 5 Minute Helpers really work best when you have fun doing them. So, enjoy!

In the next chapter, we'll explore the most versatile and powerful self-care tools there is: our breath.

11

Turn to Your Breath

When it comes to cultivating well-being, there's no greater source of support than your own breath. Your breath is a river of life and energy that is always moving through you. In Hindu philosophy, breath is also referred to as *prana*, which means "life force." You might pause to consider this for a moment: *breath is life*.

Connecting with your breath can comfort, soothe, relax and rebalance you. It can energize and renew you, help you to think more clearly, and relieve pain. Breathing consciously, with awareness, can connect you deeply to yourself, to the Earth, to Nature and to spirit. Each day, all the trees and the green plant world freely create abundant life-sustaining oxygen for all of us to breathe. Then, with each exhalation, we create carbon dioxide, or CO_2, which is an essential nutrient for plant life. In this way, through the breath, we nurture plant life and are nurtured by it in return. That deep sense of our interconnection with Nature is another gift that connecting with our breath offers.

Connecting with your breath can expand your awareness. This is why breathing has been a key element in many spiritual and meditative practices over the centuries. Another word for inhaling is "inspiration" which literally means "in spirit"— we are breathing in spirit.

All of this makes the breath a very powerful aid to self-care and joyful living.

Unfortunately, most people don't realize the power of their breath. That's why, in this chapter, I'm going to guide you to becoming more acquainted with the miraculous, nurturing aspects your breath, and show you how to use your breath to foster self-care. Most importantly, I hope that this chapter leads you to experience your breath as your friend, your constant companion and powerful ally.

The Power of Your Breath

Your breath is uniquely versatile. Compared to your other body functions, like your heartbeat or digestion, breathing is unique in that it can be regulated in two very different ways by your nervous system.

The first way is automatic. Breathing just happens, beneath your conscious awareness; you do not need to think about it. While you are sleeping, driving, or going about your daily activities, you are "being breathed."

But then there is the second way. You can *directly affect your breath by paying conscious attention to it.* And herein lies the key to its power. Just close your eyes for a few moments now and feel your breathing. Notice if this focused awareness slows or deepens your breathing. As you breathe more consciously and deeply, more life-sustaining oxygen and energy is able to pour into your being, while also releasing tension and stress. This is what I mean by connecting with your breath.

Now, consider how easy it is to connect with your breath. Did you know that you breathe about 18,000 times each day? This is why I call your breath your constant companion. This means that you have 18,000 opportunities each day to use your breath to care for yourself. That's a lot! Because you breathe so frequently, even the briefest deepening or slowing of your breath can have a profound positive effect on both your physical and emotional well-being.

All of this makes your breath a wonderful self-care tool. You can call upon it anywhere and anytime to feel better physically and emotionally. You can use it to help lift your energy and lighten your mood. That is why you will see suggestions in this book about using the breath to ease daily transitions and create calmness in stressful situations, as with my 5-Minute Helpers. For example, with Touchstone, you can turn to the breath to connect with and rebalance yourself. And the breath is not just a tool to deal with stress. By turning to your breath on a regular basis, you can enhance your overall well-being.

Breathing Activities to Connect to Your Breath

I've developed a series of activities to help you discover the power of your breath and to encourage you to experiment with breathing in new ways. Many of us constrict our breathing; it's a habit of which we're largely unaware. By consciously engaging in these breathing activities, you can unlearn old habits, remove restrictions, and experience the joy of breathing more deeply and freely.

As I wrote in the beginning of this book, *how* we do things matters; it is possible to approach anything, even a yoga class or a relaxation exercise, in a stressful manner. It's the same with breathing exercises: most people try too hard and use more effort than is required. That's why I refer to these breathing experiences as "Breathing Activities" rather than exercises. Or even better: think of these activities as simply an invitation to visit (or connect) with your breath, a call to enjoy a breath of fresh air, or to sigh with relief.

Easy Does It

To begin, let's look at how to approach breathing awareness. Again, think simple and easy; we don't have to work hard to use the power of the breath to help us in the moment, or even to transform years of tension and restriction. Here are two examples designed to show you why this is so. I think of one as an example of "working too hard" and the other as "breathing with ease." I invite you to take just a minute or two to try each of these now, and feel the difference.

1) Try to "take" a very big breath right now. Really pull the air into your nose and lungs and push out your chest and ribs. Then, let your exhale just happen. Try this a few times.

Can you feel how much effort you are using? Do you notice tension in your shoulders or neck as you do this? Do you enjoy breathing this way?

2) Now try slightly exaggerating your exhale by slowly blowing the air out of your mouth, or sighing as you exhale. Continue this for a few breaths. All the while, just let your inhale happen naturally. As you keep exhaling this way, you may notice that an easier

and deeper inhalation will automatically follow your exhalation.

Do you enjoy breathing this way?   Do you feel more energized or relaxed?

Did you feel how much easier it was to increase your exhale rather than your inhale?

Increasing your exhale has other benefits, too. It helps release tight muscles, calms and balances your nervous system, and interrupts restricted breathing. In addition, a deeper exhale automatically deepens our inhalation. These are all reasons why, in this chapter, we will focus on *increasing the exhale* (the letting go part of the breath), rather than on trying to "take" a big breath.

Now let's go deeper into my approach to the breath.

Connecting to the Breath: My Embodied Approach

It has been my experience that the beneficial effects of these breathing activities are amplified when we can also envision images based on the actual physiology of breathing. In other words, the positive effects of connecting with our breath can be even greater if we know—and can picture—what is actually occurring in our bodies as we focus on our breath. This is a key part of the embodied approach I take to my work, and it's what makes these suggested breathing activities unique. It's also why this next section is designed to take you on a little guided tour of the wonderful world of breathing.

What is Breathing, Exactly?

Simply put, breathing is the exchange of air in and out of your lungs. The physiology of breath has two major parts, which I'll now describe. While the breath is a physical process, it also transcends the physical in a way that can teach us some profound life lessons. I'll describe that aspect as well.

External Respiration: Emptying and Filling

As you inhale, your lungs, ribs and torso expand and your diaphragm lowers. All of this increases your capacity to take in the oxygen-filled air needed to nourish all the cells in your body. Then, when you exhale, you expel the "used" air, which is filled with carbon dioxide. This process—which is called *external respiration*—reflects a process found throughout all of Nature: that of *emptying out and then filling up*. Through the breath, we can connect deeply with this universal process, which has a very positive effect on our sense of well-being. Let's see how we can connect to both aspects of this process, beginning first with emptying.

Exhale and release. Besides letting go of stale air, each exhale also provides an opportunity for us to empty out. Specifically, that means that, as you exhale the stale air that you took in a few moments ago, you can also let go of anything that no longer serves you. You can release challenging bodily sensations, such as tension, tightness or pain. You can also let go of difficult emotions such as anger, or fear, as well as upsetting thoughts and frustrations. That means that you can begin right now, in this very moment, to discharge past hurts and regrets that still weigh you down even though they happened years ago:

The process of releasing through exhalation is such an important tool for me. I experience my exhalation as a pathway, a kind of road or a river, that is always there, available to me. When I exhale, I send out anything I no longer need and feel it being carried away. I call this breathing activity, "Blow It Out," and I do it often throughout the day to help me let go of anything I want to release. (Blow it Out is one of my 5-Minute Helpers. See the chapter, Return to Balance.)

Emptying prepares you to receive. This, too, is a profound lesson of the breath. The more you exhale and empty your lungs, the more your lungs can expand. You literally have a greater capacity to receive more nourishing oxygen when you inhale. It's the same in life. When you empty, you have more capacity to receive.

Inhale and receive. Have you ever felt empty or exhausted. . . wrung out like a dishtowel . . . like you've given all the attention and care and energy you have to give? In those moments, you need sustenance, but you don't want to work to get it. In those moments, remember: nourishing, renewing, life-sustaining oxygen is always freely and abundantly available to you. Just inhale, and let yourself receive fully. It's a wonderful way to practice receiving.

In sum, there is a natural resonance between the breath and the circle of giving and receiving, and you can use this to enhance your well-being. When you pair the letting go aspect of breathing with a conscious intention to release, and pair the receiving aspect of breathing with taking in specific, nurturing feelings and sensations, the effect is very powerful. Let's take a moment to experience what I'm suggesting. Here is a breathing activity that couples the physical aspects of breathing, exhaling and inhaling, with the emotional and spiritual aspects of breathing, releasing and receiving:

- First, imagine your breath as a pathway or river that can carry away what you want to release. Now, as you exhale, release and send out tension or anything else you want to let go of at this time. As you do so, release your jaw and sigh or make some other sounds. Repeat 3 or 4 times.

- Then, as you inhale, invite nourishing and uplifting feelings and sensations such as calmness, energy, hope, beauty into your body and being.

- Now, imagine actually receiving those qualities . . . Allow those feelings and sensations to seep into you and work their magic, just as a hot bath or shower penetrates and loosens tight muscles.

You can give yourself a renewing moment like this anytime during your day. Or, combine focused breathing with a short rest—that's doubly revitalizing! (This breathing activity can ease daily transitions, too. For more, see the chapter *Your Relationship to Time*.)

Internal Respiration: The Other Side of Breathing

There is another aspect of breathing, called *internal respiration*. This term describes what occurs internally in the moments *between* when we inhale and exhale. Most of us are not aware of this wonderful part of breathing.

After you inhale and your lungs fill with oxygen, that oxygen goes into your heart and your blood. Your heart then sends this oxygen out through your blood vessels to every cell in your body. In this way, your cells receive the steady supply of life sustaining, nourishing oxygen that comes in through the lungs.

As your cells use this oxygen to metabolize food nutrients, they produce a waste product, carbon dioxide, or CO_2. This CO_2 and other waste products are then carried back through the blood to the lungs to be expelled out through your exhalation.

This description of internal respiration gives you the inside picture of what happens to the air we breathe in, how it gets to nourish every cell in your body, and how the used air finds its way out to be exhaled.

The next breathing activity offers an opportunity to connect with the source of the oxygen we breathe in: the plant world.

One More Nourishing Way to Visit with Your Breath

Here is a breathing activity that connects body-mind-spirit and helps you to feel more whole and connected.

The flow of receiving and giving and interconnecting with nature

As I've said, when we exhale out carbon dioxide (CO_2), we feed the plant world, and when we inhale, we breathe in the oxygen created by the plant world. In this meditation/activity, you use your imagination to experience the wonderful exchange of life-giving substances that is always taking place between your body and the plant world. This is one of my favorite breathing activities. I often do it for a few minutes while walking, or when I feel depleted and need energy. It gives me a deep sense of connection to the earth and to myself. It also serves as a deep reminder of the importance of balancing receiving and giving. I hope you enjoy it.

- Sit or stand, either outside or indoors, near a window or a houseplant. Choose a tree, plant or anything green and alive that you can see and feel drawn to.

- Then, as you exhale, send your CO_2 to nourish that specific tree or plant along with appreciation for the plant.

- Now, inhale and receive the oxygen from that tree into your lungs. Imagine that you can also receive some of the trees energy and vitality, along with the oxygen. Remember that this oxygen goes to every cell in your body.

- Continue this breathing for a few minutes, or for as long as you wish.

Add a simple movement to enhance your experience:

- Direct your arms out to the plant or tree as you send your exhale.

- Now, fold your arms back toward your chest gathering the nourishing oxygen and aliveness of the plant world. Put your hands over your heart (Touchstone), and allow yourself to receive this goodness and nourishment. Let it fill you.

Before I share the next breathing activity, I'd like to address the importance of breathing freely in a little more depth.

Breathing Freely

The full inner movement of the breath—as in the Breath Wave activity I'll share at the end of this chapter—literally helps your body function better. The movement massages the digestive organs, increases circulation and can even help loosen tight shoulder muscles. In practicing this activity, however, you may discover that you have been *unconsciously restricting your breathing*. This is not uncommon. In fact, most adults don't breathe freely and fully in the way our bodies were designed to.

You may wonder: why is this so? Perhaps, as a child, we were told to sit still and be quiet, so we learned to refrain from moving our bodies. We might have had asthma or other breathing issues, or we simply lacked information about our breathing. I was able to see how much this lack of information could affect breathing when I taught a class called "Breathing Freely":

> *I discovered that virtually everyone in the class had an image of their lungs as being like plastic bags, an image they'd picked up in an elementary school class on biology. These "bags" had no real substance; they just filled and emptied in a very passive way. If they really understood their lungs, I thought, it would forever change how they experienced their breath. And this is exactly what happened. When they learned, for example, that their lungs consisted of at least 150 million air sacs, which, if laid out flat, would fill an area the size of a tennis court, they were amazed. Just knowing this fact gave them a sense of fullness and appreciation for their lungs that they had never before experienced—and it changed how they breathed!*

Do you hold your breath?

Many of us have the habit of holding or restricting our breath when we focus on a task. We might do this when we're performing a new task, especially one that requires a lot of concentration, manual dexterity and delicacy, but we can also do it even when we're performing a simple, routine task. I have seen this pattern many times in others and even in myself. What is the reason? That's a question that has puzzled me for a long time. Do we feel threatened or unsafe? Are we bracing for criticism or harsh words that might be hurled at us if we make a mistake? Or is it simply that working on a task somehow got paired with holding our breath, and we just go into that familiar pattern, regardless of what we actually feel about the situation? Whatever the reason for this habit, it is important to unlearn.

We may also have learned to hold our breath as a way of managing difficult feelings when, ironically, it does just the opposite. As we discussed in the *Coming into Balance* chapter, restricting our breathing has a negative impact on how we feel, both emotionally and physically. The more we restrict our breathing, the less oxygen we take in. A diminished oxygen supply leads to increased tension and fear. In turn, fear tends to quicken our breathing, which leads to even more restricted breathing . . . and so on.

Increasing the amount of oxygen that we take in, on the other hand, helps us to think more clearly and feel calmer. Relaxed breathing leads to feelings of ease and safety, which then deepens our breathing and brings in even more life-giving oxygen. By encouraging relaxed breathing, you can, at any moment, choose aliveness and vitality. In sum, how you breathe both reflects and affects your emotional state. Feeling joyful relaxes and expands your breathing, which in turn increases your joy. That is a good reason to cultivate joy on a daily basis—it leads to more joy!

Another reason that we might restrict our breathing can come from being told by authority figures that we must "correct" our posture Here's a story that shows how trying to stand up straight affected how a client breathed and caused her much pain:

> *Joyce had been in almost constant pain for a long time. She began receiving chiropractic treatments, which eased her pain temporarily, yet her chiropractor could see that Joyce was still not releasing a long-held pattern of holding her spine very tightly. The chiropractor believed that this habit was the cause of her pain, so she referred Joyce to me.*

> *As we spoke, Joyce told me that she reminded herself all through the day to hold in her stomach and to stand or sit up straight. She did this because a health practitioner had once told her that she had terrible posture and that she should hold herself erect. However, this practice seriously restricted her breath and tightened her whole back.*

> *Working with me, Joyce learned to let go of this impossible goal—one that was causing her pain—and to release her breathing. The Move and Breathe Breath activities (introduced on the next pages) were especially helpful for her.*

Lastly, I want to dispel the idea that there is a "right" way to breathe; there isn't. If you have ever been told that you breathe shallowly, or that the way you breathe is "wrong" or bad, I hope this comes as some relief. Furthermore, your breathing naturally varies during different activities; it depends on your body's need for oxygen at any given moment. If you walk up a steep hill or staircase, your muscles need more oxygen to accomplish the extra climb; conversely, your breath slows when you relax and sleep. Also, your breathing changes, depending upon your emotional state. The way you breathe when you are excited is likely to be very different from how it is when you feel sad, for example. In sum, rather than focusing on breathing "correctly," I encourage my clients and students to focus on weeding out any old habits of restriction that may be interfering with their breathing fully and freely.

Move and Breathe

Have you ever watched an infant or a cat or dog sleep? If so, then you may have seen how much their bodies move with every breath. That's how it looks when we breathe freely.

This next breathing activity brings together breathing and movement to support breathing more freely. It mimics the automatic movements of your body that physically assist your process of exhaling and inhaling—and exaggerates them to increase the benefit.

This is how it happens: When you exhale, your ribs, lungs, and torso condense, or get smaller. Conversely, when you inhale, your torso expands to create room for your lungs to fully fill up. Your chest and ribs grow in all directions, and your diaphragm lowers down to support this expansion. We are usually not aware of these wonderful internal movements happening with every breath. However, the following breathing and movement activities give us an opportunity to experience and enlarge these internal movements. These activities lubricate the joints of our spine and hips, activate the pelvic floor muscles and release the back tension, tightness and pain that comes from sitting too much. They are also a great sensual warm-up! And they only take a few minutes.

As you play with these movements, listen to your body. Always start small, do what is comfortable, and then gently begin to move more fully. This may feel different from how you've ever moved before, but don't worry about "getting it right"—having fun and being relaxed is much more important! It may seem simple, but it works and it feels good!

The Move and Breathe Activity:

- Stand in a relaxed way; allow your knees to bend slightly.

- As you exhale, follow and exaggerate the natural condensing movement of your exhale by bending your head and spine forward, and folding your arms in front of you. Continue a few times and let your whole body get smaller, and curl up like a ball.

- As you inhale follow and encourage the natural expanding movement of your whole body to grow in all directions and expand while you inhale. Open your chest and abdomen, and let your whole body expand more and more so that you're stretched out wide and tall with your fingers reaching out to the ceiling or sky above you.

- Continue doing this rhythmic movement and let it grow so that when you exhale you curl over as much as you can, and expand even more when you inhale. Enjoy the movement.

You can increase the power of this movement in two ways: Blow the air out as you exhale. Open and close your hands and arms as you expand and condense your torso.

Now here's a way to further deepen the movement of the breath through your whole body. It's called the Breath Wave. This movement begins from your pelvis and travels up to your head. It has more of the quality of a wave. I love the Breath Wave. It feels delicious.

The Sitting Breath Wave:

- Sit with your feet flat on the floor. Sit forward in the chair. Don't lean on the back of the chair.

- Place your hands on the top of your hipbones. Let your hands slide along with the forward and backward movement of your pelvis.

- To warm up your hips, first rock your pelvis forward and back in small movements.

- Let the movement become as easy and effortless as possible.

- As you exhale, tilt your pelvis back, blow out the air and curl up your body forward like a ball.

- As you inhale tilt your pelvis forward. Let you whole body grow in all directions and expand. Open up and expand your chest, arms, and torso and bring your head up towards the ceiling. Imagine that you are bringing your face up to drink in the warm rays of the sun.

I've also developed a lying down version of this Breath Wave. You can find this and more suggested Breathing Activities, on my website: lindatumbarello.com.

In closing, I hope that this chapter helps you to experience your breath as your friend, a constant companion and ally. I also hope that the breathing activities here lead you to easily and simply tap into the power of your breath. And please remember: whatever you do or feel, wherever you are, no matter what, you are always breathing—about 18,000 times a day—so you can always tune into your breath to feel better.

All you need is a few moments.

12

Cultivating a Friendlier Relationship with Food

As you come to this chapter, you might find yourself thinking, *Oh no! Here's someone else telling me what I should or should not eat—I just can't stomach that!* Maybe you even felt your stomach knot up with anxiety just thinking about the topic of eating and food.

I bet you have felt a knot in your stomach before, if not now. I sure have. That is your digestive system letting you know that you are anxious or upset in some way. You might have been in other situations that you just couldn't "stomach," or heard opinions that you didn't want to "swallow." You may also have experienced "gut" feelings that told you whether or not something was right for you, or whether someone was speaking honestly or not. Welcome to the world of your digestive system!

Yes, food is an emotional topic, so before continuing on, I want to make you a promise: This chapter will not contain the usual information about what you should or should not eat. I will not attempt to convince you that this or that particular food is better for you, or suggest that you follow one diet or another. Nor is this a recipe for an overhaul. It's not another six-week plan to lose x number of pounds—pounds that you'll gain right back. Nor is it a food plan of some sort, promising miraculous results in no time at all. There is no quick fix, and certainly not one that's long lasting or permanent.

And that's okay.

It's okay because the journey to true self-care—the journey that you're taking with me in this book—is not focused on the external; it's focused on caring for you from the inside out. Changing your relationship with food and eating is an inside job. And like the first Practice, *Cultivating Inner Kindness,* it will not happen overnight; a major change like this can take time. That's because many of the habits and beliefs we have around food and eating are long-standing—maybe decades long—and they are reinforced, often on a daily basis, by the media and other cultural influences. Lasting change happens slowly, a little bit at a time, by keeping our efforts small, easy, do-able and fun. Don't underestimate the impact of those small steps! They can have a significant positive impact on your health and well-being, not to mention your self-worth and your capacity for joy.

This chapter, I hope, will serve as a good beginning. Here, I invite you to apply what you have learned thus far about caring for you to eating and nourishment. That means creating a healthy, positive relationship with food. You see, eating is meant to be pleasurable. Maximizing the pleasure of eating deepens our satisfaction, our joy. It also encourages relaxation, which aids digestion and assimilation. I know this may seem counter-intuitive, but increasing the pleasure of food is a pathway to s-l-o-w-l-y, over time, shifting your relationship with food. For some women, it is also a gentle and successful way to improve digestion and lose weight.

Eating is meant to be a source of support, of sustenance, and joy. Yet, many of us have a conflicted relationship with food. Take a moment to ask yourself: *What interferes, right now, with the pleasure of eating?*

Here are some possible answers to this question:

- Feeling uncomfortable with your body

- Feeling guilty about eating "too much," or even about eating at all

- Feeling guilty about what you are eating—especially when you eat "forbidden" or "fattening" food

- Feeling guilty about eating whenever you feel hungry, or snacking

- Eating whatever you can grab, whether it is tasty or satisfying

- Feeling tense and harried at mealtimes; preparing food in a rushed manner and eating too quickly

- Eating while watching TV or being otherwise distracted, such as thinking or worrying about the next thing on your to do list

If you recognized yourself in any of these, you are not alone. If you have ever had negative feelings about your body, if you have ever tried restricting foods in order to lose weight, sometimes over and over again, you are not alone. If you struggle with food and eating, you can often feel like the only one who does—but it's just not true.

It is that feeling that I hope to address, and help shift, in this chapter. In this chapter I will show you how you can:

- Develop a friendlier, more nurturing relationship with food and with yourself, a relationship in which you experience freedom from dieting and unnecessary food restrictions. Remember: Practice #1 is about *Cultivating inner kindness and love.*

- Discover *what is most nourishing for you.* Expand your food repertoire, and eat with greater enjoyment, pleasure and relaxation.

- *Find your own way* to nourish yourself with food— slowly, by taking one small, easy step at a time.

So, what exactly, will we cover in this chapter? This chapter is divided into four sections. We will start first by looking at how our beliefs and self-talk impact how and what we eat. Many of the things we tell ourselves are false. As you read, I invite you to examine your own beliefs about food and encourage you to slowly release false or limiting beliefs, replacing them with new, life-affirming beliefs.

Then, we'll get to know our digestive system. Listening to your body's cues and wisdom is essential to your well-being now, and over the long term. Understanding how your digestive system works, and attuning to the different kinds of signals it sends you, can help you to *find your own way* to eat.

Most everything you have read about eating concerns "what" and "what not" to eat. In the third section of this chapter we will look at the *What of Eating* in a new way. And lastly, we'll look at the *How of Eating.* We will look at the entire process of eating, which actually begins long before we actually sit down to eat. Let's start.

Start with beliefs

"Eat when you are hungry." The message embedded in these five words, uttered by a caring physician (let's call her Dr. Sage), changed the life of one of my friends. It freed her from a false and restrictive belief about how and when she should eat, and enabled her to connect with her body's wisdom. The story began to unfold when Rachel went to see her doctor after a routine blood test showed elevated blood sugar:

I was quite upset when the doctor told me that I really needed to take this seriously, as my elevated blood sugar level could progress to diabetes. But then, I couldn't believe her advice. Not only did she tell me to eat more often, but she also instructed me to eat whenever I was hungry. I was shocked. To be given permission to eat when I was hungry was revolutionary!

For almost all of my 68 years, I had been very conscious about not gaining weight (what woman is not?!), so I'd always restricted my eating to three meals a day. I never snacked, because I thought I shouldn't—especially on foods that I thought had too many calories and fats, like nuts. Then, when it was finally mealtime, especially lunchtime, I was absolutely ravenous and tended to eat whatever I could get my hands on—to excess.

After that conversation with my doctor, I began noticing what times of day I felt hungry. I realized that I was especially hungry in the morning. I awaken early, eat a small breakfast and then take a walk. After my walk, I began noticing that I felt hungry, so I began having a protein-rich snack. Then I noticed that, because I had snacked in the morning, I was no longer famished at lunchtime.

As I continued to listen to my body, I discovered the routine that worked for me. Now, I eat a small meal, followed later by a snack. I eat less at mealtimes because I'm no longer ravenous. As I learned to listen to my needs and hungers, I became more aware of which foods actually support my well-being, and also when I feel full. When I allowed myself to snack on nuts, cheese and other fat and protein-rich foods I once considered taboo, I found that not only my blood sugar level stabilized, but so did my moods. As I continued to listen to my body around food, I found that my trust in my body's wisdom deepened.

Rachel began to eat in a new way that supported her health and well-being. She ate "fattening" foods and ate more often. However, she lost weight! My friend had never been over-weight, yet for nearly 68 years she had followed the dictum of eating only three times a day—even though it didn't really work for her. So how did she get so caught up in this limiting belief, rather than listening to her own body?

We are subject to an endless bombardment of opinions about eating and dieting. There may be more books, articles, programs, blogs, et cetera, devoted to eating than to any other single issue. The diet genre, in particular, is dominant. In fact, "diet" is one of the terms most frequently entered on Internet search engines. How many women have tried how many countless programs touted as being effective for losing weight? How many women restrict their food intake to meal-times only, regardless of when they actually feel hungry, even if they might benefit from having a snack? How many women carry around boulders of self-criticism and shame about their weight and body size? How many women continue to be chained to the diet wheel—losing and regaining the same weight again and again and again? I, too, have been chained to this wheel, as have many of my clients and friends.

Even though there are many other worthwhile concerns, weight loss seems to be portrayed as a major woman's issue in our culture. Each and every day, the media—including numerous women's magazines, ads of every kind, and websites— exploit this issue in head-spinning ways. For example, in some women's magazines, you may see articles about dieting placed right alongside recipes for decadent desserts. Then, of course, there are the countless articles describing "easy and quick" makeovers and body overhauls.

Even if the content of a magazine does not focus directly on losing weight and whipping your body into the right shape, the ads, filled with young, rail-thin women convey those very same messages: this is how you *should* look.

It is so easy to "swallow down whole" these culturally transmitted beliefs about how we should look and what we should eat. No wonder so many women struggle with issues about weight and body image, often beginning in adolescence.

Like many adolescent girls, I gained weight—though looking back at it, not very much. However, after some classmates called me "fatso" and "tumbo" (a play on my last name), I started to feel fat. This led to a long, vicious cycle of dieting, losing weight, gaining weight and dieting yet again. This self-defeating cycle consumed at least 10 years of my young life before I realized that I had lost and gained my entire body weight. So much suffering, and what a waste! There were so many more productive ways I could have used my energy. Later in the chapter I will tell you how I freed myself from this self-defeating cycle.

My experience is not unique. Though the dieting industry has been remarkably successful—the weight loss market amounted to almost $60 billion in the U.S. in 2014—it is an abysmal failure for most. Statistics have shown that 95% or more of all those who diet eventually gain the weight back, and sometimes even more. So, even though dieting rarely works, and leads to our feeling miserable and defeated, we are made to believe that we need to do it to look a certain way.

Eating and body image

Food has been linked with body image in a way that has made eating—the necessary nourishing of our bodies—problematic for many, many women. We will never, ever look like the media tells us we should look. I have encountered very few women who have not felt concern or worry, at some point in their lives, about being too fat, or having the wrong shape. This sense of "not being okay" about our weight or body image is insidious. It is like living with a persistent, negative voice that is constantly saying: "I'm not good enough; my body is all wrong." Negative body image lowers self-esteem and interferes with a sense of satisfaction and connection to our bodies. It can also be the cause of difficulties in relating to others—as well as with one's self. Body image is such an important topic for women that I will address it again in the last chapter, Growing Older, specifically with respect to sexuality. I also address it in my previous book, *Joyful Sexuality*. Specifically, I encourage and guide women to connect to how they feel on the inside, rather than how they think they should look, or how they see themselves in the mirror.

Am I a good girl or a bad girl?

There is one very oppressive belief that many women buy into: the idea that what we eat somehow defines whether we are good or bad. "I was bad last night. I ate a brownie," we might say. Or "I was so good. I ate just a small salad for lunch." We may say this even though that salad might have left us hungry and unsatisfied, or even famished, just a few hours later, prompting us to devour a bag of potato chips, which gave us a stomachache. *Sound familiar?*

> *The tendency to castigate ourselves over our food choices seems to have no bounds. We can beat ourselves up for eating foods that are fattening, as well as foods that we are allergic to or have trouble digesting. Whenever we fail to eat as we believe we "should" eat we create another opportunity to beat ourselves up. Inevitably, the strain of trying to be "good" takes its toll, and then we may rebel—and eat way more of what we really wanted to eat in the first place.*

And it can get much worse. The more we have internalized those negative, judging messages about our bodies, the more self-critical we become, and the more eating becomes linked with self-loathing. In *Women, Food and God*, author Geneen Roth reflects upon how this affected her life: "Eating what I wanted was not allowed. Wanting what I wanted was not allowed. I needed to sacrifice, atone, make up for being myself. For being fat."[18] And later in the book, she writes: "Overeating was my way to punish and shame myself; each time I gained weight, each time I failed at a diet, I proved to myself that my deepest fear was true: I was pathetic and doomed."[19]

How do we get to what is true?

The truth is that we all *deserve to eat and to be nourished, no matter our weight or our body size*. Yet, deep down, some of us may hold a belief that says this is not so. If that is the case, we have within us the power to change those beliefs—and to eat well. We can start to shift those false beliefs by telling ourselves the truth. For example, try reading the following passage aloud: *I deserve to eat and be nourished. I can give myself the foods that nurture and satisfy me, rather than depriving myself. I am the only one who can do this for me; no one else can. No one else knows when I am hungry or full. Only I know what I really want to eat. Eating is an area where I have the power to meet my own needs.*

Is there a part of this statement that speaks to you? Can you encourage yourself to make repeating this simple self-support statement a part of your day? (For a review of ways to release false beliefs, see the Practice called *Inner Support*.)

Now let's move on to exploring our amazing digestive system!

Digesting our life as well as our food

It's well known that there is a connection between our emotional states, our beliefs and our physical functions. In fact, each of our organs is associated with a certain quality or state of mind that relates to the function it serves. The organs in our digestive system are no exception.

Our digestive system is intelligent; it knows what is or isn't nourishing for us to eat. It also knows what is or isn't nourishing for us in other areas of our lives. A colleague of mine, Linda Hartley, writes this about the digestive system: "The quality of its functioning tends to reflect many of our attitudes towards nourishment at all levels of existence—physical, emotional, mental and spiritual. How we accept or reject, digest, assimilate, integrate, choose (what is to be retained and what eliminated), and let go in terms of food, nurturance, material possessions, people, ideas, and so forth, are attitudes of the digestive process. [20]

As I wrote in the beginning of this chapter, you might already be getting information from your digestive system. It might be a sinking feeling in the pit of your stomach, or some other gut feeling that tells you when something feels right or warns you that something is not as it seems. This is just some of the special wisdom our digestive system offers us. The more attuned we are to our digestive system—the more we understand how our digestive system works, how it relates to our overall well-being and how it communicates with us—the more we can perceive and benefit from that special wisdom.

Digestion involves five essential stages.

No matter what we eat, all our food needs to be digested, i.e., broken down, so that our body can absorb its nutrients. It has to be transformed and reduced to its basic parts: minute particles of proteins, fats and carbohydrates. These particles are then absorbed into our bloodstream where they are carried to feed every cell. That which has not been digested then needs to be sorted and separated so that it can be eliminated. This process of digestion has five stages:

1. Ingestion: Taking in food, chewing and swallowing
2. Movement of the food through the digestive tract

3. Breakdown of that food into tiny components that can be absorbed

4. Absorption or assimilation of these nutrients

5. Elimination of that which has not been digested.

The time-consuming process of digestion begins at the mouth and continues through the 25-foot-long digestive tract to the anus. Each stage is essential, and each stage teaches us something different about the process of eating—and about ourselves.

Your mouth – where it all starts

The process of digestion begins in the mouth. The mouth is a very important and powerful place in the body because it is where we take in food from our environment and bring it into our inner world. To understand how connected our digestion is to our whole being, let's look more deeply at the mouth.

The mouth has many different aspects or qualities. First, the enzymes there break down sugars and starches, mixing them into the near-quart of saliva that we produce every day. This saliva moistens the food, which helps to ease swallowing. The mouth also contains powerful teeth that tear food apart. Our teeth can grind food down to an almost liquid state, depending upon how much we chew. The mouth is also a sensual place. The tongue has countless taste receptors that bring us pleasure, or let us know if food is spoiled or might be toxic to us. The presence of all these taste receptors indicate that eating is meant to be a pleasurable experience.

The mouth is the primary way that infants begin to know and

explore their world. This is why they put almost everything in their mouths. The mouth also has softness. We can share love and passion through a kiss.

We also speak through our mouths. The mouth is the first place we say "yes" or "no" to what we take in—and these words are particularly crucial to eating. Infants and young children are very clear about their "no's" related to food. They shut their mouths tightly to keep out, spit out or push out food they don't want. They turn their heads away when they have had enough food. We, too, have the capacity to say "no" in this way, even to spit out food we don't like, though we rarely give ourselves permission to do so. We also have, or can regain, the capacity to say: "No more," or "No, thank you" when we have had enough to eat—or enough of a toxic situation.

We can also say "yes" to what nourishes our body, mind and spirit.

After our mouths have done their work, we swallow. Swallowing moves the food from our mouths to our stomachs through a tube (the esophagus).

Next stop - the stomach

Food arrives in the stomach, where it receives a bath of digestive acids that break it down chemically. At this point, the body still has a way of saying "no" to what we have taken in. It can send this mixture of food up and out, through vomiting. Likewise, we can still reject toxic thoughts or ideas before we take them in fully.

Food can be rushed through our systems, as tends to happen

when we are anxious or unwell, but the result is unusable food, food not adequately broken down, food that does not provide nourishment. This is analogous to what happens when we rush through our lives; we miss out on the nurturance. Alternatively, food can also just sit in the stomach—undigested—where it feels like a big lump. Our lives can feel the same way, sluggish or obstructed, perhaps especially if we are overwhelmed with tasks, information or experiences.

Our stomachs are very communicative! When we listen to the sensations in our stomachs, we are able to know when we are hungry and when we are full. Our stomachs are also sensitive to our emotional states. When we eat in a relaxed way, our stomachs calm down, and good digestion is enhanced.

Next stop—the small intestine

The rest of digestion happens in the beginning of the small intestine. Here, enzymes that break down fats, proteins and carbohydrates come into play. The small intestine also discriminates, separating that which has value to our body from that which does not.

Our small intestine has three parts, which together make up 18-20 feet of coiled tubing. That's big! The long length serves to provide as large a surface area as possible for the maximal absorption of all the nutrients in our food. The blood then carries these nutrients to feed every cell in our body.

The small intestine carries a message that goes beyond its physical task of absorbing nutrients from our food; its discriminatory nature reminds us how important it is to be able to distinguish what is beneficial to us from what is not. It also reminds us to *savor the goodness in life, to take it in and allow it to nourish us.* This lesson is applicable to many aspects of our lives.

Elimination

Five feet of our digestive system is dedicated to elimination—that's big too! The large intestine prepares to eliminate whatever has not been digested and absorbed. Some of what is designated for elimination might have actually been good quality food, but perhaps we ate too much of it, or perhaps we got a stressful call in the middle of dinner, which got in the way of our digestion.

An important lesson that we can learn from the process of elimination is to *let go of things we don't need or that no longer serve us.* This can range from unhelpful situations or interactions with people to too many material possessions that stuff our homes and disrupt a sense of peace and order. (Excess stuff needn't be thought of as bad, just more than our system can handle.)

In summary, we can use the framework of our body's process of digestion to guide us in developing a new relationship with food:

- Our mouth can teach us to speak up and say "Yes" to foods that make us feel good and "No" to foods that don't, or "No more" when we are full.

- Our stomach gives us signals to help us know when we are hungry and when we are full. It reminds us to slow down so we can fully take in our food.

265

- Our small intestine teaches us about discerning what is useful from what is not. It also instructs us about opening to and absorbing what is good in our lives, and letting it truly nurture us.

- Our large intestine is the master of eliminating that which we no longer need, or no longer serves us.

Each of these organs and stages of digestion can teach us a different lesson, opening us to experience more freedom, freedom from limiting, false beliefs and the freedom to explore a new relationship with food. Here's a client story that illustrates that:

At times, I bring different foods to sessions with clients to help us explore various eating issues. Once I brought in food for a client in her 30's who had a serious eating issue: she often made herself vomit after eating.

Before and during the food exploration, I gave her permission to spit out anything she did not like and provided paper towels for this. Having this choice gave her an enormous, and unprecedented, feeling of freedom; she could say "No" to food even after it was in her mouth. I also encouraged her to explore and enjoy the taste and texture of the food in her mouth, to say "Yes" to foods she wanted. These food explorations were key to resolving her eating issues, as they were much more powerful than speaking about them.

By attuning to the wisdom of our digestive system, we allow it to teach us. It can teach you how to experience more of the joy that comes from the true nourishment of your body and spirit. And when you commit to experiencing the joy of true nourishment, you are one step closer to *finding your own best way* to nourish yourself—by saying "No" to people or situations that don't work for you while saying "Yes" to, and fully taking in, all the good in your life.

The *What* of Eating

What should we eat? What shouldn't we eat? As I said in the beginning of this chapter, most everything you have read about eating concerns the "what" of eating, most especially "what not to eat." In this section, we will look at the What of Eating in a new way. I will begin by sharing my journey, how I learned to connect to what I wanted to eat, and how I let go of dieting.

Freeing myself from the cycle of dieting and deprivation.

After many years of dieting, by which I mean depriving myself of certain foods in order to lose weight, a saga that began in my adolescence, I moved on to "health food" diets, but little changed. I was stuck in an endless cycle: eating food I thought I shouldn't eat was followed by remorse and regret, and then by dieting and deprivation. It continued this way until one day a friend who had similar issues suggested that we read together a new book she had discovered: *The Psychologist's Eat Anything Diet.*[21] Throughout the book, the author guided readers to ask themselves specific questions, such as, "What do I *want* to eat now?" rather than, "What *should* I eat (because I am told it is 'healthy,' low-fat, or a 'diet' food)?"

At the time, the approach offered in that book was revolutionary. Before the early 1970s, almost every book about eating was a diet book. There were just a handful of books suggesting anything other than deprivation, or that dealt with the specific concerns of women. In addition, most psychotherapists in that era didn't consider the depth of women's struggle with food to be significant unless she was severely underweight or obese. This was my experience, just as it was the experience of many of my clients.

This book was life changing for me, because it helped me see how often I deprived myself of foods I enjoyed because I thought I shouldn't eat them. Somewhere along the line I'd picked up the belief that some foods were innately "fattening" and/or just didn't fit into one or another of the new healthy eating plans I was trying. Some of the foods I had denied myself were ethnic foods that I grew up eating, like pasta and Italian bread, both of which were described as containing "empty" calories. I gave these up without even considering how much these foods brought me comfort and connected me to my heritage and my family, especially when I missed them.

Over a period of time, with the guidance of that book and the support of my friend, I was able to break free from the diet cycle. Slowly, I started to pay attention to what I *wanted* to eat, rather than to what I thought I *should* (or should not) eat, or what the newest health food expert told me to eat. I began to trust my own body and to let it guide me. Most importantly, as I learned to follow my desire to eat what I wanted, I discovered that I actually ate less, because I felt so satisfied. Conversely, I became aware that whenever I ate food that I did not find physically or emotionally satisfying, I tended to eat *more*—often lots more. I realized that it *was not* quantity *that I really craved; it was that my body wanted specific foods* now. Now was the key, because my needs for food changed daily, depending on all kinds of things: the weather, my activity level, my emotional state or who knows what! So, I learned to tune in.

Much like studying a menu, I "tried on possibilities" in my head to help me discover what I really wanted to eat at that moment. Sometimes, I craved a very specific food; other times the desire was more sensual. I wanted to bite into a crusty sandwich or an apple, or experience the comfort of hot soup.

When I first started to read that book, I was concerned that if I allowed myself to eat whatever I wanted, I would gain a ton of weight. However, I reminded myself that I had already suffered too much by dieting. Clearly, that approach wasn't working! I also feared that I would only want to eat breads and desserts. But that was not the case. I still remember one evening when I tuned into what I really wanted to eat. It was a tuna fish sandwich with all the trimmings: pickles, mayo etc. Just then, a friend called, inviting me to come over to her house for dinner. I really just wanted to stay home and quietly eat my sandwich, but I said yes. I remember how unsatisfied I felt later because whatever I ate there—though delicious—wasn't what I really wanted. That evening, I ate more than usual. Then, when I came home, I made myself that sandwich, though I was too full to enjoy it.

What is the larger lesson from my story? That the "what" of eating begins on the inside. When at last I was able to reconnect with my body wisdom, my relationship to eating began to transform; eating became about nourishing myself. Each day became a new opportunity to take small steps, and slowly, those small steps make a huge difference. In time, learning to tune in and listen to myself freed me from the chain of dieting; in fact, I have not been on a diet to lose weight for more than 30 years!

The book I am talking about was invaluable, but that was only a part of the story. Opening up and talking to my friend about my feelings regarding food and eating was just as valuable. Before that, I had only chatted with acquaintances about new diet plans and calories; I had never spoken to anyone about my struggles with food, which made me feel very isolated and alone. But none of us are alone, and we have to remember that.

Much of my learning was about listening deeply to what I wanted to eat rather than what I thought I should or should not eat.

Let's look more at that and some other aspects of the *What* of Eating:

1. Identifying the feeling of hunger
2. Choosing what we want to eat
3. Anticipating our food needs

In my experience, we seldom give these the attention they deserve. Let's take a closer look at how attending to these can help us find our own "what" to eat.

1. The *What* of Eating: Identifying the Feeling of Hunger

Because it is so easy to be out-of-touch with our bodies, we may not actually recognize when we are hungry or what, specifically, we are actually hungry for. Sometimes it's not food that we want or need.

Food is only one form of nourishment. I asked a good friend what helped her cope with the eating issues she'd had years ago. She said the most important breakthrough came when she realized that she might actually be craving another form of nourishment:

> *"Whenever I felt hungry," she said, "I started to ask myself: Is it really food that I want now? Or do I want some other kind of nurturing?" Sometimes I would give myself a few moments to sit and breathe in energizing oxygen, and that felt nourishing. Sometimes I realized that what I really wanted was to rest or take a bath. Other times, I wanted to talk to a friend on the phone. And if I was certain that I actually wanted food, then I would tune into what food would be most satisfying right then, and take a little extra time to enjoy that food.*

This realization is really important. We may not be sensitive to the kind of nourishment that we really want. This is a good moment to do the Touchstone exercise. As your hand rests on the bone in front of your heart, ask yourself: *What do I really want now?* If no answer comes, keep asking questions like: *Do I want connection to a person? To nature? To spirit?* If the desire truly is for food, ask: *What food, specifically?*

2. The What of Hunger: Choosing What We Want to Eat

What food is good for me now, at this time in my life? The arena of food and eating is stuffed with others' beliefs. There are beliefs about eating meat or not, eating a low carbohydrate diet, eating raw foods, eating three meals a day, et cetera. Navigating through this mountain of information about how others think we *should* eat can seem like a daunting task.

But keep in mind that even the "experts" often disagree with each other. In addition, research findings can be contradictory and trends about what constitutes healthy eating have changed dramatically over time. Remember the example about olive oil in *Find your own way?*

And all too often, the information that is out there speaks to us as though we are all exactly the same, when in fact, we all have differing genetic dispositions and differing abilities to digest some foods more successfully than others.

> *Even now, many years later, I still remember a theatrical performance I attended about women and food. The evening involved audience participation, and at one point we were asked to honestly write down what foods we had eaten the day before, and at what times. The responses were amazing! Not one woman out of 70 had eaten three "typical" meals. Some ate more than three meals; some grazed throughout the day; some had steak and vegetables for breakfast, and others had cereal for dinner. The women there were of all shapes, sizes and ages.*

I can think of no better reminder of how unique and different we really all are! Even though this statement is in the section on the Guideline *Find Your Own Way*, I will repeat it here because it is so important: There is no one diet, exercise plan or system that works equally well for everyone. We are all individuals with different constitutions and needs; even when treated in the exact same way, we can react very differently. Even though a certain way of eating may work for your family or friends, or has been scientifically researched, it may not work for you. In sum, I think it is essential to remember the old adage that "one person's meat is another's poison." It's not really about whether a food is considered intrinsically "good"

or "bad" in the eyes of current thinking; it's about how it inter-
acts with *your body* at a given time.

Another factor to put in the mix is the fact that one's ability
to digest certain foods can change over a lifetime. This occurs
much more frequently than was previously thought, as do digestive difficulties. For example, we may discover that we have
become sensitive to wheat or dairy products, or find it difficult
to digest certain meats or fats. Often, this is due to a change
in the production of digestive enzymes. These can lessen as
we grow older, or be lacking at any age. Several years ago, I
was fortunate enough to work with a health practitioner who
realized that my severe digestive difficulties were related to a
lack of the enzymes needed to digest fats. Once I learned this,
I was able to take a digestive aid, which helped me.

Because no one approach to eating is best for everyone, it is
vital that you listen to your inner wisdom, and adapt any suggestions and programs to your needs.

You already know a lot about what works for you with regard
to food. For instance, you may have noticed that you have more
energy or feel better when you eat a certain kind of breakfast,
or eat dinner before a certain time in the evening. You may
have noted that you feel bloated after you eat this or that, or
out of sorts when you don't eat enough. You might have noticed that your joints ache the day after eating certain foods.

How you feel after breakfast, in particular, can give you important clues as to what kinds of foods help you maintain both
balanced blood sugar and mood. Whenever I eat something
like pancakes dripping with syrup (which I adore!), I find that
I am ravenously hungry shortly after, and crave more "sugary"
things all day. So, when I want these foods, I eat them later in

the day for dinner or dessert. I eat more protein-rich foods in the morning. That works better for *me*.

What about you? Do you notice your mood and physical energy level changing in relation to what you eat?

Don't eat this. Don't eat that.

We hear a lot about all the foods that we should stop eating. Have you ever noticed how focusing on *not* doing something rarely works? For example, planning to never again eat sugar (or some other food) is a guaranteed prescription for failure! Yet, some women know that if they eat certain foods, such as sugary or baked goods, they will tend to keep eating them compulsively, so it's best for them not to have any at all.

We each have to find our own way. I know this from experience. When I was struggling with digestive issues, I was told to completely eliminate certain foods that were problematic. I knew that wouldn't work for me because I really enjoyed those foods. Instead, I let myself have a little of those foods on the weekends. That's how I found my own way. In general, rather than trying to eliminate things, a more successful approach is to focus on *adding new foods* to your diet, especially if eating healthier is a concern. Let's look at that now.

Expand your food choices

Are you in a rut when it comes to food? It is all too easy to eat the same foods, cooked in the same way, over and over. However, this dulls the senses and makes food less satisfying. When our food is boring or less than enticing, it is easy to eat more in order to feel satisfied, or follow up the meal with too much dessert or something else to make up for the blandness. Eating the same, limited kinds of foods can take away the sheer joy of eating. It can prevent us from experimenting with new types of foods that might *taste and feel* better to eat. Remember the mouth? The mouth enjoys sensual pleasures!

One way to begin expanding your food choices is to think about all the different types of foods there are: fruits, vegetables, meats, poultry, fish, dairy products, nuts and seeds, whole grains, breads and pastas, spices, sweets, herbs, et cetera. Different foods can give you more satisfaction through variety and taste. Ask yourself these questions: *When I consider what I eat on a regular basis, are certain types of foods rare, or even missing altogether? Which of the foods that I rarely eat appeal to me? Can I imagine enjoying them? Can I imagine being nourished by them?*

Here's one way to easily expand your food choices:

Go on a shopping adventure. To inspire clients to add new foods to their food choices (and to have fun too!), I suggest that they go on a special shopping adventure. Whenever I do this I discover or rediscover nourishing foods that I really enjoy. Why not try it? On your shopping adventure, give yourself time to slowly walk around and look at foods in the different categories, listed above, that might be missing from your usual fare. As you shop, ask yourself: *What food looks appealing to me? What new foods would I like to try?*

Explore new kinds of places to shop like a farmer's market or specialty shop where the food is fresh, and well displayed. If you connect with your food in joyful anticipation, then the very act of shopping for food becomes a sensual experience. So, go on a shopping adventure soon!

3. Anticipate your food needs

Many women find it hard to anticipate their food needs. That was true of me as well. Over time, I have cultivated my ability to anticipate my food needs because I've learned that if I don't, I may experience a strong low blood sugar reaction, complete with anxiety and other unpleasant bodily sensations. If this occurs, it takes time for my body to rebalance. Having learned this, I now take precautions to avoid these episodes. If I notice signs of low blood sugar, such as feeling out of sorts, crabby or weak, I eat as soon as I can. Occasionally, that means I may start eating before the people I am dining with begin their own meal. Believe me, those who know me support this. They would rather I eat before them than be with a cranky, unhappy dinner guest!

What about you? Do you notice your mood and physical energy level changing when you skip a meal or wait too long to eat?

Here are some more questions to ask yourself to help you anticipate your food needs:

- Do you remember times when you didn't anticipate your food needs and were stuck being hungry or eating something that you didn't enjoy or that didn't go down right?

- Are there upcoming events, or an extra-long work day, where you know it would be especially helpful to carry snacks or prepare food ahead of time?

I know that the thought of anticipating your needs around food might seem tiresome, trivial or time consuming; however, I have found that it has a very positive effect on my well-being, and that of my clients as well. I encourage you to try it!

How often—and how much—do you need to eat? I eat often. I don't skip a meal, and when I go out, I carry snacks with me. When I get up early, I eat two breakfasts. I've also learned that I enjoy big lunches, not just a sandwich, so I cook extra food at dinner that I can heat up quickly at home or take with me. In short, I've learned to listen to my body's needs and that it's okay to nourish myself in the way my body needs. This is perhaps one of the most important lessons I've had to learn. Once you learn it, too, it will be life changing:

> *One day, I went to an all-day outdoor event. I knew I might not have access to any food that I enjoyed or digested well, so I brought hefty sandwiches and snacks with me. The woman I went with also brought food, but only a tiny amount. While I was eating my voluminous amounts, I offered her some of mine. She kept declining, saying she was hungry, but needed to lose weight. It saddened me that she couldn't allow herself to be nourished.*

The *How* of Eating

As I said, a lot has been written about the "what" and "what not" of eating. But there's not very much focus on what I consider to be an equally important aspect of eating: the *how*. The *How* of Eating has three aspects:

1. Prepare your food
2. Prepare your body and create an atmosphere that fosters both enjoyment and digestion
3. Pause after eating

1. Prepare your food

To eat delicious food, work is required. Unless you are a lucky child or spouse, have a full-time cook, or enjoy eating out all the time, (and can afford it!) you will have to buy food, cook it and then clean up. *However, you do have a choice about how you approach these tasks.* This is an opportunity to remember the guideline *Make It Enjoyable.* Ask yourself: "What can make shopping, cooking or cleaning up more fun for me?"

Often when we resist doing a task, we rush through it. The habit of rushing while doing daily activities is just that, a habit—and an unhelpful one. I know from experience that rushing doesn't save time. I often spill or drop something when I'm doing things in a hurry. Cleaning up the mess adds twice the time! The habit of rushing can make tasks unnecessarily unpleasant:

> *As I was writing this section, I realized that I was very hungry. I had postponed lunch in order to keep writing. I checked in myself to find out what would be most satisfying right now, and then started to prepare my lunch. Then I noticed that I was rushing, even though I didn't need to. I noticed, also, that I felt tight and tense. I was even holding my breath.*

> *Rushing through tasks is such an ingrained habit that I needed to remind myself several times to slow down and relax, so that afternoon I put up a 5x8 card on the refrigerator that said: "Have fun cooking." I brought some lively CD's to the kitchen and played music as I prepared lunch. I kept an eye out for when I start rushing unnecessarily, and gently reminded myself to breathe.*

Rushing is a habit we can break. As you begin to prepare your food, ask yourself these questions: *Am I having fun, or am I suffering in the kitchen? Am I rushing? If so, can I slow down and enjoy the process? What could make cooking more fun for me?*

2. Prepare your body and create an atmosphere that fosters both enjoyment and digestion

I'd now like to bring your attention to two aspects of the *how* of eating: the first is preparing your body to eat by *relaxing*. When you relax before eating, you are more able to be fully present; to connect to what you are eating and savor it. This amplifies the satisfaction you derive from your food, and also your ability to receive its nutrients. Being relaxed also makes it easier to sense when you are full.

Why is it important to take a moment to shift gears and relax before eating? There are two major parts of the nervous system: one part helps us to be actively engaged out in the world; the other encourages us to care for our inner world. This latter part helps us to relax, sleep—and digest our food. When we eat, we want to engage that aspect of our nervous systems.

Eating is a "taking in" activity, a time for our body to recharge and refuel. Often, we're still in an active mode when we arrive at the table, a holdover from the flurry of preparing food or rushing to the table after busily working or doing errands or tasks. That's why it is so important to S-L-O-W down. Even a momentary pause will help us to shift gears and go into a receptive and relaxed state so we can healthfully digest and enjoy food. This is especially important if we have digestive difficulties, a lesson I learned firsthand.

Here's what happens when you relax before eating, your body creates more saliva in your mouth, and more digestive juices in your stomach, both of which help break down food in order to absorb the nutrients from your food. So before eating, take a quiet moment to relax.

Here's what I do before I eat: *I pause and breathe before I begin my meal. I exhale out a few times and release my jaw, neck and general body tension, along with any worries, as I do. Then I breathe in calmness. That way, I can give my full attention to my delicious food.*

I love this peaceful moment before eating, but even so, I still need to remind myself to do it, especially if I am very hungry. But slowly, I am doing this more and more. (See the Guided Eating Experience at the end of the chapter for more.)

Create a pleasurable atmosphere wherever you eat. You can create a satisfying atmosphere whether you eat at home or dine out; eat alone or with others. If you want to dine out, most likely you would consider the atmosphere of the restaurant—noise level, size, lighting—as well as the food itself. Your choice might vary depending upon whether you want to have a peaceful meal, a romantic one, or a fun feast with a boisterous group.

You may not have the money to eat in a fancy restaurant but you can create an elegant and nurturing atmosphere right in your home with a candle, a nice tablecloth and other beautiful items that you already have. Can you go on a "treasure hunt" in your home to find these items? The difference between having a nice atmosphere or not, is often only a few moments of time. So go ahead and take those few extra moments to light candles, put on quiet music, use special dishes or place mats, or go out of doors and dine al fresco!

With whom do you want to eat? Can you choose whom you want to be with when you eat—whether they are with you in person, or whether you are simply thinking about them? Ask yourself this: Would you invite guests to dinner that you didn't want to be with, if you were not obligated to do that? So, don't invite unwanted guests, even in your thoughts.

My friend said this:

> *I realized from our talk that feeding and nourishing myself well was one of the few areas of my life that was only about my needs. Usually, I am so focused on caring for others and their comfort, but I began noticing that when I ate with people with whom I felt uncomfortable, I lost track of what I wanted to eat. I also had trouble knowing when I was full, so I tended to eat more. Now, I rarely eat in situations that do not feel nurturing. I prefer eating by myself, or with loving friends and family.*

Create a protective bubble around eating

Can you imagine creating a protective bubble around yourself during mealtimes? Obviously, this is a challenge if you have young children, but you can still choose to let phone calls, worries and tasks wait. Over the years, I've discovered more and more about what works and what doesn't for me around eating. For one thing, I can't talk about or listen to anything unsettling, like the news, while I'm eating. Nor can I talk about doing challenging future tasks. When I do, my stomach literally shuts down and I can't eat a bite more. It's best for me to talk about neutral subjects and pleasant things while eating. I know it's limiting, and my husband sometimes objects, but it's a real need, so it's my responsibility to maintain that boundary.

I also hate eating in noisy places or during a business meeting. I can listen to reports or someone else talking, but I can't stomach someone repeatedly asking me questions as I'm eating. I know this about myself, so instead of suffering, I've come up with ways to work around it. Often, I'll eat before or after a lunch meeting, especially if it's going to be in a noisy place.

3. Pause after you eat

After you finish eating, it is good to pause and take a moment to notice that you feel satisfied, to offer gratitude for the nourishment you've received and to *appreciate your efforts* to shift your relationship with food. Maybe you tried a new food, for example, or took a moment to breathe before your meal, or noticed when you felt full. These moments of tuning into yourself help you to develop a more intimate relationship with your body as well as with your food.

A Guided Eating Experience

Each time we feed ourselves is an opportunity to connect to our bodies, our hearts, our minds, our spirits. Right here. Right now. In this moment.

—Hale Sofia Schatz and Shira Shaiman, *If the Buddha Came to Dinner: How to Nourish your Body to Awaken your Spirit*[22]

I'd like to close this section of the chapter by taking you through a guided eating experience that brings together many of the ideas in this chapter. You can try it with a meal or a snack or just a cup of tea.

- Tune into your digestive system. Choose what you want to eat: Exhale a few times. Then place one hand on your stomach and the other near your mouth. Take a moment and stroke down from your mouth to your stomach. This helps you feel a connection between the two. Then, keeping your hand on your stomach, breathe and ask: *What food appeals to my stomach now? What appeals to my mouth? Do I want more crunchy or soft foods, light or rich foods, salty or sweet foods?* Look at the list of all the different types of food listed earlier, and feel which type of food you are drawn to in this moment. Pause and imagine eating that food. Does it taste good? How does it feel in your stomach?

- Choose a relaxing place to eat. It doesn't have to be at a table.

- Give yourself a peaceful moment: Say these self-support statements: *I have the time to eat and thoroughly enjoy my food. I deserve to be nourished and feed myself in a loving way. My body will digest this food well.* Offer gratitude for the gift of food.

- Breathe out any tension. *Blow it Out* works well here. Open your mouth and sigh. If you need to, breathe out any unhelpful beliefs about eating. Let your belly and whole abdomen relax. Receive your nourishing breath.

- Appreciate your food. Savor the smell, look, taste, and texture.

- Pause and breathe a few times during your meal. Look out the window or at something beautiful in the room. Ask: *Am I still hungry? Am I still enjoying eating? If not, what would bring back the joy?*

- Appreciate your efforts to explore a new way of eating.

As we come to the close of this chapter, I suggest asking yourself these questions:

- *Do I want more joy and ease around eating?*

- *Do I want or need to eat differently for my health and well-being?*

If so, what suggestions from this chapter resonate most with you? You might:

- Begin to examine—and challenge—your beliefs about what and when you "should" eat.

- Use encouraging self-talk to assist you.

- Play with different eating experience ideas.

- Re-read the part about the digestive system.

Wherever you choose to begin, remember to *Keep It Small*. For example, in the next week, choose to feed yourself *one* meal in a way that feels really nourishing and enjoyable.

In conclusion, I would like to confess that it's difficult for me to believe that I have even attempted to write about women and food! For me, as for so many women, food had always had so much emotional baggage attached to it. But when two friends suggested that I forego writing this chapter, I was stunned. How could I *not* write about the numerous issues relating to eating in a book focused on self-care for women? How could I not address an area that has caused so many women—including myself—so much confusion and misery, an area that affects so many aspects of health and well-being? So, I decided to forge ahead. But then another question arose. What did I have to offer that was different from everything else out there? I believe the answer is simply this: laying a foundation for lovingly caring for you, and then applying that foundation to eating and nourishment.

13

Growing Older with Vitality and Ease

I don't know about you, or how old you are, but the fact that I am growing older can still catch me by surprise. I'm sometimes downright shocked when I walk by a mirror or store window and catch a glimpse of a woman with white hair looking back at me. Who is this person? I don't *feel* old! And yet my reflection says I must be . . . What does this mean?

That last question is especially tricky because the experience of being older is not the same as it used to be, and how it looks is a lot more varied. For one thing, many of us are living longer and healthier lives. Secondly, we have more choices as to how to spend our later years. Because retiring at 65 is no longer mandatory, many folks continue to work. Some stay in their current jobs; but more and more, older people are willing to shake things up. They change careers, go on adventures, start singing or dancing lessons, divorce or find new loves. For many of us who feel healthy and vital, age does not seem to be a factor at all. Yet, while "60 is the new 50" (and "70 the new "60," et cetera) in many ways, this doesn't mean that those of us "of a certain age" should ignore the fact that we are growing older altogether. So, getting back to our question, what does it mean to grow older today?

I believe that each one of us must come up with our own answer to that question. That's because there is no longer any one-size-fits-all response—and that's a very good thing. But it also means that each us has to *Find our Own Way*. In our extremely youth-oriented culture, it is tempting to ignore the fact that we're growing older and to keep challenging ourselves to look or act youthful in ways that are unrealistic or even harmful. On the other hand, we might succumb to pervasive, but often incorrect, cultural myths about aging.

Growing older is a process, not a static state, so we need *to listen to our bodies* and keep adjusting as we go. This requires a balanced approach. That's why in this chapter I offer you guidance for finding your own, unique answer to the question: *What does it mean to grow older?* I also want to inspire and empower you to keep feeling as good as you can for as long as you can, whatever your age. Yes, growing older brings changes, and some of them can be challenging, but we can develop the resilience to respond creatively. I encourage you to adopt a *perspective on growing older wherein you don't deny these changes, but neither do you define yourself by your age.*

This topic is worthy of a book in itself, as growing older touches on all aspects of our lives: physical, mental, spiritual and emotional. There is simply no way to cover everything in this one chapter, so I will focus on some of the most important dimensions, discussing how you can use the guidelines and practices in this book to help you grow older with the joy and well-being that you deserve.

A Matter of Belief

I'd like to begin by making a distinction between *growing older* and *aging*. When I first started writing this book, I had named this chapter "Aging Gracefully," but the more I thought about it, the more I felt compelled to rename it "Growing Older." That's because the words we use to name or describe something effects how we think and act with respect to it. We all grow older every day; it is something that we all have in common. But when you hear the word "aging," what comes to mind? If you're like most people in our society, you may believe that aging means losing abilities, going downhill, et cetera.

Because our beliefs about aging are so strong, I want to offer a little reminder about the power of belief, backed by research. Medical research has shown that patients who believe that their treatments or surgeries are effective are more likely to heal and recover more easily than those who don't hold that belief. Over the years I have seen this firsthand with clients that I have helped prepare for and supported their recovery after surgeries and treatment. That's the power of belief; our beliefs and thoughts can profoundly affect our well-being. As Christiane Northrup, M.D. puts it in *Goddesses Never Age*, "The most important thing you need to know about your health is that the health of your body and its organs does not exist separate from your emotional well-being, your thoughts, your cultural programming, and your spiritual outlook. Your thoughts and beliefs are the single most important indicator of your state of health ... This is the part of health that western medicine always leaves out, but trust me, it's where your power resides, with no exceptions. Your beliefs and thoughts are wired into your biology."[23]

It follows, then, that what we believe about growing older—and how we talk to others and ourselves about what we believe—can affect how we actually experience it, for good or ill. Here's a story that's illustrative of the power of belief:

A relative of mine had exercised regularly for most of her life: several times a week while she was still working, and then daily after she retired. That sounds great until you realize that she was only doing exercises designed to keep up her strength; she was doing nothing aimed at maintaining her flexibility. In addition, she always did the exact same exercises; she never updated or expanded upon her routine. Knowing this, I tried to encourage her to add some simple flexibility exercises, especially as I saw her neck movement becoming more and more restricted, but unfortunately, she didn't believe in trying anything new.

Then, over time, my relative began to lose even more flexibility. Soon, things began to cascade. She eventually lost the ability to turn her neck at all, requiring that she sleep only on her back, which then stiffened her whole spine. Most importantly, this rigidity made it difficult for her to bend her head down in order to see well while descending stairs. It was only a matter of time before this led to a fall and an injury. Luckily, the injury was not serious. However, the fall shook her confidence, and she began to fear going out. For years she had walked to a number of stores to do her shopping, but now she hesitated. As time went on, she went out less and less, and the less she went out, the more fearful she became that she might fall when she did go out. And so it went. First her movement, and then her life, became extremely restricted. And whenever we spoke about her situation, she would shrug and attribute it all to "aging."

This story illuminates how beliefs about aging can create a self-fulfilling prophecy. When my relative first began to experience a problem, she didn't listen to my suggestions or look for solutions herself; instead, she gave up. Why? Because *she believed something about aging that just wasn't true.* To her, growing older meant having aches, pains and limitations. The truth is that it is possible to prevent or alleviate much of the suffering that has been associated with growing older. In her case, spending just a few minutes each day "oiling her neck" (see the *Joints* chapter) could have *prevented* the limitations she later developed, especially since she already had a lifetime habit of exercising to build upon. In addition, she could have easily worked with a movement specialist to update her routine and incorporate new flexibility exercises.

You may think this story unusual, but I have seen many preventable situations starting just like that: a person encounters a fixable problem, but instead of being open to solutions and looking to discover what actions they might take, they just tell themselves that these things are an inevitable result of aging. That attitude stops them from trying to find solutions or seeking help; it prevents them from even considering that things can change for the better. In effect, they are saying to themselves, "I am powerless, I just have to suffer with this or that…for the rest of my life." To make matters worse, doctors can collude in this thinking. Some doctors also believe that their patients' difficulties are simply due to their getting older. If they believe certain issues or difficulties are just an inevitable aspect of aging, they may hesitate to refer their patients to practitioners who might be helpful. In addition, many doctors are operating under time constraints that preclude their exploring more creative options with their patients. And without their doctor's support, many patients tend to do nothing about their situations. This is unfortunate, because time is often of the essence. It is important to act while there is still the possibility of alleviating the condition.

Growing Older and Empowerment

The antidote to an attitude of powerlessness is self-empowerment, recognizing how much power we have to affect our well-being, no matter our age. One of the keys to self-empowerment is resisting the temptation to blame issues or problems on our biological age. Here's a story to illustrate:

I have had a bone spur in one toe for about 10 years. I only notice this when I walk barefoot or wear shoes without adequate cushioning. Once, I loved going barefoot and wearing nice looking sandals, but I decided it wasn't worth the pain. However, one day when I was working at a sales booth at a conference, I decided to wear sandals instead of my usual cushiony sneakers in order to appear more fashionable. After standing all day in my sandals, I had such severe foot pain that I could hardly walk. Then my back started to hurt because I was limping to take the weight off my painful left foot. That night, I barely slept since my foot and back pain kept waking me. The next day, I wore my sneakers and a pair of thick socks. I also circled my ankles a few times throughout the day, did five minutes of back movements, and I was fine! No pain after standing all that day and the next day as well.

Later, I realized that if I had assumed that my foot or back pain was a new, but inevitable result of aging, I would not have felt empowered to seek a solution. Instead of listening to my body, I might have kept wearing the wrong shoes and continued suffering. Soon, I would have developed serious back problems. Then I would have walked less because I was in so much pain, thus decreasing my mobility. Because I was moving less, I would have less energy, and on and on. In short, this could have been a very unnecessary trip down the slippery slope into limitation. I felt fortunate that I avoided it, because not everyone does.

I will say it unequivocally: it is essential that we resolve *not to immediately jump to blaming problems on growing older* because doing so leads to powerlessness. Instead pause, and look for a specific cause, and be open to seeking a solution and getting any help you might need.

Growing Older with Serenity

Do you know the Serenity Prayer? *Grant me the serenity to accept the things I cannot change, the courage to change the things that I can, and the wisdom to know the difference.* This prayer provides guidance for how to navigate this stage of our lives. With that as our guide, I'd like to explore some very important questions: What is inevitable about growing older? What is not? How do we acquire the wisdom to know the difference?

What do we need to accept about growing older? Are some things really inevitable? Yes, but perhaps not as much as we think. And even with these, we have more power than we realize. To drive that point home, let's look at a few of the more common assumptions we have about getting older:

- We get stiffer; our movement becomes more limited.

- We have a tendency to fall or injure ourselves

- Injuries take longer to heal

- We don't have as much energy as we used to.

Cultivate Flexibility in Body, Mind and Spirit

Yes, we can experience a tendency toward stiffness as we become older. There are several reasons for this, including habitual ways of moving, i.e., moving some joints too much and restricting the movement of others. As I stated earlier, reduced physical flexibility can make daily life movements—such as getting in and out of a chair, bed or car—difficult, painful or even frightening. You might worry about suddenly finding yourself on slippery surfaces, and about whether you can protect yourself or regain your equilibrium if you stumble or trip. It can also make you more prone to injury, and the injuries you sustain may be more serious.

Inflexibility can creep into our lives without our noticing; it can happen when we cease to pay attention to how we feel, when we stop listening to our bodies, and instead do things out of habit, because we've always done them that way. This often happens with exercise. Remember the story of my relative? I have seen many women like her who are doing the same exercises suggested to them decades earlier by a physical therapist or an exercise teacher. Exercise is a great habit, but as we grow older, our approach to exercise needs to be periodically re-evaluated and re-designed to better address our current abilities and needs.

The root of many of the problems associated with growing older is a lack of flexibility, whether of joints, arteries or mental habits. So, beside keeping our bodies flexible and our joints oiled, it is important to keep our minds and spirits flexible as well. If I tend to avoid new experiences and become closed to learning, my life will narrow. But if I am flexible in mind and spirit, if I am open to new ideas and possibilities, my approach to life will be more expansive and my experience of life will be richer. In addition, a bounty of research tells us that new learning is good for our brain, especially as we grow older. So actively *tend* to your flexibility in all its dimensions:

- "Oil your joints." (See Joints Chapter.) This is easy to do and enjoyable.

- Do gentle warm-up movements before engaging in more strenuous physical activities.

- Stay open to new experiences.

- Avoid stale routines. Try different kinds of activities to discover something new and enjoyable.

- Whenever you face a challenge, develop the habit of looking for creative solutions—don't give up!

Now let's look at another assumption: growing older means we have a tendency to fall.

You Can Prevent Falls

As we discussed earlier, our beliefs affect our reality. Believing we are more likely to fall obscures the truth, which is that *most falls can be prevented*. It's extremely important to become proactive about preventing falls because the consequences can become more serious as we grow older, especially if we have osteoporosis. For example, a common home accident involves falling down stairs. After a client fell down the stairs while carrying a laundry basket because she couldn't see a slippery object at the bottom of the stairs, I decided it was time to be more proactive about preventing falls. Here are a few import-ant tips for preventing falls:

- Remove anything that might cause you to trip or slip from stairways and all commonly walked pathways in your home.

- Switch to carrying laundry in bags. They are safer to carry than laundry baskets.

- Use handrails while going up and down stairs.

- Avoid climbing on stools or chairs. Instead use a sturdy step stool.

- Check that showers and tubs are safe.

- Check on-line for more precautions you can take to prevent falls and other household injuries.

- Now let's take a look at another assumption.

Injuries take longer to heal.

Indeed, it is quite guaranteed, if not inevitable, that we will heal more slowly as we get older. There are many factors that can contribute to this, including a tendency to be sedentary, circulation issues, diet, stress levels and our overall level of self-care. *Thus, you need to be proactive if and when you do become injured.* It is essential to seek help early in the process; do not postpone treatment until injuries become a chronic condition. Make sure to seek out therapists who are sophisticated and experienced, and who know how to work with older clients; ask for referrals from friends or trusted practitioners. Finally, it is essential that you take an active role in supporting your own healing. This might include encouraging circulation with gentle movements (see oiling the joints), elevation if needed, and making sure to get sufficient rest.

So, yes, injuries do take longer to heal. But injury is not an inevitable part of growing older. There is a great deal you *do to prevent injury*—you can become more aware of the common causes of injury and take precautionary steps. Here are some suggestions:

- **Pay Attention. Slow Down:** A common cause of injury is that we were not paying attention, or being mindful. Rushing especially makes us less careful.

Because I was in a hurry to get home after a trip, I carried too many things to the car at once. As a result, I injured my elbow in one arm and my wrist in the other. In trying to save 10 minutes, I ended up spending lots of time and money getting help to heal from two totally unnecessary injuries. And, yes, I was surprised about the length of time it took to heal. Even six months later, I still had some pain when I do certain activities. So, the lesson to me was to slow down and be more mindful! It's a lesson that I keep working on. I especially remind myself to slow down when I'm getting ready to leave the house.

- **Don't Overdue. Guard against Unrealistic Expectations:** Many injuries occur because of overdoing physical activities and exercises. I'm sure you've heard of the "weekend warrior" syndrome. This is a term for what happens when someone decides to suddenly tackle sports they haven't played in years, hikes three times as much as they have or works in their home or garden until they drop. While it's important to stretch and try new things, we also need to exercise good judgment. To reach *too far beyond* what we actually know we're capable of may cause harm. When we have unrealistic expectations of ourselves, we can overdo, which can lead to injury. Here's an example:

A friend needed to switch her clothes from storage to her closet for the summer season. It was a huge job as she has lots of clothes. So, she kept putting it off. Then one day she decided that she was going to do it all right then, no matter what. Unfortunately, she had a lingering issue with her hip that she had been managing well. However, after spending hours bending and carrying clothes, her hip was hurting more. Soon after, her back started hurting, too.

That evening, we went for a walk. After 15 minutes of walking, she was in extreme pain. She had to lie down, take ibuprofen, and ice her hip for a while, just to be able to drive herself home.

My friend recovered, but this is a lesson for us all, one that is especially important if you already have a vulnerable situation, such as my friend's sore hip. Pain is a signal to listen to your body.

- **Become Aware of False Beliefs of Perfection.** My experience with injury as well as that of my friend, and many of my clients as well, has made me wonder: How many of us expect ourselves to be Super Woman, to be invulnerable, to push ourselves to keep doing, to not have needs and limitations, to not need help or support—in short, to be perfect? Beliefs such as these don't serve us, especially as we grow older. So be aware if you find yourself getting caught up in them.

At root, preventing injury is about being grounded in our bodies, in the present moment and in the real (not imagined) demands of the task at hand. It's about being centered and making sensible, mature decisions based upon our capabilities at any given time. Hopefully, we are not just growing older; we are growing wiser!

Cultivate your Energy

Now we will look at another assumption: that we don't have as much energy as we used to. Your life force energy, your vitality, is like a lantern that lights you up—and it's essential to joyful living. Throughout your life, your vital energy ebbs and flows, sometimes unpredictably. Now older, if you feel it ebb at times, you might assume there is nothing you can do—but there is. We can cultivate our energy by attending to ourselves.

For months now, I've been asking everyone I know who's "older" how they get their energy going. I love one answer in particular. One woman I asked is 80, and has had a lot of health challenges and physical limitations for a great deal of her life. This is what she said:

> *I don't give in. It's hard, but I keep moving. That's what gives me energy. The best thing I've discovered to do is to wake up every morning to a new song, "Happiness." I get out of bed and giggle buck-naked to the song. What a great way to start my day!*

> *To get myself going one morning when I felt especially tired, I put on that song and danced around. This time, though, I kept my clothes on, as it was cold!*

This story reminds me about the importance of starting my day out right to optimize my energy. Movement is key to my vitality, as it is for many, so I walk each day, whatever the weather. I used to walk at different times of the day, but I've discovered that moving in the mornings is what best feeds my vitality and productivity; walking in the afternoon does not give me the same lift. When I brought this up in a group of women, my age peers, everyone nodded. They confirmed that the Guideline, *Make Your Day Work for You,* is an important key to growing older with vitality for them.

Here are some other things you can do to cultivate your energy:

- **Anticipate energy changes**

One night, I found myself wanting to go to bed at 8pm! "Oh no . . . I'm going down the tubes," I started to think, but then I remembered that this had happened before, last fall, especially right after the time change. My body, like most bodies, needs time to adjust to seasonal changes.

Anticipating changes in my energy at this time of year helps me to better plan my time and avoid misinterpreting my tiredness as an inevitable sign of aging. I also know that exercise helps with the transition of light at this time of year, so rather than going to bed at 8 p.m. that evening, I knew I would sleep better if I took a walk. It took some effort and encouraging self-talk, but it worked. I enjoyed the walk and slept well. Then, the next night, it felt right to go to bed early instead—reminding me that there is more than one way to tend to my energy.

- **Allow yourself time to rest and renew.** Rest and renew: it was probably a good thing to do all your life, if only you could have managed it and given yourself the time! Now, however, it is essential. Lie down, rest your muscles and your mind. Listen to a relaxation tape. Think of it as giving yourself a delicious treat;

instead of a piece of cake, a rest. A short nap or rest of 20-30 minutes added to your day may restore your energy. Even if there's something pressing that has to be done, it is still possible to find time to rest and renew. It is such a small price to pay for renewed energy, and you don't have to fall asleep to gain benefits. (For more inspiration to rest and to counter the belief that resting is only for "old folks", see my chapter on Rest and Renewal.) Also, one of my 5-Minute Helpers, *Revive,* will be especially helpful.

- **Discover what drains your energy.** I've noticed that I feel particularly drained when I do one thing while thinking that I ought to be doing something else. Whenever I do that, I'm not present, and that leaks energy away. I also feel drained when I get caught up in feeling like a victim and acting like life is "all work and no play." These are some the things that drain me. What drains you?

- **Invite your inner child to play.** Take a moment to listen to your body, and tune into yourself. I find it helpful to ask myself questions like these: *What makes me feel most vital and alive? What would lift my energy now?* If you ask yourself these questions, the answers can show you how to tend to your energy. What you hear might surprise and delight you! For example, you might be reminded of things that brought you great joy as a child. That's what happened to me. I re-discovered my inner child, and invited her to play. When I'm in touch with my inner child, I find, for example, that I want to move more, to squiggle around in the water as I swim, to walk just a little longer to see what's around the next bend, to dance around my kitchen. I feel vital and alive!

Now let's look at another assumption, and how to empower yourself to deal with it.

What Really Is Inevitable? Change Itself

Everything must change.
  Nothing stays the same. Everyone will change…
    Mysteries unfold. Nothing—no one goes unchanged.

—Song by Bernard Ighner

One thing that seems inevitable is that we experience more change as we grow older, and many of life's transitions are likely to be major.

Some of those changes will be by choice. We may change jobs, go part-time or retire. With retirement, we may consider other options: a choice to move nearer to family, into an elder community, or to a better climate. Then, of course, there are the changes that we did not choose. Even if you are able to keep many things the same such as staying in your home, working in the same way, etc., you have no control about changes others make that affect you. For example, the training program where I taught for 30 years moved to a different location, and as a consequence, my work life changed. Though I was considering moving on to other things, I was still thrown off because this change did not happen on my timing!

Change, even change that we want or have looked forward to, frequently brings a sense of loss. A decision to move to a warmer climate or downsize involves saying goodbye to favorite neighbors, friends, or to your beloved home. Even little things, like letting go of your comfy favorite chair or a couch that won't fit in your new place, can stir those bittersweet feelings.

The longer we live, the more probable it becomes that we will experience changes affecting what we often see as the very bedrock of our lives: our finances, our relationships, our health. It is likely, for example, that we will lose our parents and older relatives, and before that, we may have to be become their caretakers. Such changes can bring a profound sense of loss, especially if they may seem to come all at once. The Buddhist teacher Pema Chodrin wrote a book entitled *When Things Fall Apart*.[24] I can't think of a better way to describe how it feels when a cascade of events, demanding a series of adjustments, seem to all come at the same time. To deal well with such experiences you may need to call upon a whole new range of skills. (This is a huge area, one that I will address in detail in my next book, *Self-Care during the Hard Times*.)

Often the hardest thing to accept is change itself. That's particularly ironic, because change is the very nature of life. The further irony is that when we resist change—or resist anything, for that matter—we suffer. Because of this resistance we may stay "stuck" in a situation, clinging to the status quo even if it is ineffective, painful or even harmful. This is a lesson we need to learn: how to anticipate, prepare for and adapt to change, not resist it.

The Good News: You already know how to adapt to change. Whether or not you still menstruate, you did at some point. When you menstruate, you expect to feel different during that part of the month. Whether PMS, cramps, mood shifts, heavy bleeding or a sense of relief at the onset of your period, you experience—and learn to adapt to—significant physical and emotional changes. Because you've had this experience, you already have the ability to adapt and come back into balance. This is a solid foundation you can draw upon as you encounter new changes in your life.

A Note about Change and Menopause

If you haven't already, you will learn even more about dealing with change during menopause. In fact, menopause was once called "the CHANGE," and spoken of with dread. Now, thankfully, attitudes are improving.

Menopause is a profound transition, affecting both body and mind. As you go through the process, unexpected changes may occur, some of them quite intense, weird or unpleasant; others, hardly noticeable. If you compare notes with women you know, you may find your experience is unique to you. Menopause is an important time for self-care. Use your self-care tools to adapt to these changes, and remember that you can talk to other women, ask for support, and learn more about menopause when needed.

As I said, change is an inevitable part of growing older. Here are some ideas to help you prepare:

- **Expect Change.** Instead of resisting out of fear or insecurity, expect, anticipate and accept change. An attitude like this is especially helpful when presented with change that is sudden or especially challenging.

- **Remember your Previous Successes.** Think of some of the changes that you have had to accept and adjust to. We've already discussed menstruation and menopause. I bet many of the others have been technological!

For a long time, I resisted getting a smart phone. Then, at some point, I felt I had to. Now I love the additional features. I also resisted purchasing the new computer that I am now writing on. The underlying reason for that is clear to me now; I was clinging to a situation that was ineffective and caused me stress because I was afraid of dealing with change. I dreaded having to transfer my files, and was anxious about needing to learn a new system. The good news is that the new screen is much easier to see and the file transference was handled for me.

- **Move!** What helps coping with and accepting change? Movement. Yes, I said "movement." Movement is not only exercise for your muscles; it is also a model for change. In fact, movement is change. Walking is a good example. With each step you take, you change which leg your weight is on, where you look as you walk, what sights you see, your pace as you go up and down hills and more.

- **Breathe In, Breathe Out.** Your body is a model for change because, internally, even when you are lying still, there is always movement. Do you remember, in the breathing chapter, when I said that we breathe about 18,000 times a day? That's movement. That's why we can turn to our breath for support with change. As the Serenity Prayer advises, each of us must learn to "Accept the things I cannot change." How do we develop this capacity? Start with your breath. With every exhalation you have an opportunity to let go of something you don't need, whether that is stress or, most relevant to this chapter, your resistance or refusal to accept change. With every inhalation you can breathe in acceptance and calmness.

Besides your breath, there is also the constant internal motion of your heart. Your heartbeat and breath are your lifelong companions, and yet breathing and heartbeat change constantly, depending upon activity level, your mood, your emotions, your state of relaxation or tension, and so much more. Do you see how change is always happening in your body and your life?

- **Use the large ball to help you adjust to—and enjoy—change.** You may have noticed references in this book to the large exercise ball and some enjoyable ways to use it. Here's another: you can use the ball to train yourself to adapt to change. Sitting and moving on the ball gives you a direct experience of responding to a changing, moving surface. (See the *Joints* chapter for an exercise for your hip joints involving sitting on the ball.)

- **Cultivate support within your community and yourself.** If you have ever gone through a difficult change in your life, you may remember how very helpful it was for you to talk with someone who had gone through a similar experience. Just hearing about how they felt, and the surprising solutions they may have come up with, helped you feel less isolated and more hopeful. Draw upon that experience and reach out to others. Community or religious organizations may offer support, including discussion groups that might work for you. Cultivating your Inner Support is important too. Engage in encouraging self-talk, such as: *"I remember that I dealt with this well before"* or *"I can ask for and receive help."* (For more, see my chapter on *Cultivating Inner Support*.)

- **Work through Transitions.** We can build our capacity to handle larger changes by finding positive ways to deal with and smooth out the daily transitions in our lives. (I address this in *Your Relationship with Time*.) Change is always an opportunity to work with, learn about and enhance your power. When you set change in motion, you will feel empowered. When change feels forced or unanticipated, you can empower yourself by observing and modifying your responses, using the tools in this book, especially those in the *Returning to Balance* chapter including the 5-Minute Helpers.

- **Cultivate a spiritual perspective.** Our connection to spirit is an important companion along life's journey that helps us to deal with change. Having a spiritual outlook can help us walk the fine line between enjoying the present and looking forward to a long, healthy life, while also acknowledging the reality that illness or death could happen at any moment.

Each time I hear about an age peer or someone younger who dies suddenly, I ask myself questions like this: How can I more fully absorb the goodness, and the abundance of my present life? I turn to my breath to help me connect deeply with myself. I also imagine that I'm looking at my life or a challenging situation from a mountaintop. This perspective gives me a sense of serenity and helps me to be more accepting of both the situation and myself.

Cultivate your spirit by connecting to spirit in a way that is meaningful. It could be through nature or a spiritual practice. Taking time to reflect upon your life can also be part of a spiritual practice. Time is precious, and it becomes even more precious as we grow older. Again, I want to emphasize the importance of *time to be,* because our need for this time increases as we grow older. Time for reflection is critical to absorb life's goodness and to think about what you need to feel more fulfilled. As I said, many of us are living longer - longer than our parents and much longer than our early ancestors. This is a tremendous gift, and with this gift comes a responsibility to ask ourselves important questions, such as:

- How do I want to spend these bonus years? How can I make these quality years?

- What kind of shape would I like to be in: physically, mentally, spiritually and emotionally? What am I willing to do to prevent the unnecessary aspects of aging?

- How might my self-care shift and change as I grow older? What do I need to prepare for, to plan or anticipate? How do I keep tuning in and tending to myself?

- Have I given myself permission to dream about what I want? Am I postponing doing those things? Am I hesitant to give myself what I need? Am I postponing joy?

Look at *Time to Just Be* for inspiration and ideas to quietly be with yourself, and any of these questions that call to you.

- **Cultivate Gratitude.** Not so long ago, I met with a friend who talked about what a miracle it is that she is so healthy and able-bodied at 76. She said that she doesn't take any aspect of her life for granted, and neither should we. Having that attitude sets up each day to be a good one. Each day is a gift, a blessing, and tomorrow we get another! We all have difficult days. I sure do. Even with my 5-Minute Helpers and other tools, some days just don't work out, but tomorrow presents us with a fresh opportunity.

Things We Can Change

What *can* we change? You can do many things to cultivate more joy as we grow older. You can:

- **Change your Beliefs.** As we discussed previously, beliefs and assumptions about growing older can make a huge difference in how we experience this stage of our lives. If we have negative beliefs about growing older, if we think of it as "aging," with all that implies, it is more likely that we will experience the fulfillment of those negative beliefs. Become aware of your own beliefs, and question what society tells you is inevitable.

- **Change your Self-Talk.** A friend recounted how she had invited an old friend from out of town to lunch with her local friends. Afterwards her visitor reported being amazed that none of the women at the lunch had complained about their ailments. It was so refreshing and lively! And unusual. She said it sometimes seemed that was all her friends back home talked about. My friend responded by saying: "I prefer not to listen endlessly to what's *not* working, in other's lives. I have my own aches and pains, but it is not where I choose to focus my energy."

We need to be aware of what we say to others and especially what we say to ourselves. We need to replace unhelpful self-talk with encouraging self-talk. Here are some examples of things you might say without thinking: "I can't bend down anymore because I'm getting old" or "I can't walk much anymore because my back hurts" or "That's because I'm getting old ..." or "You can't teach old dogs new tricks..." You fill in the blanks. You've heard others say things like this or you've said them yourself.

You might think that saying such things is a form of acceptance, in keeping with the Serenity Prayer. But while it's true that the Serenity Prayer talks about accepting things you cannot change, this is not true acceptance, which requires careful thought: it is more like fateful resignation.

- **Focus on what you *can* do.** Focusing on what you can't do can lead to feeling like a victim, which can quickly spiral down into powerlessness. That's why it is so much more helpful—and enlivening—to focus on what you can do. Maybe you can't hike in the woods because you know you could stumble on a root and wrench your knee, which is still healing from an injury, but you can take an energizing walk on the nicely paved, flat and beautiful bicycle path just a short drive away.

- **Re-evaluate your habits.** In a sense, as we grow older we tend to become more of who we are. That's because we've had more time to "practice and perfect" our habitual ways of thinking, being and acting. However, not all of our habitual ways of being are so helpful; many can actually cause us physical or emotional pain as we grow older. Fortunately, we can acquire the wisdom to know if our habits are helpful or hurting us, and then choose to do something about them. To do that, sometimes we need a little help:

A new client assumed that her ankle movement was permanently restricted after a surgery that occurred more than 30 years ago. Because of this belief, she had long ago stopped trying to move her ankle fully. My instinct and experience were both telling me that her lack of mobility was not a result of the surgery, but rather the result of her habit of holding tension in her ankle because she believed that the restriction was permanent. So, as we talked, I gently began to move her ankle. My instinctive perception turned out to be true, and in a short time she regained much of her flexibility.

Can you see how protecting her injured ankle turned into an unquestioned habit? This kind of thing happens all too frequently. If you sustain an injury, it can be helpful to protect that injured area by limiting your movement for a short time. Often, however, these self-protective measures become habits that last far too long. Here's another example:

One of my clients began restricting her neck movement after she sustained a neck injury at age 40, and she never stopped. Now, at age 60, she has 20 years of practicing that same habit—and a stiff and painful neck!

It may seem impossible to change a long-standing habit such as this, but I have seen many clients regain flexibility, even after enduring years of restricted movement. With time and the proper guidance encouraging us to do good, helpful movements such as "oiling the joint," plus a belief in new possibilities, we can regain flexibility. (See the Joints chapter.) And by the way, the same principle applies to our emotional lives. After a psychological "injury," we can develop a habit of protecting ourselves against future hurts by shutting down. This can limit our access to joy.

Some unhelpful habits may be due to old patterns of thought. If I habitually tell myself how miserable my life is, for example, that way of perceiving the world will limit me; I won't be willing to think out of the box to find creative solutions. The consequences of repeating these unhelpful patterns of thinking and self-talk increase as we continue to do them over the years. The same is true if I have a habitual tendency to believe that there are no solutions for my difficulties. That belief only leads to powerlessness. Telling my "story" over and over in discouraging ways, using phrases like "I'll never be organized" or "I'll never get more physically fit" or "I'll never find any help for my condition" will make it much more difficult to shift to a new way of being when circumstances call for it. Other unhelpful habits may be patterns of action, such as rushing through activities, trying to do too many things at once, restrictive moving and breathing, tightening muscles, or discouraging self-talk. A habit is like a path through a field of tall grass; the more it is walked upon, the more it is padded down, and the easier it becomes to walk that same path over and over again. If that path leads us to places we no longer wish to visit, it is time to create new pathways, ones that lead to greater health and well-being.

Saying "Yes" when you want to say "No," another unhelpful habit. This habit can really zap your energy and get in the way of doing what's important for you. Certainly, there are times when we have to care for or help others and can't say no, but many times we say yes just out of habit, without stopping to think about it. Learning to say "No" is an important skill for women of any age to learn. However, as we grow older, it becomes even more important.

An easy and effective way to begin to change this unhelpful habit is to create a new one: instead of responding right away, practice creating some space between when you receive a request or invitation and when you answer. This will give you time to consider whether this is something you really want to do or not at this time. To create that space, you'll need to say something like:" I will get back to you after I... look at my appointment book, check in with my partner, my family or co-worker, etc." If your answer is ultimately "No," you may have to repeat your "No's" many times. I have had to repeatedly remind people that I write on Tuesdays and I'm not available for social occasions or other activities. If you wish, you can present an alternative such as, "I can't help with that event, but I can ..."

- **Increase your commitment to self-care.** As we get older, the consequences of ignoring our body and neglecting self-care becomes more pronounced, and costs more in time, money and pain. If you want your life to include good health, independence and minimal limitations, now is the time to begin making self-care a central focus. The practices and guidelines in this book are here to make taking good care of yourself easy, effective and enjoyable. Remember, the prevention of injury and illness, along with early detection, are critical to maintaining your best health, and these become more imperative as you grow older. Do not hesitate to get a checkup, take extra care, or seek support from a health professional. Please listen to your body.

The Wisdom to Know the Difference

We've talked about some of the things we can change about growing older, and some of the things we can't; things we must accept—without falling into "false acceptance." Now, how do we develop the wisdom to tell the difference? This takes positive thinking and a willingness to seek a solution. Here's an example to illustrate what I mean:

A couple of weeks ago while I have been finishing this chapter, I started to have pains in my joints. The pain was moving around to different joints. One day, my right knee hurt; then one hip and then the other. Then the pain moved to my elbow, which I had previously injured. I became alarmed. Here I am, writing a chapter about how you can keep flexible while growing older, I thought, and my body is falling apart! Not great self-talk! I also started worrying that maybe I had Lyme disease again.

Because of the shifting nature of the aches and pains, I was reluctant to get a bodywork session. So, instead, I "oiled my joints" and did self-massage, which helped ease some of my aches. Then, I called an old friend who is a massage therapist to ask for her advice. She asked me when the pain began. When I told her, she laughed and asked: "How many bushels of tomatoes are you eating a day?" she asked. Indeed, I love tomatoes. I only eat them in season, and it was a bumper crop this year. In fact, the only veggies I grow are tomatoes!

My friend then told me that many of her clients come to her this time of year with complaints of roving joint pains just like mine. It's a reaction to nightshades plants like tomatoes that some people have, especially when they eat a lot of them. Learning that this was a temporary situation caused by something I was eating was a great relief. As I stopped worrying, my aches and pains began to diminish. Slowing down my tomato consumption also helped. I kept moving and, most importantly, I didn't accept this as an "inevitable symptom of growing older".

Now let's look at another very important area where we need to cultivate the wisdom to know the difference: sex.

Sex and Getting Older: What's True?

Probably most of us believe that growing older will affect our sexuality, but what's really inevitable about that? And what can we change?

It's important to acknowledge that women's sexuality is so individual that we can hardly assume that growing older is the only major factor. For one, while very real hormonal changes do take place as a consequence of menopause, changes that specifically affect libido, it's not the same for everyone. For some women, the increased level of testosterone that comes with menopause can actually *intensify* their sexual appetite. In addition, finally being beyond concerns about an unwanted pregnancy can bring a new sense of freedom. For others, the specific, spontaneous hormonal desire to be sexual may substantially diminish with menopause. But the truth is that some women hardly have ever had much spontaneous desire. So, what is "normal," really?

In my book, *Joyful Sexuality for Women*, I debunk the myth that there is some way we "should" be with respect to our sexuality. I also inspire women to *cultivate* their sexuality, whether with a partner or by themselves. Can you think of your sexuality as a living part of you that needs to be nurtured, especially as you grow older?

One issue with which we have to contend as we get older is how the media reflects or ignores older women. We see few images of sexy older women in the media; in fact, we seldom see older women making love at all on stage or screen. We are much more likely to see older men having sex with younger women. This pattern of systematic omission sends a false message about how things are or should be. If we are not careful, we might take these messages to heart, perhaps even giving up on our own sexuality. Don't! As authors Deidre Fishel and Diana Holtzberg state so powerfully in their book, *Still doing it— The intimate lives of women over 60*: "What's so sad is not only are older women being denied images of sexuality and romance that reflect their reality, but the rest of us aren't seeing the joy our older years can bring. We're so inundated with the image of sex as two hot pumping young bodies that even thinking of women in their seventies or eighties having sex seems foreign, if not distasteful."[25]

We very much need those images of older, powerful, passionate, sexy women! I strongly believe that seeing them can help women of all ages feel better about their sexuality. That's something we can change by speaking out and bringing pressure on the media. We can also seek out those women who embody sexiness at any age as role models.

Mirror, mirror on the wall. How we relate to our own appearance is another aspect of our sexuality. It is undeniable that we don't look the same as did when we were younger, but in reality, that has nothing to do with our innate sexuality. Once again, however, culture has an impact. We are certainly not brought up to view the realities of aging, like wrinkles, as beautiful; rather, the media floods us with images of young women, telling us that they are what "sexy" looks like. It is strong conditioning but here, again, we have choice. We can select where we put our attention. Again, and again, we can choose to focus on our increased capacity for joy, our shining eyes, our inner strength, the daily pleasures of being alive, rather than the wrinkles or sags that have begun to appear. Do we want to focus on what we have lost or what we have gained? As I am getting older I am coming face to face with these vital questions:

- How do I love and respect my body, both as I am now, and as I change through my life?

- How do I shift the focus from how I look from the outside to how I feel on the inside?

Recently, as I was about to go out, I stopped to comb my hair. Standing in front of the mirror, I saw a glow on my face and in my eyes from the excitement of going to my favorite restaurant. I appreciated how good my hair looked. Then I also noticed the growing wrinkles and the sag under my chin. In that moment I realized I had a choice. Which do I focus on? Both the glow and the wrinkles exist, I thought, but I can choose where I put my attention. Focusing on one will keep me feeling good, whereas focusing on the other will make me feel miserable. Which did I choose? I bet you can guess!

In that moment, I realized that I could also shift my focus from how I look on the outside to how I feel on the inside; that was also a choice. As I did this, I noticed how sexy and attractive I felt in my dress. I enjoyed how the dress moved, so I did a few delicious stretches and sexy movements to feel even better.

I successfully *changed the channel!* The effect was magical.

Good News

Despite the very real issues concerning sexuality and growing older that I have mentioned, the reality of older women's sex lives may be much better than the youth culture hype would have us believe. Here's an inspiring quote from *Still doing it – The intimate lives of women over 60* "… whether it's been documented or not, the truth, and what we should all be shouting from the rooftops, is that the reality of older women's lives is a hell of a lot better than the images we're exposed to." Most of the women the authors interviewed said that when they were younger, they were unaware of what they either wanted or needed sexually, and were often too intimidated to ask. Now older, that's no longer the case: "Many said maturity and sexual confidence have made them more comfortable with letting go and seeking their own pleasure."[26]

More Good News

You may have read that one needs to be continuously sexually active throughout one's life, or risk losing the possibility of ever being sexual again. However, the stories of many debunk this myth. Women who have met a new lover in their 70s or 80s are quite able to resume (or even begin) their sexual lives, even if they have not had a partner for years, or even decades. And women of any age can begin to explore self-pleasuring.

That means it's never too late to reclaim our sexual selves—and more and more of us are doing just that. In fact, many of the women I see in my practice express the wish to rekindle their interest in sex along with a sense of their own sexiness. Yes, as we grow older, we may experience vaginal dryness and thinness, but lubricants and suppositories can help. In addition, exercises for the pelvic floor muscles can strengthen and enliven the pelvic area.

In sum, while some women feel that their libido has diminished as they've grown older, we have the power to cultivate desire, and our anatomy of arousal can still work at any age. Isn't this great news! For ideas on how to cultivate desire and more good news see my book: *Joyful Sexuality for Women.*

As we close this section on the wisdom to know the difference, I again urge you to question your beliefs. Even if you are faced with some rather obvious signs of growing older (like joints "wearing out"), you still have choices along the way, including joint replacement. I have supported clients to ensure good recovery, and will address that as well as healing with ease in my next book, *Self-Care in the Difficult Times.*

The Gifts of Growing Older

Finally, I want to remind you that *growing older does bring forth many pleasures*, not the least of which is feeling more comfortable in your own skin. Many women speak of caring less—or not at all—about what others think and say about them, and what a relief that is. Here's how one woman spoke of how she felt turning 70:

> *I suddenly no longer cared about how I looked. After disliking my looks for years and after a number of attempts to look younger with plastic surgeries, my vanity seemed to disappear almost overnight. What a feeling of freedom!*

Another friend said she felt that "*At 70 it was time to focus on me and my needs, and to let go of helping out my daughter financially after so many years.*" And as for me, at every birthday I ask myself this question: Would I go back to a younger age if I had to give up what I have learned in the last years? So far, the honest answer has been a big NO! Using the guidelines and practices in this book to support my self-care along with the blessing of good genes and a dash of luck, I am able to still move the way I want to. I am able to do the activities I love, including dancing, biking, and lots of walking. I dance more gently, now. I no longer do it barefoot, but I still dance. I know what I need to do to feel good. I know how to *change the channel* to shift my thoughts and feelings towards light, love, life. I have more appreciation and acceptance of myself. I have learned to cultivate more joy and have more fun!

As we come to the end of this chapter, I invite you to take the opportunity that each day offers to live as joyfully as you can. You do have the skills to do that and to cultivate vitality and well-being. So, take that opportunity! Enjoy the gifts of growing older for as long as you can.

Conclusion

As we come to the end of this book, I want to remind you about a few things, and also share a little about what I've learned from working with the material in this book, because the two are interconnected.

I offered an approach to self-care that is, first and foremost, about being kind, accepting and compassionate towards yourself—because that is the heart of self-care. My approach is also practical because I understand firsthand the challenges, setbacks and obstacles that can occur when you choose to bring more self-care into your life.

To support you on your journey, I offered you five Practices designed to strengthen and empower you from the inside out: *Cultivate Inner Kindness and Love, Cultivate Joy, Discover What You Really Want and Need, Listen to the Wisdom of Your Body,* and *Cultivate Inner Support.* In naming some of them, I deliberately used the word "cultivate" because the results only come over time—but they do come. The more we keep doing the practices, the better they work. There is seldom a lot of "doing" required with these practices; for me, it is often simply a matter of shifting my self-talk, or remembering to ask myself, "What would bring me joy today?"

I developed ten 5-Minute Helpers: easy fun and effective ways to relieve stress, shift and lift your energy and mood, and rebalance your body and mind. I always carry the Helpers with me as I find many occasions to use them. I encourage you to do the same.

I explored many different aspects of self-care, bringing to them what I hope was a unique and inspirational perspective. And to make your self-care both sustainable and joyful, I offered five Guidelines: *Keep It Small, Make It Enjoyable, Find Your Own Way, Make Your Day Work for You, and Appreciate All Your Efforts.* These Guidelines have been like my secret formula, supporting me to do what I truly want, whether that was to find a new way to enjoy more physical activity, create an especially nurturing day for myself, or complete this book. For example, each time I simply appreciated my efforts—acknowledging myself for what I did, however small, rather than focusing on what didn't get done—I was able to keep going forward. Please use them! In the introduction, I invited you to use your inner wisdom to choose from all of these offerings those that speak to you and offer you the support that you need. Now that we come to the end of the book, I encourage you to keep this book nearby. As new areas of self-care become appealing to you, and especially as issues arise, come back to it for support. Turn to it as you might to a kind friend. Let it keep reminding you about the 5-Minute Helpers, the Practices and Guidelines.

I sincerely hope that this book supports your capacity to live a balanced and joyful life; to feel empowered, flexible and re-silient, both now and as you grow older. I know from personal experience how it can be hard to challenge the false beliefs and other obstacles that get in the way of a joyful life, so please use the guidelines and practices to help with those; I had to break through my false belief that you, dear readers, would not find this book helpful unless it was "perfect."

I hope that the love that compelled me to write this book comes through, and that I keep inspiring you to love yourself just as you are, even as I, too, struggle with that one more time. And although this book focuses on your relationship to yourself, I encourage you to reach out to others. You may find that friends or acquaintances have similar challenges and would welcome the opportunity to talk with you about them, or hear what you have found helpful.

And please reach out to me. Though this is the end of this book I look forward to a continued relationship with you, dear reader. I'd love to hear from you about what has supported you, and what other support that you need. For my part, I will continue to create ways to stay connected, both individually and as a part of a *Heart of Self Care* Group. In addition, I will keep writing. In writing this book, I realized I had more I wanted to say about sexuality than would fit here, so I created a small companion book, "Joyful Sexuality." Delving into that topic has inspired me to work more with issues around sexuality. My next book will address self-care during difficult times, such as recovery from illness, surgery and loss. I look forward to working on that, and on creating guided meditations and relaxations, and other audio "helpers" for you. So please check out my website for these, and for information about upcoming classes, workshops and talks.

In closing, I started this book with a dedication to the heart. Let's end with *Touchstone*.

Place your hand on your heart and let these words from my heart fill your heart: May you continue to develop a kinder relationship to yourself, and enjoy each day more fully, despite the challenges and obstacles that present themselves. Your heart knows that you deserve to have all the joy, well-being and nurturing you want, so remember to connect to your heart with touchstone, anytime, anywhere.

Endnotes:

[1] Nachmanovitch, Stephen, *Free Play: Improvisation in Life and Art* (A Jeremy P.Tarcher/Putnam Book, 1990), p. 43

[2] Nachmanovitch, p. 43.

[3] Ibid, p. 118.

[4] Freydberg, Peggy, *Growing Up in Old Age* p.37

[5] Frederickson, Barbara, *Positivity: Top-Notch Research Reveals the Upward Spiral that will change your Life* (Crown Publishers, 2009), p. 184.

[6] Oliver, Mary, "A Summer Day," *New and Selected Poems, Volume 1* (Beacon Press, 1992).

[7] This Huffington Post article, "13 Mental Health Benefits of Exercise" by Sophia Breene, provides a good summary (03-27-2013, accessed 10-13-2016): http://www.huffingtonpost.com/2013/03/27/mental-health-benefits-exercise_n_2956099.html

[8] *8 Weeks to Optimum Health: A Proven Program for Taking Full Advantage of Your Body's Natural Healing Power* by Andrew Weil (Ballantine Books, 2013), p. 58

[9] http://www.pnas.org/content/112/4/1232.full.pdf, referenced at http://www.digitaltrends.com/mobile/does-blue-light-ruin-sleep-we-ask-an-expert/#ixzz4BfijJb3r

[10] http://www.medicaldaily.com/mobile-technologys-blue-light-still-suppresses-sleep-hormone-melatonin-affecting-326534

[11] https://sleepfoundation.org/ask-the-expert/electronics-the-bedroom

[12] Note: Some say 30 minutes(?)

[13] http://www.northwestern.edu/newscenter/stories/2014/08/natural-light-in-the-office-boosts-health.html

[14] Pogrebin, *Getting Over Getting Older*, pp. 93-94

[15] Frederickson, p. 51

[16] Frederickson, p. 51

[17] https://www.bharatbook.com/healthcare-market-research-reports-467678/healthcare-industry-healthcare-market-research-reports-healthcare-industry-analysis-healthcare-sector1.html

[18] Geneen Roth, *Women, Food and God: An Unexpected Path to Almost Everything* (Scribner, 2010), p. 64.

[19] Roth, p. 83

[20] Linda Hartley, *Wisdom of the Body Moving: An Introduction to Body-Mind Centering* (North Atlantic Books, 1995) p. 198.

[21] Leonard Pearson and Lillian R. Pearson, with Karola Saekel, *The Psychologist's Eat Anything Diet (Gestalt Journal Press, 1973).*

[22] Hale Sofia Schatz and Shira Shaiman, *If the Buddha Came to Dinner: How to Nourish Your Body to Awaken Your Spirit (*Hachett Books, 2004*)*, pg. 29

[23] Northrup, Christiane, *Goddesses Never Age* (Hay House, 2015) pp. 9-10.

[24] Chodrin, Pema, *When Things Fall Apart – Heart Advice for Difficult Times* (Shambhala Publications, 1996)

[25] Fishel, Deidre and Holtzberg, Diana, *Still doing it— The intimate lives of women over Sixty* (Avery, 2009)

[26] Fishel, Deidre and Holtzberg

Acknowledgments

This book was written over a period of ten plus years. During that time, many people supported me at different times and in various ways.

I am grateful to the clients, colleagues, friends, and other women who shared their personal stories, and wisdom about self-care. Their names and circumstances have been changed to protect their privacy.

I am very grateful for my editor, JoAnne O'Brien-Levin, who deeply heard my voice, and my heart, and made this book better and clearer, while keeping my true voice. This book would never be in your hands without her skill, support and patience.

Also important in making this book a reality is my friend, Rochelle Lipkind, who from early in my journey with this book offered to read what I wrote, and through her feedback helped me to become a better writer. Many times when I felt alone at points in my long journey, she sat right next to me and read aloud what I wrote.

I deeply appreciate: my sister, Isabella Caruso, who offered much needed encouragement and feedback for my early writing, and along the way; and my brother, Angelo Tumbarello, who supported me through his photographs and in many other ways.

I am grateful to Emily Feit, who first helped me to organize the form and structure of this book.

I want to thank these friends who spent hours listening to me talk about the book, and giving me feedback, ideas and encouragement: Donna Dragon, Kim Jessor, Myra Avedon, and Martha Eddy.

Also, I want to thank friends who supported me through different parts of this long journey: Nuria Vallandingham, Ariana Shelton, Carol Beauvais, Mary Ingari, Marlene Potter, Nina Barwell, Carol Magrone, Joann Lutz, Kathy Freshley, Lenore Grubinger, and Sara Hostetler.

I greatly appreciate Barbara Simons, for believing in me and offering me a grant to support my early writing.

I am grateful to Martha Eddy, Blake Middleton, and Christina and Jim Bethin for opening their homes for my writing retreats.

I am grateful to Jacki Jacobs, for her beautiful photographs on the covers, and the many ways she has supported me to get this book out.

I am grateful for my book designer Deana Riddle for her patience and skill in creating this beautiful book.

Thanks to Glenna Collett, who supported me in getting the book ready for publication and helped me navigate the world of publishing.

Thanks to Kerstina Avedon-Tresselt, who offered her time and expertise as a photographer when this book was in a different form. Also thanks to Leslie Cerier, for her photography on an early writing project.

I would like to thank my teacher, Bonnie Bainbridge Cohen, for her gift of Body-Mind Centering ® and for the opportunity to share this wonderful work at the School for Body-Mind Centering® with many students for 30 years.

I thank my mother, who always encouraged my work as a healer and therapist. I wish she was here to see this book. She would be proud of me. I thank both of my parents for giving me the perseverance to complete this book.

In keeping with the spirit of this book I want to deeply appreciate myself for all my efforts to go through this long journey to bring this book to completion.

Most of all I want to thank my life partner and love, Ron Freshley. You supported me even as I spent time away to write, and money we didn't have to publish this book. You listened when I shared my difficulties and obstacles again and again. You knew my heart and soul needed to write this book, so when I wanted to stop, you encouraged me to keep going. I am so glad to be living my life journey with you.

About the Author

Linda Tumbarello is a Licensed Mental Health Counselor, and Certified Body Mind Centering® Practitioner and Teacher, and Dynamic Embodiment Practitioner, Continuing education provider, and Self-Care Coach.

Linda conducts workshops, private retreats, and is a sought after speaker. She teaches classes and has a private practice in Northampton, MA where she specializes in body-mind healing.

Linda has developed a powerful way of working with the body and mind using hands-on work, body-centered psychotherapy, embodiment practices, and movement. Her therapy work is especially helpful for clients who are highly sensitive or who have experienced trauma or abuse. She helps clients to regain a sense of ease, comfort and safety in their bodies.

In her coaching work, she has supported many women to create sustainable self-care, and to stay vital and moving, especially as they grow older.

For 30 years, Linda was a faculty member in The School for Body-Mind Centering® Practitioner Training Program, and taught in the Dynamic Embodiment Training Program with Dr. Martha Eddy.

Linda develops and offers advanced trainings to Psychotherapists and Bodywork Practitioners. She offers coaching to, and provides supervision to massage therapists and bodyworkers.

She is also the author of "Joyful Sexuality for Women: a little book on a big subject."

Linda lives with her husband and her 2 cats in Northampton, MA where she enjoys being outdoors, puttering in her garden and dancing.

To find out more about Linda's workshop, talks or retreats, or about her Heart of Self-Care group, visit her popular website:

www.lindatumbarello.com